ETHICS, VALUE, AND REALITY

ETHICS, VALUE, and REALITY

Selected Papers of
AUREL KOLNAI

Hackett Publishing Company
Indianapolis

Library of Congress Catalog Card Number 77-83145

ISBN 0-915144-39-5
ISBN 0-915144-40-9 pbk.

For further information address Hackett Publishing Company, Inc.,
Box 55573, Indianapolis, Indiana 46205

FOREWORD

The papers in this volume appear in chronological order.

The paper entitled 'Aesthetic and Moral Experience' is an amalgamation of two papers published separately. These two papers were meant to be two parts of a single paper, and we have accordingly taken the opportunity of presenting them in what we understand to have been the form intended by the author. The changes this entailed are confined to the wording of titles and sub-titles, the numbering of sections and the creation of one new sub-title.

'Deliberation is of Ends' is the only paper whose text is appreciably different from the originally published version. The author himself made a fair number of deletions from his own copy, and made one or two brief insertions. These changes have been incorporated wherever the author's intention was clear.

The only papers previously unpublished are the two parts of 'Morality and Practice'. They form what would appear to be the first two of six projected chapters of a book with this title. Chapters three to six were never written. A fair number of minor changes and corrections have been made to the text, and the titles have been slightly modified to accord with the presentation. Dr Kolnai was awarded a grant from the Pilgrim Trust Fund of the British Academy for this work.

'The Sovereignty of the Object' was originally published in the U.S.A., in a *Festschrift* for the seventieth birthday of the Catholic phenomenologist Dietrich von Hildebrand. Certain minor changes have also been made to the text of this paper, many of them indicated in the margin of the author's copy.

All important editorial changes have been mentioned in notes at the end of the book and are indicated in the text by a, b, c, etc. We have made changes only where we deemed it to be absolutely necessary.

The other five papers remain as they were originally published, apart from minor corrections. The author's footnotes appear at the foot of the page, numbered in the usual way.

The index was compiled by Francis Dunlop.

Thanks are due to Mrs Elizabeth Kolnai for the work she has

done in the preparation of the bibliography. Because of the scattered nature of the material, it has not proved possible to check every reference thoroughly.

Grateful acknowledgement is made to Bedford College for a grant towards the cost of publication.

Francis Dunlop
Brian Klug

CONTENTS

ACKNOWLEDGEMENTS

The editors and publishers wish to thank the following for their kindness in granting permission to reprint material that has previously appeared:

The Aristotelian Society for 'Erroneous Conscience', *P.A.S.* (1957–8); 'Deliberation is of Ends', *P.A.S.* (1961–2); 'Existence and Ethics', *P.A.S.S. V.* xxxvii (1963); 'Moral Consensus', *P.A.S.* (1969–70); and 'Forgiveness', *P.A.S.* (1973–4); The Royal Institute of Philosophy for 'The Concept of Hierarchy', *Philosophy*, vol. xlvii, no. 177 (July 1971); The British Society of Aesthetics for 'Aesthetic and Moral Experience', *The British Journal of Aesthetics*, vol. 11, no. 2 (Spring 1971); and 'Contrasting the Ethical with the Aesthetical', *The British Journal of Aesthetics*, vol. 12, no. 4 (Autumn 1972); the Fordham University Press (New York) for 'The Sovereignty of the Object', from *The Human Person and The World of Values* (1960).

Aurel Thomas Kolnai
(1900-1973)

1. This volume commemorates, by a small collection of papers chosen for their quality and for their representativeness of a large and various output, Aurel Kolnai's philosophical work and activity in England, his final home in the long succession Hungary, Austria, France, U.S.A. and Canada.

Kolnai came to live in England only in 1955, but he had been deeply interested, ever since his Budapest childhood, in English literature and English political institutions. He took readily in 1955 to analytical philosophy, saw no incompatibility between it and the exercise of the imagination, and conceived an admiration for the eighteenth-century British moralists, for the intuitionists G. E. Moore, H. A. Prichard, E. F. Carritt and W. D. Ross, and for J. L. Austin. In the case of Moore, admiration bordered upon passion, which did not exclude sharp criticism. He distinguished seemingly without effort between the virtues and the vices of analytic philosophy, which had dominated the English academic scene since the Second World War; and he discerned in it a variant of the phenomenological method in which he had been trained in Austria.

Kolnai was an extremely clever and intellectually ingenious man, more imaginative, better read and experienced by life itself in political history, and far better versed in the history of moral and political philosophy, than almost all the members of the analytical school which he joined.[1] But his arrival caused no great splash. John Findlay and Stuart Hampshire appreciated his gifts. H. B. Acton became a lifelong friend and created a visiting post for him at Bedford College (where the writers of this introduction encountered him in turn). But he did not have the influence he deserved to have, or which the critical acclaim accorded in 1938 to his political philosophical masterpiece *The War Against the West* might have led one to expect. At least in part, this was because political

---

[1] And except that it would have been hard for him to match the late J. L. Austin's ear for English, he had a finer ear for language. (Languages rather—he was on intimate terms with at least five living languages and two dead.)

philosophy (where his reputation was secure—if anyone had wished to recall National Socialism) was in temporary but near total eclipse. More important, he despised all success which was not won on his own unconditional terms. (One recalls the peculiar scorn which he reserved for the philosophy once called Evolutionary Ethics.) It was a psychological and physiognomical impossibility for him to act or write with the aim of making friends or influencing people. He wrote down his thoughts as he himself wanted to read and reread them. If more thoughts came on some point he often made room for them within the sentences which he had already written. He expected the readers (whom he passionately wanted to have, but only on these terms) to make the same effort in reading that he had made in writing and thinking. It is to be hoped that the appearance of this volume at a time when some moral philosophers have begun to sense the need for a broader and much more inquisitive interest in the history of their subject, will have brought closer the day when more readers will overcome the obstacles which it may be complained that the author himself put in the way.

2. Kolnai was from 1959 until his death Visiting Lecturer in Ethics at Bedford College in the University of London, an office which the College was persuaded by Kolnai's seemingly inextinguishable intellectual vitality to regard as renewable without limit of age. He was writing and teaching up to the end, and the two editors, Francis Dunlop and Brian Klug, were among his last graduate students. Kolnai's appeal as a teacher was far from universal. He spoke in his lectures without regard for the limits of time, timetable or the philosophical or historical incompetence of his audience—and with a degree of sophistication, indirection, qualification and playfulness which was always beyond the comprehension of at least half the student body. Within another and smaller group, however, his lectures and classes became the object of dogged and loyal persistence, even cult. The period during which we each knew him was an increasingly political period in the University. It is questionable whether the subtlety of Kolnai's philosophical method was as keenly appreciated at that time as the fact that he was a very political moral philosopher. His view of the relationship of politics and ethics was both complex and old fashioned, as 'The Moral Theme in Political Division' (1957) makes clear:

The basic moral intuitions of mankind—which Right and Left alike cannot but take for granted as a premise for their moral appeal—provide no solution, except in a prohibitive and limiting sense, for the permanent or topical problems of political organization and choice.

But what mattered was that he had a view, and that he declared it, however displeasingly pluralist it must have been found by some of his listeners at that time.

Alain is said to have said that 'anyone who is not an anarchist at sixteen will not have enough energy at thirty to be a fire chief'. Different university teachers have done different things with this thought. Kolnai's approach was polite but the opposite of conciliatory or condescending to all 'radical subversionism'. We can reconstruct it best for the reader by quoting from certain earlier writings the views which we know that he retained and continued to express until the end of life. They will illustrate also the perfect consonance which Kolnai saw between *qualification* and *candour*.

The most characteristic stigma of 'social conscience' as a disease consists, neither in the absence of 'selfishness' nor in a lack of due respect for one's social or intellectual 'betters', but in the mind's incapacity to take a genuine interest in objects, things, problems, artistic tasks (and the immanent correction of their possible solutions) or similar themes *as such*, which requires a phase—though not a final or comprehensive attitude—of complete indifference to any 'welfare' or 'service' interest as such, social as well as private; . . . The victim of the 'social obsession', incapable of such a mode of behaviour, is by the same token incapable both of true citizenship and of true charity: he can neither be true man nor be a true Christian. . . . Many of our more estimable contemporaries, who are by no means typical sophists or lovers of tyranny, yet succumb to this highly subtle trick of the Enemy, an ostensibly Christian or ethical appeal to their 'social conscience' . . . Here is an attitude significantly devoid of patience, humility, freedom of mind (with the consciousness of limitations that underlies it) and of generosity (not as an equivalent of 'altruism' or 'cooperativeness' but in the sense of a readiness to sow without being assured of harvest) . . .

('Privilege and Liberty' (1949), p. 102)

For most of his student adherents in the period of the 1960s, Kolnai was no ally in politics (still less in well-meaning suggestions of syllabus reform towards greater 'relevance') but an eccentric, resolute and formidably long-winded adversary, who aroused strong affection. His most sympathetic traits were the physical frailty of a refugee, an exact sense of the academic worth of individual students and a sense of humour. He was not open to compromise concerning the autonomy of philosophy, and yet he had a profound sense of the interpenetration of philosophy and economic and political history.

3. The passage about social conscience as a disease comes from a work published ten years before Acton was able to appoint Kolnai to Bedford, and written when he was at Laval in Quebec.

(The second piece in the volume represents his reaction to what
he called in correspondence to Hayek 'the intolerable Thomist
and tribalist atmosphere prevailing there'.) That these were still his
opinions, however, can be documented in detail, and most clearly
from the book he left three quarters finished at his death, *The
Utopian Mind* (cp. *Crítica de las Utopías Políticas* (1959)), and for
which he had come in 1955 to research in London, with no certain
prospects of regular academic employment. It is a familiar criticism that utopian thinking is irrelevant to practice because it is
unrealizable in practice and distracts attention from the attainable
second best. Kolnai's criticism was quite different. It was that
utopia cannot even be described or thought out in theory: and that
this makes utopian theorizing not less, but more dangerous. *The
Utopian Mind* was to have been the exhaustive and definitive exposure of the obstinate refusal to see everything for what it is
(notably brutality as brutality, whatever the utopian impulse from
which it was descended), of the inability to comprehend the separ-
ateness and irreducibility of all distinct intrinsic values, of infantile misconceptions of liberty which Kolnai claimed to see at
work not only in totalitarian states but also in a wide variety of
attitudes and policies everywhere to be encountered (in milder but
incipiently recognizable form) in the liberal democracies of the
west.

4. To the convincing treatment of such themes lived experience is as important as imagination and historical learning. Kolnai
was as well qualified in this respect as almost any other twentieth-
century philosopher who has survived to tell the tale. Kolnai
narrated the story of his life up to the time when he came to England in his autobiography *Twentieth Century Memoirs*, an unpublished work originally commissioned by a Catholic publisher who
went bankrupt (by a turn typical of the bad luck which Kolnai
stoically encountered throughout his life) even as the manuscript
was to be handed in to the printer. Kolnai described the work for
the publisher as follows:

The book, autobiographical in form and devoted to a number of political,
philosophical, religious and cultural as well as local and personal subjects
runs to a length of 700 typed quarto pages. The title refers to the present
century (and an individual life starting with it), seeing its unprecen-
dented promise of human progress and perfection, and the dramatic, if
not perhaps altogether definitive, stultification of that promise. Though
definitely Catholic in its religious outlook, the book is utterly unlike any
kind of current Catholic literature and explicitly critical of certain
tendencies more or less inherent in the Catholic attitude. As regards its
political colour, the book may be described as markedly Conservative,

in a broad and reflective fashion linked to its general 'common-sense' outlook. It is radically opposed to all forms of Utopianism or Totalitarianism. The Introduction and Chapters I–III contain a good deal about Hungary up to the twenties; Chapters III, IV and (partly) VII, about the Austria of the twenties and thirties. Subject to his firmly rooted British loyalty, the author reveals much sympathetic interest in Switzerland, France, and especially Spain. In philosophy, he has been influenced by various objectivist, realist, intuitionist, and analytical schools of thought.[2]

[2] The bare chronological record of Kolnai's life was set down by Kolnai in a *Kurzer Lebenslauf* which he prepared in 1970 in the official style, leaving a blank for the date of his death:

Born	Budapest, Hungary	5th December 1900
Died	[London, England	28th June 1973]

Of Jewish extraction; father in banking. Married 1940. No children.
Education: Four years of elementary school; eight years at the Royal Lutheran Gymnasium, Budapest. Matriculation *magna cum laude* May 1918. University studies in Vienna 1922–1926. Main area of studies; philosophy under Professors Heinrich Gomperz, Robert Reininger, Karl Bühler, Moriz Schlick, Hans Eibl, Felix Kaufmann. Subsidiary studies in modern history under Professors Alfred Francis Pribram and Heinrich von Srbik. Classes under Professor Ludwig von Mises in political economy also attended. D. Phil. July 1926 with agreed distinction from both faculties. Thereafter (1928) further study in philosophy in Freiburg in Breisgau under Prof. Edmund Husserl and Martin Honecker; and in Berne in Spring 1938 with Professor Herbertz.

Until 1945 I worked for preference as writer and journalist. From 1926–1936 I was a regular contributor to the weekly review *Der österreichische Volkswirt*, Vienna; and from 1926 to 1931 I contributed to the weekly *Der deutsche Volkswirt*, Berlin. For short periods I served with several Catholic periodicals in Vienna (1928–1936). In the period 1927–33 I published longer papers on sociological and philosophical topics in specialist journals. Between 1933 and 1939 I was engaged on the preparation of a comprehensive critique (written in English) of National Socialism and related doctrines (*The War Against the West*, published in 1938), and on a critical discussion of pacifism in the West (unpublished). During World War II I worked on newspapers in London and North America. In 1944–45 I did some translation work for the American Office of War Information.

Nationality: Until 1929, Hungarian; 1929–1938, Austrian; thereafter stateless; 1951–1962, Canadian; thereafter British.

Residence: Until 1919 Budapest; 1920–1937, Vienna; 1937–40, London, Zurich, Berne, and mainly Paris; 1940–1945, New York and Boston, Mass.; 1945–1955, Quebec, Canada; thereafter London with frequent visits to Madrid and Brussels.

Conversion to Catholicism resulted from various influences, mainly that of G. K. Chesterton and the writings of the German Phenomenological School of Philosophy from 1923. I was baptised in Vienna in 1926.

Teaching duties: 'Chargé de cours' and later 'professeur agrégé' at Laval University, Quebec from Autumn 1945–55. Visiting Lecturer at Bedford College, London from Autumn 1959. In 1952 and between 1956–61, guest speaker at the Madrid Ateneo and several other Spanish 'Ateneos'.

5. Kolnai's philosophy does not emerge in his writings as formally or insistently religious. But his Christianity, more specifically his Catholicism, expresses itself powerfully in the shape and direction of his thought. It is a Christianity which takes the secular world and its less highflown concerns as the proper focus of human life. Only in relation to these is there any prospect of making sense of practical reason or of morality—two things which Kolnai refuses to follow the Aristotelian tradition in identifying. The impulse to reject that world as depraved, to regard the aspects of human nature which find themselves at home in it as beyond rational or unaided human hope, he found corrupting and the source of a destructive despair. There is a revealing passage in *The War Against the West*:

Personally I am inclined to think that in spite of its Christian polish, Luther's pessimism is more pagan than Hegel's pagan optimism, the latter being not entirely foreign to nineteenth-century progressive and constitutionalist views. For black despair is the very core of overweening arrogance. It is true that with Luther this is wrapped in the thread-bare guise of reckless belief in God's grace independent of man's conduct. Hegel, on the other hand, preserves some elements of actual morality . . .

(p. 127)

For Kolnai, all attempts to transcend the everyday world by rhetorical elevation of human powers into an image of success which could command unqualified satisfaction were a constant object of distrust, criticism and reasoned contempt. When that image took on more heroic pretensions, his reactions extended to the utter condemnation which informs so many pages of *The War Against the West*. The words of the poet of the *Winterreise*, 'Wenn kein Gott auf Erde sei, sind wir selber Götter', express a thought whose enactment Kolnai deeply feared. The active distaste for success which was a feature of his own life colours his reaction to writers and philosophers alike, most conspicuously perhaps Aristotle whom Kolnai commended for some (but only some) of the things he said about practical reason, but distanced and mocked for his moral elevation of mere success or social superiority. Kolnai would have had Napoleon exiled not to Elba but to a chair of philosophy for having seen (what Aristotle did not) that 'Etre grand, c'est dépendre de tout' (p. 200 in this collection).

This concern for the commonplace is not negative: for one thing, there is no trace of cowardice in it. It is sustained by the understanding, lacked by Nietzsche, that the signs of health are themselves commonplace. It is also balanced by the same ability, which was manifested in Kolnai's recreations of the past, to transform the commonplace—for instance, by hearing its words for the first time, as in the fine passage on Heidegger's 'das Man' and death:

I can see no peculiar frivolity in death being sometimes decorously, but not incorrectly, referred to in such terms as 'If something happens to me': most people in fact do not die either as suicides or as centenarians submitting, having spent every particle of their vitality, to the law of nature, but death 'happens' to them with an aspect of contingence about it, and sometimes pretty unexpectedly. Even the boorish Hungarian squires of old who in their noisy carousals used to shout 'Yo-ho! We'll never die!' were not necessarily, for that reason, self-deluded fools or inauthentic cripples.

('Existence and Ethics', p. 137 below)

Kolnai goes on to give some exceedingly good reasons why an unreflective involvement in the commonplace can be the condition of serious life and thought.

Kolnai's Christian imperfectionism opposes not only the glorification of ideals and the elevation of morality beyond everyday life, but even the elevation of morality within it, the exaggeration of morality into being the whole fabric of life. Obligation has priority and morality comes first; but, for all that 'life is subject in its entirety to moral judgement, direction and evaluation', life is primarily a conjunction of non-moral practical concerns. (Cp. 'The Thematic Primacy of Moral Evil' (1956) *ad fin.*) The urgency of morality in fact depends on the negative character of its duties, such as the duty not to lie or the duty, as he puts it in a passage which makes typical use of his love of language and languages, to keep off others' property:

It should be noted that when we speak of 'respecting' alien property (as also life or rights) we use that word in its weak sense of 'leaving alone', 'not touching', 'not interfering with', much as it is used in French medical language (the rash of typhus fever 'respects' the face, i.e. in the soberer style of English textbooks, the face 'escapes'), not in its strong sense of positive appreciation for something distinctively noble and respectable . . .

('Morality and Practice II', pp. 105–6 below)

6. Imperfectionism or anti-Utopianism is one of the many links between the moral philosophy expressed in this collection or in the unfinished book on Utopia and Kolnai's pre-war work, notably *The War Against the West*, already mentioned. This was unique in its time, and is still unusual, in both attacking Nazism as a total and radical assault on humanity or civilization and emphasizing that that assault was being launched to some considerable extent in the name of heroism and 'higher' values. An ideology of over-

reaching perfection was conspicuous among the mass of ideas and images which Kolnai painstakingly sought to separate and expose. Kolnai had been putting material together for the book from 1926 onwards. He wrote most of it in a Vienna cafe which was a favourite haunt of Austrian Nazis. An almost incredible feature of this fluently written and powerfully expressed work is that English was for him a literary language, largely learned by reading and rereading G. K. Chesterton. (He wrote in a letter to one of the present writers: 'It is too little known that Chesterton was largely a phenomenological analyst in the informal guise of a copy-producing and prejudice-airing journalist; and characterologically the polar opposite of Belloc, an oracular non-argumentative prophet and a great artist'.)

Kolnai sifted in the book a gigantic and terrifying range of Nazi writers, to produce a densely documented account of all major aspects of Nazi ideology. It is a book about the literature of Nazism, rather than about Nazism as it politically gained power or socially organized itself. Though it is a deeply political book, in the sense in which Kolnai's moral philosophy was by implication political, it is not a book about politics, and it contains little hint of what distinctively political means might be used to avert or combat destructive totalitarianism. He stresses the antiperfectionist theme that the despised, shabby compromises of bourgeois life are actually closer to spiritual values:

. . . even a society of hucksters and stockbrokers (however unjust and arbitrary this picture of liberal civilization may be), could infinitely more easily be imagined as a ground-plan of a mankind morally united, self-responsible and persistently cooperating, than could a society of irregular military bands and self-enclosed tribes with demi-gods for leaders.

                                        (p. 109; cp. 180)

Civilization, in a society free from myth or overarching political aspirations, is centered for Kolnai on rationality, and on patient public discussion. He quotes, with ironic approval, a Nazi writer:

'The plea for public discussion can only be understood as something reared in the soil of rationalism . . .: it was thought that in this way the right thing, or at least the relative truth, could be found, and fixed socially.' We confess, blushingly, that we are still not wholly weaned from so monstrous a superstition.

                                        (p. 131)

The addition is typical of him; and it is revealing of his thought that the word 'rationalism', as he indicates, is here his translation of *Aufklärung* ('Enlightenment'). The hope that by public rational discussion the right thing could be 'fixed socially' seems for Kolnai to be virtually *the* hope, the only possible alternative to overblown fantasies of social life on the one hand, and on the other the despair which he regarded as both a mistake and a sin.

7. Commenting on one of the mottoes of Nazism, 'not classes but types divide humanity', he wrote:

At bottom this means that ... conflicts are not caused by evils generally acknowledgeable and remediable according to any moral evidence; that the breach in human society which induces struggle is not founded in moral wrong or insufficient thought, and allows for no redress before a supreme tribunal of human consciousness. Not a struggle for the interpretation and shaping of social order, but a turmoil of tribal life-forces beyond discussion and persuasion, *beyond the possibility of solution*!

(*War Against the West*, p. 114)

His liberal rationalism provides the implication that if conflict is a matter of class and not of race, then it is remediable according to moral evidence. But there is something else that is behind the final emphasis of the passage—a demand which is not to be met entirely or even principally in political terms, if those are taken to be the terms of strategy, institutions, or reforms. Kolnai's belief in rational discussion—his belief that rational discussion offered the only hope there was—rested on a fundamentally Christian understanding of what room for hope there could possibly be. The secular cannot redeem and it is not its business to try; but it can and must preserve decency. Practical thought aimed at political measures is of course not excluded. And Kolnai recognized that democracy must itself evolve. But it is the spirit of decency which has to support the struggle. Something must, and nothing else can.

'Daemonic evil' is a phrase Kolnai more than once applied to Nazism, and he totally disbelieved that its existence could be adequately explained by the effect of economic sanctions or any similar cause. He gives us to understand that it is better understood as a glimpse of what we are always up against—something which only the resources of human decency can ultimately combat. The notion of *human* decency, for Kolnai, intrudes no note of external assistance. Yet his understanding of what human decency is, what it might be capable of, and what it cannot attempt without destroying itself, is certainly a Christian understanding. Though his ideals resembled those of a man of the *Aufklärung* to the extent that he opposed obscurantism, arbitrary authority, mythological politics, blind obedience, fanaticism and *Schwärmerei*, his confidence in his own ideals itself rested in a Christian understanding of why those ideals were necessary, and why they were possible.

8. At the time when Kolnai wrote *The War Against the West* he thought Nazism a far greater threat to civilization than Communism. He wrote approvingly (p. 323) of socialist principles of equality, and of bringing public control and co-operative responsibility into the fabric of class relationships and the organization of production. These were the terms in which he had welcomed the victory of the Allies in the Great War. But as freedom diminished in Communist countries he became more and more concerned with reaching a fresh understanding of the psychic meaning of totalitarianism. He emerged from the process as a conservative. At its beginning he wanted to understand how, in spite of the plain facts about restriction and negation of freedom, the Communists could claim that Marxist freedom was superior to bourgeois and conservative freedom. According to the analysis which Kolnai arrived at (cp. 'Privilege and Liberty' (1949)), the only thing which could make plausible or even possible such a claim was a profound deformation of the human soul, the childish inability of many human beings to accept or even understand the divide between the notion of *participation*—or the idea that *response* not *fiat* is the prime gesture of the human person—and notions of identity which tempt men into absurd ideas of 'positing' or 'generating' a reality of their own and of absorbing the infinite into one human Consciousness (cp. 'Privilege and Liberty', p. 73), and even into metaphysical subversion of the individuality, plurality and contingent inequality of men.

To the 'common man' every human face in which he does not recognize his own reflection as in a mirror appears crazy, uncanny, in some way impure; in short, it might be said that any face endowed with a personal character, with 'contours' or a 'profile' is an irritant to him.

When the tension between Participation and Identity is not respected the ideal of freedom requires that supreme power should both embody the power of everyone—with the exception of course of those unfit for identification with the will of society—and be unlimited.

Kolnai's writings in politics and ethics insist that there is a constant human tendency towards infantile oversimplification of facts and foolish reductionism of values; they also display a gift rare in British or American philosophers for diagnosing the elusive logic of the illogic from which great political creeds of the modern world are so often fabricated.

9. For Kolnai moral and political philosophy were distinguishable subjects, but practically all the dominating political and religious concerns we have so far identified have their roots in his moral

philosophy. To this subject he brought the training of a pheno-menologist, but he was not complacent about the all too often rather faint and conflicting conclusions which the method had achieved. (His reservations about some of the ideas that the method had issued in with Heidegger—and less directly Sartre—can be seen in 'Existence and Ethics' in this collection.) And, to judge from his practice, which involved extensive use of both analytical and phenomenological methods, it was as if he thought them com-plementary, indeed mutually dependent, and as if he saw in some happy combination of the analytical approach at its most imagina-tive and the phenomenological approach at its soberest, the only hope for rational philosophy.

By phenomenological training and by gift of nature, Kolnai had a singular capacity for narrative description, and a power few philosophers possess to fix some moment of experience in its cen-tral significance, yet leave it intact in its life. He could bring the past to the present in a way which made it immediate while it still remained of its time. One winter afternoon in a dark room in Bedford College, when Kolnai had been listening with his usual courtesy and modesty to some discussion in the theory of know-ledge, he illustrated a point, now forgotten, by telling how a boy was in a boat on Lake Balaton one hot afternoon in 1914, fishing, when he saw a figure on the shore, gesturing and shouting words he could not hear at all. He rowed across the flat water, to hear that war had broken out. This tiny fragment of Kolnai's experience— or rather his telling of someone else's experience (for we learn from the *Memoirs* that he himself learned of the outbreak of war when in a tram and read it from an Italian newspaper held upside down in another passenger's hand)—is more vivid in the memory, from his quiet, careful narration, than most memories of one's own. The relation to the past of the image he called up seems very pure. It is indeterminate, obviously, in almost all respects, yet it embodies completely a certain time and place, and preserves an experience which, whatever significance it gains from the knowledge of later events, emerges in Kolnai's recreation of it, quite undistorted by that significance.

But there was a special reason for offering description, and Kolnai offered a special kind of description, for purposes of moral reflection. The aim can be documented from several of the essays in this book but perhaps the most striking combined expression and exemplification of it is to be found in the introduction to *The War Against the West*:

If objectivity means the faithful presentation of a thing according to its own essence and undistorted by one's own feelings, then I may claim that I have at least made a sincere attempt to be objective. . . . I have taken great pains to do justice to the object of my inquiry; but to do someone justice does not necessarily imply that one justifies him. Let us suppose, for example, that we have to characterize an eroto-maniac, a sombre, tragic, insatiable and dangerous Don Juan. It would be unjust to describe him from sheer dislike as a thief when in fact he scrupulously respects the property of others; or as a vulgar profligate, which again he is not. On the other hand, it would not be in the least 'objective' to interpret his actions as a harmless pastime, a sublime quest for friendship, or a cult of beauty, notable for its high educative value. This also answers to the charge of over-estimation. Both the refusal to see unpleasant, horrible and minatory things in their true colours and the refusal to see the relative virtues and achievements attached to them, are symptoms of that intellectual cowardice and self-complacency which are bound to bear sinister fruits, and which I am more than ready to condemn. . . . I set myself the task of proving, not disproving, that National Socialism is a thing of grandeur.

Description did not exclude the description of value. Kolnai did not confuse objectivity and indifference. But the description of value had to proceed feature by feature, concentrating on the goodness or badness of those features in the many modalities of good or evil, not hastening to some overall prescriptive conclusion or verdict. In his intercollegiate lectures on Phenomenology (1970–2) Kolnai claimed that whenever we take a *pro* or a *con* position towards anything with a note of objectivity or intrinsicality, 'as distinct from the pure and mere "it suits us" or "it thwarts or vexes us", we attribute to it value or disvalue (often several values or disvalues, or indeed both: "this is a right action but apparently done from two or three indifferent or even objectionable motives"; "this is a crime but obviously reveals courage, or ingenuity, or an aspect of distinterested nobility . . .")'. Kolnai thought that if we will view the thing axiologically, and assess it first in the'currency of value' ('I know that this is a rather bad and misleading analogy', he said, 'take it *cum grano salis* then it may not be wholly useless'), as opposed to the language of 'ought' or 'must', then we are protected as best we can be from certain premature fixations. We are provided with 'a realm of approbative or disapprobative insights . . . without stressing the unbridgeable gulf between *Is* and *Ought*'. Kolnai held that if it proceeds in this way then value ethics

. . . precludes the classic pitfalls in Ethics: Hedonism or Eudaemonism; Utilitarianism and Consequentialism of any kind, i.e. the interpretation of moral in terms of allegedly more evident primary, natural conative experiences; and various kinds of Imperativism: 'duty' cut off from Good and Bad, and its interpretation in terms either of a concrete (social, monarchical, fashionable . . .) authority, or the 'rational ego', or of 'Conscience'.

According to his view

axiological ethic directs our attention, not only to the plurality of moral values and disvalues, but to the falseness of every monism in regard to the *object* of moral valuation: be it action, intention, maxim or motive, virtue and vice, character, and all the more of course wisdom or again ontological perfection.

Kolnai's conception of the work of the moral philosopher, and his obsession with the need not to warp our 'genuine response to value', were akin to the novelist's or poet's conception of the novelist's or poet's work. Auden once claimed that 'Poetry is not concerned with telling people what to do but with extending our knowledge of good and evil, perhaps making the necessity for action more urgent and its nature more clear, but only leading us to the point where it is possible for us to make a rational and moral choice.' The difference Kolnai might have stressed, in the mature London period, between his own view and these words of Auden lies only in their apparent faith in a unitary and uncontestable rationality.[3] How could there be a unitary conception of rationality when 'in the real world we experience—rooted in the tension between Value and Being—a diversity, in many ways discordant, among *Values*; a thing is better than an alternative thing in one respect but worse in another . . .—the prime ground for the "oppressiveness" of the Utopian atmosphere; from such a world all personal choice between incompatible, or at any rate competing, values appears excluded' (*The Utopian Mind*).

10. When so much is said, it will be unsurprising that the philosophers whom Kolnai warmed to in the Anglo–Saxon tradition were the intuitionists Moore, Ross, Carritt and their intellectual forbears. In the twentieth as in the nineteenth century, philosophers of moral intuition have been put aside principally because the intuitionist could provide no principles—'not even the most rudimentary decision procedure'—by which to adjudicate between competing moral or political claims.

Faced with a person demanding such a decision procedure

---

[3] Cp. 'Privilege and Liberty' (1949), p. 105. 'Whoever revolts from having to submit (in any sense concerning his social environment) to the "whims of Chance" will in due course be called to submit—in a way incomparably more abject, total, and final—to the whims of the tyrant, whoever would cleanse the map of social relationships about him from the manifold islets of "irrationality" with which they are interspersed will pay the penalty of having his life "planned for him" by a human "rationality" which his own reason, if he has any left, may recognize as madness.'

Kolnai would surely have tried to make the questioner think what
he was asking for. Is the demand that hard questions should be
somehow rendered easy? That a theory worked out by a philosopher with a few dozen cases at his imaginative disposal should
provide him with principles which he can then apply to *absolutely
every* case?[4] A standard reply to this will appeal to the idea that a
theory is designed to save certain fixed points among the phenomena, and that from these it can serve to provide decisions.
Kolnai's reply can be found in 'Morality and Practice II':

The pitfall to be avoided is the assumption or postulate, that a unitary,
constructive concept of ethics may *supersede* our direct apprehension of
the data of moral experience and our receptiveness to moral emphasis in
its various dimensions. The endeavour to render moral consciousness
intelligible is justifiable so long as it does not degenerate into explaining
moral intuitions away in order to get rid of their residual obscurity.

(p. 119 below)

Kolnai made repeated attempts to hit on a good name for the
moral philosophy he had in mind. At the beginning of his paper
'Moral Consensus' he writes that his investigation implied for him
'a defence of the intuitional view of morality—in the broad sense
of the not very felicitous word "intuitional", for which I might
substitute other words such as "intrinsicalist", "non-naturalist",
and above all "non-reductionist".' It is plain that by intuitionism,
or what was good in it, Kolnai did not mean a sterile doctrine of
cognition but 'an analytical ethic based on the phenomenology of
value consciousness'. If it is true that

In general our vision of things as they are is largely dependent on our
emotive and valuational attitudes; and conversely, our valuations, including our moral views, are largely contingent upon our perception and
construction of reality and our appraisal of the factual importance of
various things and forces in its order

('Erroneous Conscience', pp. 8–9 below)

then is the demand (implicitly conceded by doctrines of moral
'inspection') for a separate reckoning of the cognitional and
affective aspects even coherent?

By intuitionism, or whatever it was to be called, Kolnai also

---

[4] Some philosophers addicted to the language of principles have stressed the
element of particular judgement which is involved in applying and simultaneous-
ly refining principles. But if this is thought of as an exercise of the moral
consciousness or feelings, or as a fresh response to a concrete situation etc., then
there is here an unacknowledged reliance on precisely what Kolnai wanted to
insist upon.

meant a certain programme for the elucidation of the content of value judgements (aesthetic, hedonic, moral etc.), and an elucidation of the relationship of their truth-grounds both to experience and feeling and to *consensus*, which is not for Kolnai a mere epistemological source of moral valuation but intrinsic to their content. Our awareness of consensus or the need we feel for it, is an integral part of the consciousness underlying moral valuation.

On these matters the reader can do no better than study the 'Moral Consensus' paper, leaving behind the preconceptions of the textbook attacks on intuitionism, giving the doctrine which emerges the benefit of a theory of mental experience which is not in itself absurd (either in the behaviourist or the traditional introspectionist fashion) and conferring upon it, if that is important to him, a new name. Where he may find he wants collateral information is Kolnai's understanding of the phenomenological method.

Kolnai used to explain phenomenology for English audiences by defining it as the opposite of phenomenalism, as the reasoned rejection of Ockhamite preferences for minimum presuppositions, and as the study of the *appearing of evidence* (of different degrees of certainty and different qualities)—of evidence as it presents itself as opposed to evidence as *mere appearance*. And of the merits of the method he claimed:

Subtlety, deep introspective analysis, and passionate concern about cautious distinctions are the forte of phenomenology at the expense of convincing rigour or handy standard formulations or directly applicable moral (or more generally practical) guidance. In some respects phenomenology presents striking analogies with Moore, with the later Wittgenstein, and with linguistic analysis, . . . in spite of the so-called Idealistic and Cartesian turn of the later or middle later Husserl, the central attitude of Phenomenology is emphatically objectivistic and typically anti-Cartesian. Nothing could be farther from it than the Cartesian myth of the *Cogito* (the attempt to understand the world starting from *one* incontestable truth—or alleged or supposed truth) . . . From spurious and misleading intuitions and simulacra of evidences we have no recourse other than to rectified intuitions and valid evidences.

(Intercollegiate Course 1970–2)

In its application to ethics and value-theory this may remind the reader of Aristotle's conception of phenomena—that which is or appears *manifest* (τὸ φαινόμενον ὄν). Speaking of Aristotle Kolnai said

The so-called *Philosophus*, whatever his defects and unworthy snobberies or tricks, had the deepest knowledge of the somehow incurably *circular* character of our cognition of things: whatever the thing or theme in the focus of our attention, some vaguely familiar atmosphere of *other* things must somehow surround and support it.

(Intercollegiate Course 1970–2)

The allusion to circularity links up with two important remarks Kolnai made about Husserl:

Without being an expert on Husserl, I entirely support the realistic and ordinary consciousness interpretation, especially on the ground of the posthumous work *Erfahrung und Urteil* (Hamburg 1948 and 1954) . . . [the] insatiability to stop anywhere constituted [Husserl's] *tragedy*, not the Titanistic tragedy of aspiring to human omniscience and omni-potence (which would not interest him at all) but the Sisyphean tragedy of stamping eternally on the spot . . . trying to pry behind every evidence into something more directly given.

(Intercollegiate Course 1970–2)

and more encouragingly,

What is wrong with Phenomenology is its one-sidedly Socratic tendency to concentrate on the Mind—although in the realist intention of coining out and discussing in rational terms its objective world-experience—taking too little interest in natural reality and man's place therein. . . . [But Husserl's] posthumous book *Erfahrung und Urteil* propounds a grandiose vista of absolute anti-Cartesian[ism]: in other words, the dis-covery, as original as it is epoch-making, but Aristotelian in spirit rather than anything else, that our valid and strict 'scientific' or 'philosophical' knowledge proceeds not from a 'minimum' knowledge of certain and evident truth, the prime error of most philosophies—inspired by prig-gish didacticism—but from our inexplicit *world knowledge* in all its wealth, manifoldness and implication of *order*. Husserl's pet words in this context, 'world', 'horizon', and 'perspective', are by themselves suggestive of an atmosphere as alien to Descartes as can possibly be conceived.

(*Twentieth Century Memoirs*, Ch. VI)

There is a general point about the whole of philosophy here—and a wise one—but there is also a point with peculiar and special application to moral philosophy. In science, theorists hope to find a few principles from which everything else will be deducible. There are more serious reasons than purely aesthetic for wanting that—clarity, the hope that the drive towards it will reveal error wherever it exists, the subsumption of many diverse phenomena under one satisfying description. But in the case of moral philo-sophy what defines the subject is a highly heterogeneous set of human concerns, many of them at odds with many others of them, many of them incommensurable with many others of them. In this case there is no reason to think that what is needed is a theory to discover *underlying order*. This is not a subject after all where very much is hidden. Or rather what is hidden is hidden in a psychological or interpretive sense. There is no question of a secret axiological ordering principle. There is no deeper level of reality comparable to the microscopic or submicroscopic level explored by chemistry and physics which it is the moral philosopher's duty to probe. And where one can make no sense of there being such a level, the idea, urged by some moral philosophers, of finding the 'simplest theory' which will 'save the phenomena' (in the normal acceptation of the phrase) is nearly meaningless. In a physical subject matter where people speak in this way, the word 'simplest' can in the respectable case (where theory is more than a mere curve-fitting exercise) be provided with an independent (but subject-bound) elucidation; and the equations which yield the required curve on a graph can then be thought of as homing, as it were, upon an independent physical reality. In the moral theory case it seems perverse in the extreme to look for anything like this—unless we think of the theorist's principles as homing upon a mental reality, viz. the moral and valuational consciousness from which the whole construction originates. But that is not something hidden or unobservable. It can be consulted at any time and it may be that it can be improved: but not by the regimentation of a theory whose sole claim to authority resides in its fallacious title to express the underlying and hidden laws of that consciousness.

The firmness and decisiveness and human interest of some of the results Kolnai was able to achieve from such a starting point suggest not only that the subject must be begun here, but also that it can be.

David Wiggins
Bernard Williams

I

Erroneous Conscience

1. THE PROBLEM: SUMMARY OF ITS ASPECTS

(a) On the common-sense suppositions that moral judgements are true or false, and that, therefore, conscience can be correct or erroneous, whereas on the other hand it is morally right to follow and wrong to disobey one's conscience, we seem to be faced with a paradox in ethics. That some kinds of conduct are morally right, while some are wrongful and blameworthy, is presupposed in moral discourse and in conscience itself ('I am ashamed of having broken my promise'; 'My patriotic duty commands me to . . .'); yet if the agent is doing what he in entire 'good faith' thinks to be right his conduct cannot very well be immoral, while if he is doing what he thinks to be evil his conduct *eo ipso* is immoral. The traditional solution of the puzzle is that one ought to follow one's conscience, whether correct or erroneous—the agent, anyhow, cannot possibly know that his conscience is erroneous, so long as it is his conscience—but that to hold an erroneous conscience denotes, so far as it is not reducible to mere 'invincible' ignorance of *fact*, a moral defect which implies some degree of guilt. From this we may conclude to a general duty for men, but especially for such as hold a *dissentient* conscience and again for such as find themselves confronted with moral dissent not obviously preposterous, to allow for the possibility that their conscience may be erroneous and to examine loyally the arguments against their moral opinion.

In actual practice, at least in our capacity as appraisers and advisers, if less perhaps as agents, we nearly always take this dualist view, commending a person's moral insight as well as a person's conscientious 'integrity', and blaming moral misjudgement or lack of percipience as well as the various types of unconscientious behaviour. We expect a man to behave rightly, rather than either merely appraise rightly or merely behave according to his appraisal, and thus we consider 'sinning against the light' essentially guilty but also attach a moral disvalue to a person's following his errant lights. And a conflict between these two apparently disparate points of view would strike us as more shocking, more paradoxical, more in need of a special elucidation, than the tension we continually experience between different moral criteria, all on the same level of intrinsic moral appraisal. We find it natural enough that a man's morality should be, not worthless indeed but imperfect, in that he, say, displays a strong sense of justice but little human sympathy, or yields to his generous impulses at the expense of justice; but if a man sticks to his conscience, we feel tempted to regard his morality not merely as better than nothing but as *perfect*, and yet if at the same time he thinks right what we and the like of us think wrong, we again feel tempted to regard his morality as *invalid* rather than merely imperfect.

(*b*) Theorists fond of neat system and sturdy simplification may, of course, try to get round the dilemma by applying 'Occam's razor' to either of its terms. I propose to call 'formalism' the view that the agent's acting or not in conformity with his conscience is the only test of his behaving rightly or wrongfully, though apart from that his conduct may be prudent or unwise, and socially useful or harmful. The converse view I propose to call 'intellectualism'. On this view, subjective 'good faith', regardless of *what* the agent believes to be right or wrong, has no tangible meaning; right conduct depends on true moral knowledge (and, perhaps, on a normal capacity for action) alone, and all wrongful conduct expresses a moral error (or perhaps weakness of will, but never a wilful disregard of what the agent thinks right). I shall argue, in Section 2, against formalism, and in Section 3, more briefly, against intellectualism—endeavouring to show that both Erroneous Conscience and Ineffectual Conscience exist, and that, while distinct from each other, they reveal a certain interdependence.

The point I am chiefly concerned to bring out is that the moral status we feel inclined to concede to erroneous conscience is attributable to it, not by virtue of Conscience representing an inscrutable and unjudgeable supreme principle of 'formal' morality regardless of its 'material' contents, but inasmuch as that genuine Conscience, however erroneous we may reasonably deem it by reference to a specified province of morality, expresses and presupposes the agent's general response, assent and submission to the valid intrinsic principles of morality as we know them. Accordingly, in Sections 4 and 5 I shall try to establish a distinction between genuine Erroneous Conscience and the type of comprehensive principles of conduct to which this description no longer applies. Such principles, seeing the eminently 'conscientious' attitude (in a technical sense) they may command in those who profess them, seem to pose the problem of Erroneous Conscience in a particularly baffling and paradoxical form, claiming as they do the respect due to consistent devotion of self, while at the same time arousing moral revolt. I shall distinguish, then, Erroneous Conscience proper from what I propose to call Overlain Conscience informed by the agent's surrender to a 'non-moral absolute'. I cannot, in the limits of this paper, deal with Dissentient Conscience as such—its argumentative and social aspects, its relation to the moral consensus and traditions of mankind, its possible reformatory and exemplary functions—nor with the interesting topic of supererogatory moral aspirations and of moral obligations experienced with a non-universal, personal or vocational, emphasis.

(c) It is well to bear in mind that—owing to the problematical *sui generis* status of moral truth and the impossibility of grasping it adequately and especially of applying it to the actual moral governance of conduct except through personal insight, reflection, emphasis and judgement—every conscience is virtually dissentient and we constantly live in the presence of at least mild and marginal forms of what impresses us as erroneous conscience, including often enough our own states of conscience reflected upon at some distance. But it is only in certain conditions that erroneous conscience confronts us with the necessity for a practical decision between conflicting moral claims—tolerance or responsibility, respect for conscience or prevention of a public danger, and similar dilemmas—thus making us more keenly aware of the underlying philosophical problem. Apart from such obvious distinctions as that between a conscientious position with a purely private range of reference and one essentially implying public pretensions, between an explicit or rigid and a doubtful or undecided state of conscience, and between various modes of *pro* and *con* attitudes on the spectator's or the public's part (e.g. tolerance and admiring respect, or essential contempt for some kind of dissent and the conviction that it calls for coercive measures), it may roughly be said that the classic conflict only arises between *contrary* positions of conscience: that is, when neither dissentient conscience nor consensual opinion about the controversial point is merely permissive but both are imperative, one being prescriptive and the other prohibitive, or inversely. Even for the philosopher, however, a greater interest may attach to antithetical posisions like 'Fairness to our adversaries is the mark of high morality.—No it is a detestable weakness, a sign of degeneracy' than to anything in the way of mere disagreement about degrees or limits.

(d) In the context of Erroneous Conscience, we use the word Conscience chiefly in the sense of sustained moral opinion, i.e. of moral rules which the agent professes as obligatory or moral standards he recognizes as valid. In so far as the agent feels committed 'in conscience' to principles not properly or purely moral (for example, religious, political or expressive of whatever particular loyalty or appreciation of value), or again, to some particular standard of conduct he would not conceive of as universally binding (cf. *'noblesse oblige'*, *'aliis licet, tibi non licet'* or the various forms of vocational 'ethos' and of gentlemanly ideals), these are still, more or less in the nature of specified contractual or professional duties, derived from universal moral rules or at any rate referable to universally meaningful moral standards, seen in conjunction with the particular circumstances and previous acts of the agent. However, Conscience primarily and properly means, not moral convictions but moral awareness and self-criticism—remorse, warning, acquittal or approbation—in reference to one's own conduct: past, present or tentatively planned. Conscience means, further, moral judgement in the shaping of one's conduct. It is the office of my conscience, not only to enforce my concrete obligations under a permanent and universal body of moral laws it apprehends as binding upon me, but to apply, to specify and to supplement them so as to fit the moral aspect of any actual situation I find myself in; in other words, not only to represent my general knowledge of right and wrong on the one hand and to prod me to do right and to shun wrong on the other, but to tell me what is right or wrong here and now, and thus to inform the morality of my actual conduct.

No doubt, it is easier to discuss correct and erroneous conscience in terms of the agent's express moral beliefs, which are a more solid, knowable, communicable and arguable thing than is the succession of his single moral decisions or of his single states of moral self-awareness; but in speaking of conscience we should not lose sight of the original and of the full meaning of the word. Morally relevant beliefs are not all morally centred beliefs, and a man's quasi-moral beliefs, both express and operative, are not all conscience, nor all his conscience. If one who has carried out in strict obedience the monstrously unjust and cruel decrees issued by an authority to which he is subject by a kind of ideal conviction maintains that he has been acting 'according to his conscience', this may be a very inaccurate description of the real state of affairs. Again, dissentient conscience, in the full force of the term, amounts to more than a mere unusual moral belief: it may connote a significant moral experience, unknown or repressed in the dominant social ambit of the agent, and open up a valid but hitherto undiscovered or evaded new dimension of moral sensitivity.

2. THE EXISTENCE OF ERRONEOUS CONSCIENCE

(*a*) On the formalist view, Erroneous Conscience—except in the trivial sense of conscience as moral decision *hic et nunc*, misinformed as to facts—is logically impossible, seeing that Conscience is the ultimate test of morality, with no standard above it by which it could be verified or falsified. There is one apparently formidable argument in support of this view: the intuitive evidence of the reflection that nothing can be more obviously moral than to intend to do the right thing, and nothing more obviously immoral than to intend, from some non-moral motive, to do a wrongful thing. The argument does prove something, but decisively less than what it purports to prove. It is indeed never morally indifferent, but always highly important, whether the agent believes himself to be acting rightly or wrongfully. But the assumption that the most *obviously* good or bad feature in the agent's conduct exhaustively defines its goodness or badness is nothing but a plausible fallacy. It is somewhat like believing that, say, any even number must have more factors than any odd number. In fact, the moral rightness of an action I perform with a wholly satisfied conscience may be greatly impaired by the defects of my conscience, e.g. my failure to understand that even a scoundrel must never be judged unfairly; and the badness of an action I perform with an uneasy or guilty conscience may be slighter than it would otherwise appear if I have a morbidly scrupulous conscience or if my illicit action is inspired by a morally good motive, e.g. compassion or righteous indignation.

In a recent novel about intelligence-service intrigues, I read the sentence: 'It was obviously Dr Thompson's duty, as a patriotic British citizen, to announce his discovery to Major Macpherson.' This sounds so peculiarly silly, not because it is slightly redundant, but because, though in fact it is only a piece of careless writing, as it stands it seems to invite a formalist interpretation: there are two classes of British citizens, patriotic and nonpatriotic; for one of the latter, it would not be a duty to inform Major Macpherson; but the hero, unfortunately for him, happened to belong to the patriotic set, wherefore in his case that duty with its attendant discomforts did arise. This strikes us as preposterous because 'to be patriotic' is not a distinctive natural characteristic or a matter of taste, entailing moral obligations when it is present, but is itself a moral obligation of men by reference to their respective countries. It is true, none the less, that if Thompson had had a nonpatriotic or unpatriotic, a defective or erroneous, conscience, his omission to inform the Major would in one sense have been less wrongful, in that he would then have acted 'in good faith' as contrasted with prevarication. As it was, this act of disloyalty to his conscience might have marked the beginning in him of a process of moral backsliding; whereas, if he had not been a patriot anyhow, he would have suffered no such moral 'fall'. And yet, do we, as patriots or even on general moral principles, prefer the 'integrity' of a nonpatriotic to the guilty lapse of a patriotic Thompson? Hardly; at least, certainly not *a priori* and regardless of the possible qualifying circumstances. Our conscience tells us that we ought to be loyal citizens not because we have that kind of conscience but because men, including Thompson and ourselves, ought to be loyal citizens; it tells us that we, including him, ought to obey our consciences, but also that we ought to have the right kind of conscience, which among other things implies a patriotic conscience.

(*b*) As I have just admitted, Conscience is *also* reflexive and self-emphasizing. I may have the remorseful feeling that in a certain complex and morally charged situation I did not listen to the voice of my conscience, or warn myself, in view of an impending practical decision, in terms like 'Well, this course seems to offer great advantages, and something might be said for it on moral grounds; still, in some essential way it would go against your conscience'. But all such modes of conscience are secondary; they presuppose a primary reference to moral categories outside conscience—similarly as my promise to pay £100 to Jones does indeed create my obligation to pay £100 to Jones but does not create my obligation to keep the promises I make. My conscience of yesterday which I am now sorry to have silenced or cheated, or the present one which I am now telling myself to obey, was not or is not a conscience about conscience but a conscience about duties of honesty, loyalty, neighbourly love and the like, and about offences opposed to such duties or virtues. The moral qualities and rules thus referred to are not a function of my conscience but prior to it and constitutive of it, even though my conception of them has been shaped and amplified in a way involving the workings of my conscience. Just as a General whose orders did nothing but enjoin upon his subordinates the duty of obeying his orders would not actually command anything, a conscience demanding only to be always obeyed would in no wise direct the agent's conduct and would not in fact be conscience at all, but merely a phantom of misguided philosophical lucubration.

Any attempt to save formalism by propounding a weaker variant of it, which would no longer entail an infinite regress, is doomed to failure; for it must either surreptitiously bring in objective moral standards over and above conscience, or lapse into arbitrary naturalism and immoralism, superseding conscience by the agent's or somebody else's good pleasure. Thus, if we construe the sovereignty of conscience in the sense that a man behaved rightly in conforming unhesitatingly, from moment to moment, to the random hits and improvised glimpses of his conscience, we no longer imply that right conduct *means* conduct in conformity to conscience. We have switched to the gratuitous assertion—wholly out of accord with experience and common sense—that conscience *finds* what is right and what is wrong here and now by a succession of unreflective intuitions and unarguable decrees; or else, abandoning this mystical and unanalysable object of inerrant intuition, we simply mean that what a man ought to do is what he wants to do, and that conscience is nothing but the dominant impulse, craving, fancy or whim of the moment.

Again, if we suggest that the agent should adopt as rule and incarnation of his conscience some extraneous interest, system or authority, serving henceforth that objectified Principle with punctual fidelity and unflinching zeal, we are no longer holding on to a morality of Conscience. For, if the agent chooses to lean on a specified authority for intrinsic moral reasons, his conscience is no longer the definition but merely, as in the common-sense view, the guide and director of his morality, dependent on objective standards of right and wrong which it is meant to represent and to divine, not to supplant or freely to invent; whereas if the agent decides to subordinate his conscience to some outside concern or entity from any vital or historical, morally irrelevant and contingent motives, he will be adjusting his conduct not to his conscience but to something else. A conscience thus put out to lease is not conscience but the evasion of it, except for that specious semblance of conscience which may be discerned in one's blind obedience to the authority that happens to be in command.

Conscience that cannot hope to be correct, and accordingly cannot fear to be erroneous, is not Conscience in the established and dignified sense of moral self-criticism, judgement and belief—which essentially aspires to truth and tries to escape from error, and in fact expresses the agent's endeavour to ponder and argue his decisions in universally valid terms and to make his conduct *justifiable* in the open court of objective morality. Mere 'conscientiousness' as a habit of discipline, a descriptive psychological feature opposed to impulsiveness and whimsicality, is indeed one moral requirement and is independent of true or false moral beliefs; but it is only a subordinate aspect of Moral Conscience and anything but a supreme directive principle of conduct. A 'conscientious', i.e. painstaking, methodical and devoted, secretary or accountant of a burglars' association is hardly a better man than a generous and high-principled but somewhat self-willed and unpredictable servant of an estimable philanthropic cause.

(*c*) Another argument for the existence of Erroneous Conscience lies in the fact that we sometimes feel remorse over such past

2

actions of ours as we performed not against our conscience but with a definitely assenting conscience. True, in regard to some moral mistakes in our past history we may feel shame and annoyance rather than remorse proper; this points to Erroneous Conscience not through any fault of the agent's but operating guiltlessly in perfect good faith: 'invincible ignorance', as traditional language has it. But whether I say 'What a fool I was to believe that! Alas, I couldn't help it!' or 'Damned fool that I was! I ought to have known better', my present conscience criticizes not only my past conduct but my past conscience. More, when at grips with a present or recent moral problem of some complexity, I am likely to say in a tone of bemused hesitation, 'My conscience tells me I'd better do this, and mustn't do that'—revealing a tinge of reserve and doubt, an admission that my conscience might be mistaken. Indeed, when we feel very certain in a moral matter we rarely invoke our conscience: 'My conscience tells me I mustn't forge bank-notes' is less natural language than, say, 'My conscience tells me I ought to inform Smith that Brown is plotting against him'. We recognize, then, that we are responsible not only *before* our conscience but also, within limits, *for* our conscience; that we are obliged to 'apply reasonable care' in shaping our conscience (*se faire une conscience*) so as to keep it sensitive, enlightened and well informed, and to safeguard it from error.

(*d*) Finally, Erroneous Conscience exists in virtue of the intimate linkage between our moral judgements and sensibilities on the one hand, our knowledge and interpretation of facts on the other. Of course, owing to a gross error of fact a person may commit grievous 'material' wrong without any trace of guilt or erroneous conscience on his part. But sometimes the position is altogether different. Erroneous conscience may lean on intellectual delusion or misconception as a kind of collateral support, or indeed be occasioned by it. In such cases, theoretical error not only causes the agent's conscience to be misapplied in fact but colours its intrinsic content and distorts its emphasis. Thus, the moral error that it is not wrong to maltreat animals is often fused with, perhaps conditioned by, the factual error that animals are scarcely more than unconscious automata and incapable of feeling pain in any sense comparable to human suffering. The erroneous conscience of Pacifists is mostly linked up with false opinions about the nature and causes of war; that of nationalists and racialists, with certain historical delusions; that of Marxists, with their sham-scientific theory of social institutions. In general, our vision of things as they are is largely dependent on our emotive and valuational attitudes; and conversely, our valuations, including our moral views, are largely contingent upon our perception and construction of reality and our appraisal of the factual importance of various things and forces in its order.

Perhaps it might be said that misinterpretation of facts as distinct from isolated errors of fact will, in a morally relevant matter, contextually imply erroneous conscience. For the connection of our more specific and psychologically more vulnerable moral intuitions with the more general and more incontrovertibly evident ones implies our knowledge of facts and their connections. Therefore theoretical error may not only alter our actual conduct, inducing us to misapply our valid moral insights, but interfere with some of our more specific moral intuitions, depriving them of their central support—their resonance in our more general moral experience as it were—and thus cause them to wither or force them out of our dominant consciousness. Thus, for example, my spiritual infatuation for a man of brilliant qualities (including, perhaps, some moral accomplishments) may mislead me into overlooking the fact that he is mainly an impostor. By virtue of this neat error of fact I may further be goaded into the moral error of believing, not indeed that imposture is right, but that there is nothing morally wrong with the habitual use of specious persuasive rhetoric in furthering some magnificent sounding design, failing as I do to realize the categorical nexus of this looseness of discursive practice with the cruder and more blatant forms of dishonesty with which it is frequently and significantly, though not necessarily, associated.

3. ERRONEOUS CONSCIENCE AND INEFFECTUAL CONSCIENCE

(a) I shall take for granted, rather than argue at length, the thesis, opposed to intellectualism, that conduct can be at variance with the agent's conscience, and that, accordingly, a correct conscience may not ensure right conduct: '*Video meliora proboque, deteriora sequor*'. Whoever is unable to confirm this from his own experience is entitled to our boundless admiration either as a born saint or as a prodigy of erroneous conscience. The intellectualist view originates, I think, from three main sources: (i) the pedagogical postulate that right conduct should be 'teachable'; (ii) the failure of moralists—a Greek heritage still far from wholly discarded—to distinguish in a sustained manner between morality and practice; and (iii) the false assumption that the agent's conscience must be a simple thing all of a piece—for it seems logically odd that one should, even for a moment only, 'choose evil' unequivocally and wholeheartedly. I will forgo (i) altogether; but (ii) and (iii) are more relevant to the subject of Erroneous Conscience.

(b) How can one possibly choose what one believes to be wrong, reject what one believes to be right? Ineffectual conscience might appear to be an unreal, a merely conventionally pretended conscience; and all wrongful conduct, based on erroneous conscience (including complete lack of moral awareness in certain respects). But the fact is that we constantly choose on some grounds what we would reject on some other grounds, or conversely. This is precisely what choice means: our numerous, and in part changing, concerns clash mutually in various ways, and we cannot pursue them except by restricting and postponing them, by choosing to favour one and renounce another temporarily or perhaps definitively. The mutual attunement, scaling and ordering of our concerns, with 'ends and means' as one of its aspects, is called Practice. The course of action we thus choose as practically best, or better than the nearest possible alternative, would appear analytically to constitute our actual conduct. If I have decided that *this* is the best thing for me to do here and now, how could I go and do something else?—unless, betwixt the cup and the lip, some change in circumstances supervenes or some factor which I forgot when taking my decision, now makes itself felt. Suppose I decide to undergo an operation, or to approach a person in authority, but panic fear then prevents me from carrying out my resolution, whether I formally revoke it or just leave the matter in abeyance; in this sense, even practical decision may turn out to be ineffectual.

Moral approval, however, is not practical choice. My moral concerns are only one among my classes of concerns, although it is true that the practical ordering of my concerns as a whole is itself to some extent a moral requirement, and that, on the other hand, moral obligations as expressed in my conscience essentially connote an overriding claim to absolute validity—analogous, in this, to the concern of self-preservation. Yet an imperious claim, demand or command is not (and is strictly inconsistent with) an irresistible motion. However perfectly my will may conform to my conscience, my conscience is not my will. It is bad, but quite possible, that my sense of a moral obligation should be outweighed by non-moral concerns (and awareness of this possibility lies at the root of Conscience). There is such a thing as a hypocritically pretended or a weak and vague conscience; but ineffectual conscience in itself is no more unreal than, say, my craving for this or that pleasure is unreal because, for reasons of morality, health or economy, I refrain from satisfying it.

However, the habit of living with a defeated conscience may wear down the vigour of conscience and thus indirectly lead to a displacement of moral emphasis, sophistical self-justification, and a form of erroneous conscience: Aristotle's 'incontinent' deteriorating into an 'intemperate' man. Again, erroneous conscience may come to involve ineffectual conscience in that it may dislocate, without altogether uprooting, the agent's stock of sounder moral sensibilities: a fanatic who believes it to be his duty to kill heretics or to kill kings and presidents may yet be keenly aware of the general evil of murder, and in perpetrating or planning his misdeeds act in some fashion against his conscience, albeit prompted by his prevailing erroneous conscience. In fact, though it is certain that he is not acting unconscientiously like a teetotaller who in cheerful company yields to the temptation to drink, it is open to question how far his conduct is governed by erroneous conscience proper and how far by a *sui generis* type of non-moral concerns loaded with a high spiritual tension, i.e. emotive dedication of self to a set of abstract concepts, and varnished with a tint of moral overtones. For non-moral concerns, whether morally rightful or objectionable, are by no means all of a self-seeking, sensual or material order. To this I shall presently return. Let it suffice now that if the force of non-moral concerns obviously accounts for Ineffectual Conscience, their intertwinement with moral accents and aspirations accounts, in part, for Erroneous Conscience; and that ineffectual and erroneous conscience, though plainly distinct, may coexist, and, as it were, conspire mutually.

(c) Conscience is a composite thing, so much so that we precisely speak of conscience in a more exquisite sense of the word when referring to the agent's moral decision or judgement in the face of conflicting obligations than when referring to conduct in obvious accordance with an unequivocal moral belief. The more, in a given context of behaviour, the agent's conscience is called upon to *decide*, not merely to register and to emphasize, what he ought to do, the more likely is it that he will be expressly obeying the dictate of *his conscience* (as distinct from a straightforward moral imperative) *and* doing so with a slightly uneasy conscience, seeing that he has to silence or to argue into consent some protesting voice within his conscience. No doubt, a really conscientious decision (warped or not by moral error) may be reached, and may forthwith determine the agent's practical decision; but moral conflict provides a special point of application for the pull of non-moral concerns, and this makes it even easier to understand the possibility of ineffectual conscience and of its interblending with erroneous conscience.

Immoral conduct, particularly of a more consistent kind, is usually underlain by a guiltily falsified conscience implying both moral errors and a more or less robust disregard for the muffled protests of such elements of conscience as have been relegated to the margin of consciousness: a state of affairs that might be called 'specious conscience'. The point I am trying to make here is that Erroneous Conscience does not necessarily imply 'good faith' but may, without therefore being a mere conventional pretence alien to genuine conscience, connote an aspect of Ineffectual Conscience and thus embody a state of *mauvaise foi*, in the sense of self-deceit as contrasted with mere 'labouring under a deception'. Neither is Conscience *a priori* endowed with inerrancy, as formalism would have it, nor is Erroneous Conscience *a priori* exempt from blame and merely in need of material rectification, as it would appear on the intellectualist view.

4. SOME FORMS OF ERRONEOUS CONSCIENCE

(*a*) What we call an eccentric, cranky or idiosyncratic conscience may be described as an arbitrary over-emphasis or extension, a supersensitive and obsessive application, or a disproportionate observance, of some recognized moral rule or standard; in some cases, indeed, as a fictitious moral emphasis attached to what is normally considered a moral adiaphoron. Thus, beliefs such as that (moderate) drinking, or smoking, or meat-eating, or dancing, is sinful; that all violence and all participation in war are sinful; that one always ought to be not only honest but completely sincere; or again, that one ought never to enjoy anything that all or most people on earth are not yet in a position to enjoy. These and similar errors—so far as they *are* errors—mark a deviation by excess, though of course they may impel the believer to offend against some more plainly valid moral rule which he comes to disregard or at any rate to under-value. Such consciences, though often a social irritant and sometimes perhaps a social danger with grave moral implications, are not *per se* opposed, that is, *contrary*, to current standards: we do not think that peace or a gentle behaviour are evil, or that smoking is a moral duty.

Erroneous conscience of the foregoing kind does not essentially interfere with the agent's general conception of morality; his moral consciousness as a whole may be much like the normal, though it is vitiated by obsession or irrelevancy and by some displacement of accent. But let us not forget that no two of us, either, are likely—or obliged—to maintain exactly the same proportion between our respective moral emphases. My own conscience is anything but sure about the moral legitimacy of meat-eating; some of you may disagree with my moral disapproval of pleasure hunting or fishing, or even of bull-fighting; whereas my conviction that it *may* be necessary to deal sternly with the wicked might expose me to censure under certain Christian, Buddhist or humanitarian standards. Very often, anyhow, a supersensitive conscience will compel our moral respect, even if it appears to us to be tainted with error and a practical nuisance; and it may always be worth pausing to reflect whether, perhaps, it heralds a new moral truth—in however over-stated a shape—or, rather, a moral truth badly neglected, under-estimated, or flouted, in the agent's social environment.

(b) Primitive, undeveloped or crude conscience, or again, a con-science shrunken and obliterated in some respects, may be said to err by defect. Thus, some people tend to believe that whatever is not illegal is morally licit; that they are morally at liberty to do anything they please so long as it does not actually harm others; that if they only comply with their strict duties their morality can leave nothing to desire; that, say, mercy, or intellectual probity, or courtesy and good manners, have no moral significance at all; and so forth. This defective type of erroneous conscience is closely re-lated to rank unconscientiousness or to ineffectual conscience; pre-cisely for that reason, it is less of a problem theoretically, and more open either to intrinsic mending by instruction or at least to correction by social pressure. Deficient morality, so far as its range *does* extend, is still much like ordinary morality, with el-ements of genuine, unfalsified moral consciousness in control of the agent's behaviour. For example, a person who disbelieves that there is anything wrong with sexual licence *may* nevertheless as scrupu-lously refrain from lying and cheating as any of us, and from the same motives. It may also happen that an apparently defective, like a supersensitive, conscience is not actually erroneous but, rather, justly critical of some set or other of conventional moral attitudes; for there may prevail, in a given social medium, rigoristic attitudes one-sided in emphasis and largely sustained by non-moral concerns of doubtful legitimacy.

(c) I would define as 'immoralistic conscience' a type of errone-ous conscience informed by a *doctrinal* negation, explicit and operative, of the intuitive and consensual standards, traditions and rules of ordinary morality. Immoralistic conscience can, so far as I am able to see, only exist in an incomplete sense, seeing that moral appreciations, with a feeling of obligation, inalienably belong to the constitution of man (as does, also, at least a virtual reluctance to comply with the moral demand). An integral and consistent 'Evil be thou my Good' attitude—or, say, a 'morality' of the Ten Commandments professed with an opposite sign—is, I think, quasi-logically inconceivable, in that consistency as such has a positive moral aspect akin to honesty, and the self-transcendence implied in '. . . be thou my Good' could not but work out in a way involving some elements of true conscientious morality. In fact, immoralistic moods are often directed, concretely, against the servitude of moral *conventions* (valid and legitimate as these may be) and fasten on positive and recognized moral motifs like honesty and sincerity as opposed to hypocrisy, or responsible personal decision as opposed to routine devoid of moral experience.

Again, an immoralistic conscience informed by the philosophical doctrine of hedonism—as distinct from the Christian-gentleman conscience of a John Stuart Mill, spuriously interpreted in utilitarian terms—will at any rate compound with various standards of ordinary morality, accepting them as ingrained canons of taste or respecting them as social facts one can only ignore at one's peril. In the most typical case perhaps, immoralistic conscience is a proud ego's way of putting up with ineffectual conscience: suppose the things, decried as immoral, which I practise or want to practise are not really immoral but the mark of a higher morality, or of a higher perfection of man which soars above morality, beyond good and evil; petty philistine minds may call me immoral and confuse me with a common rogue, but this is only the ransom of being actually a superman. This type of character will usually develop a compensatory over-emphasis of some moral standards against which he is not tempted or not able to offend; utterly depraved rakes may nurse a deep moral contempt for homosexuals, and corrupt people take great moral pride in not being like the Pharisees.

Apart from its express revolt against some classic contents and some formal aspects of morality (e.g. traditions and conventions, the concept of obligations, or the distinction between 'my good' and 'the good'), immoralistic conscience implies the general subordination of conscience to some non-moral concern installed in the position of a supreme maxim of conduct. This mental state of affairs is what I call Overlain Conscience, and I am going to devote the remaining Section to its most characteristic and important 'totalitarian' form.

5. OVERLAIN CONSCIENCE

(*a*) By this I mean that the agent subjects and adapts his conscience to some non-moral 'absolute' which thus comes to usurp the office of an ultimate and comprehensive moral authority—taking the place of the recognized universal rules of morality as interpreted, modulated and particularized by personal conscience. What is best fitted to play the part of such a non-moral absolute is a concrete human entity, individual or collective and more or less institutionalized, with an impressive display of values or 'perfections'—seen in terms of vitality and energy, power and success, aesthetic and even moral qualities—and, in the most complete and typical cases, connoting a high 'ideological' pretension: an inherent claim to intellectual and practical direction, to power and influence, and to educative action by inspiration and example. The agent's conscience will accordingly be disconnected from its proper background of overt and discursive moral appraisal, and mediatized or overlain as it were, by a kind of 'possession', that is, infatuation for a concrete human object; possibly, by ideological and institutional loyalty erected into an ultimate criterion of value and a supreme rule of behaviour.

Such a state of conscience is obviously different from mere laxity of conscience and de facto predominance of non-moral concerns over the sense of moral obligation; and it is plainly compatible with a keen response to some moral demands, with moral effort and performance, and, in particular, with conscientiousness in the technical sense of discipline and subordination of self. The personal or social entity to which the agent clings in idolatrous attachment will be experienced by him as embodying, also, certain objective moral values; the religious or political authority to which he fanatically adheres in unreserved surrender will necessarily exhibit genuine moral features and lend itself to some interpretation in terms of morality.

Again, the salient characteristic of Overlain Conscience is not erroneous judgement or displacement of emphasis concerning such-and-such intrinsic moral points, though this is inevitably implied, but the wholesale supersession of Moral Conscience proper by an overriding principle of, shall we say, supra-moral devotion to a concrete being. This principle, whatever spiritual or other values it may represent, and whatever moral references it may enclose, ex suppositis cannot stand for Morality as such: just as Jones's will, character or temperament, be Jones ever so enlightened, conscientious, virtuous and saintly, cannot be the definition, standard and principle of morality. The agent's conscience, of the type here considered, will be erroneous by excess, defect and disproportion in various ways (by conscientious over-emphasis of devotion, 'orthodoxy', discipline and zeal, and a corresponding disdain for 'abstract' moral standards like honesty, fairness, kindness or propriety). It will, also, be ineffectual in that the agent has to suspend, dispossess and repress many a residual or rudimentary, but not wholly absent, element of his ordinary moral conscience: for it is connatural to man to act morally and immorally, in awareness of the fact; to think and to appraise in moral categories. Totalitarian language itself, though kept carefully distinct from current usage so as to impress on men's minds the superior validity of the special mode of being it is meant to convey and to subserve, abounds in ordinary moral references whose meaning is independent of the ideology in question; these ostensible moral appeals are systematically and unscrupulously misapplied in a tactical design but are by no means necessarily and invariably fallacious or irrelevant to the subject they bear upon.

However, unlike erroneous or ineffectual conscience proper, Overlain Conscience means an abdication of Conscience as moral judgement: as a representative and interpreter of universal moral demands. In developing an overlain conscience, the agent alienates the sovereignty of his conscience, transferring it to a concrete Being, Force or Will to whose dictate he chooses to submit or with which he emotionally identifies himself. At the price of his morality's being a radically falsified and degraded one, a sham morality thrown out of focus as it were, he may have secured some psychological advantages: a feeling of greater and more tangible certitude as to the rightness and meaningfulness of his single actions; a feeling of splitless unity between his conscience and his deepmost emotive self; and the feeling of acting on behalf of, and of being pervaded by, a superior Force which embodies 'the Good' or 'Perfection' in an objectified and fully real sense of the word.

(b) I need hardly insist that there is a close correspondence between a moral attitude of this kind and the philosophical position that is termed the Naturalistic Fallacy. There is, on the practical plane, something attractive in the idea of leading a life more infallibly insured against error, moie at one with itself and more 'sublime' by virtue of its communion with a thing metaphysically superior, at the cost of a mediatized conscience: in a word, of evading conscience with a satisfied conscience. This moral temptation is matched to, and partly, I think, identical with, the philosophical temptation of construing morality in terms of more manageable sets of concepts, assimilable to the order of facts and of logical evidence (thus, concepts biological, prudential, legal or psychological, etc.) with the slight inconvenience only of explaining something else in place of morality, while implying morality, at the opportune moment, in a surreptitious, casual and question-begging fashion. Whereas Erroneous Conscience proper is not necessarily linked to any particular philosophical position, Overlain Conscience entails a doctrinal error *about* morality.

(c) It seems to me that Overlain Conscience cannot, in general, like Erroneous Conscience proper, claim intrinsic respect on the strength of its expressing a fundamental allegiance to Right as such and opposition to Wrong as such. For, precisely, the agent's supreme allegiance is not, here, owed to Right but to a particular interest he has espoused, *a priori* other than Right as such; and his distinctive, 'conscientious' hostility is not levelled at Wrong as such but at that which is in the way of the interest he is upholding. Somebody's supreme *pro* and supreme *con* attitudes, even though associated with some moral biases and with the use of various moral words, do not define right and wrong. Right and wrong may not hinge upon this or that specified precept or taboo of the Decalogue or of some similarly apposite code of genuine morality, but they lack all meaning in severance from such codes of rules—or tables of moral intuitions—in general. Formal morality (the sense of obligation) and material morality (the sense of kinds of conduct intrinsically right or wrong) can be distinguished but cannot be separated as if there existed a deontic blank, to be filled indifferently by any contents fancied at random or pleasing on whatever grounds, or inversely, as if right and wrongful kinds of things could be described without a reference to their deontic force.

I respect what I believe to be erroneous conscience in virtue of its being genuine conscience, that is to say, of its interlacing with the rest of the agent's conscience, which for the most part I know or presume to be correct conscience. The moral error to which he is a prey nevertheless reflects his stock of authentic morality. Thus, a total abstainer or a non-violence pacifist may agree with me on most of the other main points of morality. More, though I am definitely opposed to both these attitudes, I appreciate the abstainer's 'erroneous' conscience also in virtue of my own moral aversion from drunkenness and abhorrence of enslaving passions, and the pacifist's, also in virtue of my own moral aversion from violence and abhorrence of wilful killing. But Overlain Conscience is a conscience in inverted commas only; it is erroneous in its basis and ensemble and correct by accident—though, as the case may be, correct perhaps on many important points.

I do not expect a religious person of the fanatical, obscurantist and sectarian type, a totalitarian partisan, or a nationalist or racialist idolater—or, indeed, the infatuated disciples of 'great men' erected into spiritual idols—to display a sound and valid conscience in all kinds of indeterminate respects Rather, I should be prepared to find the obsessive concern emerging at any moment: invading, mutilating, falsifying and throwing out of proportion whatever fragments of true moral insight and sense of obligation may be present, and possibly discarding or blurring today what was overemphasized yesterday in a different pragmatic context That erroneous conscience proper may in its turn connote an obsessive feature and exercise a distorting effect in its area of emphasis, and that overlain conscience may itself have sprung originally from excessive attention to one genuine moral theme, is beside the point. What matters is the differentia of overlain conscience, namely, its transfer of sovereignty from moral awareness, insight and judgement to a concrete object of loyalty and infatuation; even though, in the agent's formal belief, this may still be underlain by a kind of syllogism with an impeccably moral major premiss. The mechanism of overlain conscience, with its naturalistic bent, is superbly, if somewhat indirectly, depicted by Coleridge in a passage of *Aids to Reflection*: 'He who begins by loving Christianity better than Truth, will proceed by loving his own Sect or Church better than Christianity, and end in loving himself better than all.'

'Himself', i.e. the particular attachment of self to the idolized object as a natural fact, in contraposition to the self-transcendence implied in the agent's relation with truths, values and imperatives not defined in terms of the vital and historical context, situation and incorporation of his self. Again, overlain conscience essentially tends to afford an enlarged scope to *derived* obligations at the expense of the intuitive evidence and discursive appraisal of intrinsic right and wrong. I feel I ought to act in such-and-such a way, not because it is the honest, humane, decent or earnest, or even the high-minded, the prudent, or the courageous, way of behaving in a given situation (though it may be all that), but because it is in keeping with the decree of a particular authority, suits a particular 'higher' interest, or distinctively expresses the style of behaviour proper to a particular human type or community to which I belong. Inasmuch as the idol in question is supposed to represent an intuitively evident moral ultimate, e.g. the due response of man to Divine perfection, or social justice, or lawful authority, or the imitation of high examples of moral virtue as known to the agent, the special duties thus recognized by him may be described as derived moral obligations. They are derived from a moral ultimate through the intermediary of his attachment to a concrete entity. Normally, however, they (or the most important among them) would have their place among the direct intuitive data of conscience; and their possible connection with moral principles of a higher order, even though implying various kinds of factual knowledge, would be of a quite different, a far more intrinsic, nature.

One of the most prominent instances of overlain conscience, seen from this aspect, is the Communist 'party-line' rule of thought and conduct; another, always somehow mitigated of course by the Christian affirmation of intrinsic and universal moral standards, is the totalitarian form of the Roman Catholic attitude and conscience, often called *intégrisme*. It is well defined by Lord Acton's distinction between asking 'What is true?' and asking 'What shall I believe?'; in the words of Jean Domenach, a contemporary French Catholic writer, '*L'intégrisme consiste à toujours majorer l'orthodoxie*'.

(*d*) The test of genuine Conscience lies, not in the agent's profession of a universal moral principle or in his rejection of concrete, particular and embodied moral guides, authorities, exemplars and ideals, but in his recognition as a moral basis and standard of the open consensus of mankind. That consensus is not accurately or exhaustively represented by any specified system, creed, person or collective. It is laid down in the universe of moral intuitions, traditions and codes, which are necessarily incomplete and fraught with ambiguities and inadequacies, and are therefore in need of being interpreted, supplemented, re-stated and re-emphasized by Conscience. Without this primary assent to Consensus—to 'what men think to be right and wrong': the classic standards of intrinsically right and intrinsically wrongful kinds of conduct—the agent's morality is out of focus. To apply the term 'morality' or 'conscience' to a private set of maxims and loyalties, not thus grounded and accredited, is a misdescription. Again, this primary acceptance of Consensus entails a secondary acceptance of a critical and active participation in it: in other words, the selective and statutory task of Conscience. It also entails, far from excluding, a manifold of positive references to concrete authorities, models, depositaries of value and means of orientation in the agent's spiritual and social environment.

The religious, doctrinal, institutional, personal, and various other inspirations and allegiances of the agent are not irrelevant to his morality; rather, they are a condition of his keeping in touch with the moral consensus of mankind and of his building up a conscience of his own. The Naturalistic Fallacy is not *all* fallacious: morality, for all its distinctive emphasis and claim to sovereignty, is confined within the context of Practice, and, however irreducible to other concerns or to the all-round management of concerns, it overlaps in all kinds of ways with non-moral concerns, needs and endeavours.

What constitutes overlain conscience is not the fact of this interdependence, or the agent's awareness of it, but the arbitrary marking-out of one determinate allegiance as a supreme rule of life, over and above intrinsic—intuitive and consensual—morality. It is not, for instance, the attitude of a Jewish or Christian believer whose moral consciousness is centred in the Ten Commandments, but the attitude of one who were to believe that the moral prohibitions of perjury, murder and so forth would be meaningless or trivial *if considered outside their nexus* with particular historical circumstances, metaphysical beliefs, salvational superstructures, and devotional practices.

In a purely formal fashion, arbitrary monism and infatuation can easily be dressed in the deceptive cloak of a universal moral rule 'containing no reference to a proper name': thus, 'Act always in conformity with the instructions, and so as to further the interest, of a specified and identifiable social Force, highly representative of human perfection and effective for human improvement' is, so far, strictly universal. The agent's choice may then fall (or have fallen) on such-or-such-other Entity, according to his 'inscrutable' taste or the contingencies of his history—and, of course, to the different aptness of different social entities to claim and to command a totalitarian kind of loyalty. Such an attitude, though connected with some moral ideas and achievements, is one of spurious morality, not because the prefacing rule is not universal but because the preface is not the substance of the book; because the detour implied in a supreme principle thus fashioned is out of accord with the basic moral intuitions of mankind and entails an alienation of conscience.

(*e*) The objection might be raised that 'different moralities' were possible, 'each as justified as the other': in especial, totalitarian surrender to a particular 'absolute' as well as the morality of intrinsic intuitions and consensual tests. But this is a misuse of language and an attempt to muddle and confound our vision of things as they are. Men, when using moral language—moral and immoral conduct, right and wrong, good and bad character, honesty, knavery, and so on—mean, not an esoteric appraisal by reference to any of their respective and divergent 'absolutes', but an appraisal they suppose to be virtually universal and arguable in the open forum of mankind, of certain types of conduct and their decisive relevancy for judging a person's worth. And they keep on using moral language thus even if they profess some totalitarian loyalty, though they will then inconsistently mix it with distorted totalitarian idiom. Moreover, the philosophical relativism of 'several moralities equally justified' is incompatible with actual adherence to one of *these* alleged moralities.

The relativist philosopher may take an aesthetic delight in the devotion of all manner of sectarians to their respective 'absolutes', but he cannot himself be, say, a Communist, a Nazi, an *intégriste*, and an Anthroposophist at the same time. Indeed, should he choose actually to make any one of these causes his own he must cease to be a relativist philosopher; for the rival absolutes exclude not only the ordinary outlook but one another as well, as also the

broad-minded relativism which commends them on an equal footing. The real sectarian will naturally withhold *his* appreciation
from the abstract admirer of the 'concreteness' of his self-
commitment. Certainly my morality and my moral philosophy are
not the same thing; but a doctrine that precludes its professor
from really adopting the morality it is meant to supply with
philosophical credentials can hardly escape the charge of logical
oddness. (It should be noted that the mutual exclusion of rival
'absolutes' is quite unlike the clash of conflicting obligations in
ordinary moral conscience, or the points of divergency between the
genuine consciences of different persons. It belongs to the essence
of infatuations and idolatries to assert the unique validity of their
respective objects and to evade *bona fide* argument under consensual standards.)

(*f*) On the philosophical plane, the relativist doctrine of 'different moralities, equally legitimate' issues from the plausible over-
extension of the concept of morality: the inveterate confusion
between morality and the higher forms of emotive attitudes and
practical maxims as such. We all cherish more or less strongly
particularized—personal and collective—convictions, loyalties and
aspirations, of high import and manifoldly linked to our moral
beliefs; but these are not so many 'moralities'. It is part of their
meaning to support, to safeguard and to bring out more effectively
our moral positions according to our various temperaments,
histories and circumstances; if they take the place of morality it is
by way of moral aberration.

Thus, the social entities to which we naturally belong or which
we join by free choice embody, among other things, certain distinctive moral features, performances, and accents. Again, our loyalty
towards them conforms to a general moral demand, and in its turn
begets certain derived moral obligations: from our familial,
national, religious, political, etc., affiliations will arise for each of
us a set of moral by-laws, as it were. But our loyalties, though *per se*
a morally valuable and to some extent a morally obligatory attitude,
are at the same time, materially speaking, a non-moral fact of
natural inclination and personal taste, perhaps passion.

For example, the moral obligation of patriotism is different in
logical structure from the moral obligation of honesty. The latter
does not in any way raise the various indeterminate Joneses,
Browns and Robinsons (to whom I tell the truth and hand genuine
cheques, or whom I judge fairly) to the status of a permanent
moral term of reference or quasi-absolute or epitome of value. To
the normal patriot on the other hand his country will be, not just
an incidental point of application for the moral rule 'Be loyal to

your country' but a permanent object of devotion, framework of life and centre of a sphere of duties. Patriotic loyalty may thus come to hold a disproportionate place in the agent's conscience. 'My country, right or wrong', at least as a consistently applied maxim, marks a typical and frequent case of erroneous conscience; beyond that, it may degenerate into an actual rejection of the moral concept of patriotic duty, in that the agent fails to recognize its validity in regard to other countries, and denies respect to patriotism in foreign nationals. This attitude means an inchoate form of infatuational overlain conscience; the totalitarian stage is reached by the kind of nationalism whose devotees look upon the interests or the peculiar genius of their nation, or both, as the supreme standard and test of morality. Here we have a species of overlain conscience, never perhaps so comprehensive and so fundamentally distorted as that which goes with Sect or Party totalitarianism, but philosophically important for being more generally intelligible and observable. National affiliation is a more universally and inevitably given aspect of life than are ideological positions, and few of us who recognize patriotic loyalty as a moral obligation may be free from all traces of the state of conscience warped by nationalist moods and habits of thought.

It is thus, by contrasting overlain conscience as vestigially present in ourselves, together with our normal and valid conscience in regard to the same matter, that we can best gain an insight into its nature. Overlain Conscience is not conscience standing for 'another morality'. It is falsified conscience under the spell of a non-moral 'absolute', and grafted onto that irrecusable interpenetration between moral demands and natural or preferential loyalties which may in certain conditions give rise to a submersion of morality by non-moral concerns usurping its imperative accents and its *sui generis* dignity, and which we all know from our own experience.

2

The Sovereignty of the Object: Notes on Truth and Intellectual Humility

I. THE SUBJECTIVISTIC DEGRADATION OF THOUGHT

Thought, in the sense of thinking, is always somebody's thought. But again, by its very nature, it aims at Truth as such, and not at somebody's truth. This ineluctable paradox—this dialectical tension inherent in the finiteness and the embodied condition of Man's mind—lies at the root of huge difficulties and grave aberrations in our thought-life, and particularly, in that more explicit and elaborate (but virtually all-pervading) form of it which we commonly call Philosophy.

In philosophy, indeed, including every philosophical type of knowledge, vision or reasoning, the difficulty is greater and the temptations are more persistent, not to say more 'classic', than in the types of knowledge that bear upon either mathematical objects or questions of 'pure fact'. In the former domain, we are endowed with a clear intuition of essences and with unequivocal concepts on which we can reason in a mode of sovereign certitude. In the latter, we may well rely upon the direct evidence of the senses and its conceptual fixation, which is safely within our reach. In both, we are capable of unequivocal definition (though this is so because in mathematics we have the power of essential definition, whereas in the strict recording of 'facts' we content ourselves with sheer designation), and employ terms exempt from ambiguity. We employ concepts, that is, whose intended and communicable meaning can be detached easily and completely—at will, we might say— from overtones and associations, from secondary and subjective connotations. Therefore, subjectivism in the field either of mathematics proper or of fact-knowledge proper is limited to the trivial realm of gross error. It constitutes no problem involving doubt about the validity of thought itself. Apart, perhaps, from certain nationalistic myths based on vulgar fraud or rank lunacy, it has not been upheld as a doctrine and has hardly ever given rise to a discussion of principles. Within certain bounds, this holds true even of applied mathematics and in regard to the techniques, at least, of experimental science as well as to the more modest attempts at historical generalization. I am using the caution 'within certain bounds', precisely because these types of research are no longer absolutely separable from interpretation and appreciation, from the sifting of data and the weighing of their 'importance', from the craving of the human mind to descry universal causes behind singular things and to discern a meaningful order in their workings and their interrelationship. Whenever thought passes from the sphere of mathematical objects and their conceptual pliancy into that of existent realities, or again, whenever thought on objects of reality reaches the stage of being properly 'interesting' or 'worth our while' and possibly conducive to wisdom, philosophical implications arise. And with them, subjectivism as well as the wrong method of averting subjectivism—pseudo-objectivism, to put it briefly—are all too likely to creep in.

It is not suggested that we should believe the circumference of the circle to be exactly thrice as long as its diameter, because this would make us (or many of us) feel happier. Nobody contends that Napoleon won the battle of Waterloo, because this would fit in with a more fruitful conception of history. Patients afflicted with sensory infirmities, as a rule more intelligent than the philosophers capitalizing on them, do not proclaim it to be *their* truth that, say, pink and turquoise are one and the same colour. Even the worst professional sophists refrain from challenging the 'trivial' belief that July in the northern hemisphere is a hotter month than January, or advancing the 'original' view that on Monday and Thursday water is heavier than lead. But, were such absurdities put forward, those waving them aside with indignation and impatience would not be accused of purblind dogmatism or stubborn conservatism, anxious to halt the free flight of 'living' thought. Nor, on the other hand, would they invoke against these antics of subjectivism the system of such and such an authority which embodies 'the Truth' and which cannot therefore be called in question without madness, impiety or 'temerity'.

As soon as philosophy enters—and the doors are thrown open to it by the most innocent-looking questions, which the humdrum man in the street and the drab specialist of this or that science are equally liable to ask, nay, unable not to ask—the situation appears wholly changed. Opinions will diverge and will irksomely elude any hard-and-fast test of immediate and incontrovertible evidence. They will show a humiliating dependence on the taste and temper, the interests and traditions, the personal or collective circumstances and antecedents of the subjects who happen to hold them.

Such elements as fashion and *Zeitgeist*, variable degrees and modes of intellectual sensitivity, different 'optics' or 'perspectives', different proportions of stress and of response to values, will inevitably contribute towards their shaping. Argument will continue, no doubt, and indeed grow more heated, but this is because it has come to represent the clash between more or less irreconcilable tempers and mental coinages, and for the same reason it will also tend to be indecisive. The very formulation of the problems, the selection of the objects, the language in which their initial apprehension is couched, seem to bear in them already part of the answer and to be so fashioned as to admit of no other answers sensibly at variance with the preconceived one. Thus the fight of tongues and pens may easily degenerate into a mere exhibition of mutual alienness and dislike. The very use of the terms often makes them reminiscent of different legal tenders with no common standard of exchange between them. Is an 'irrational' number 'given' in experience on a footing with the 'natural' numbers? Or again, are perhaps all numbers but human works of art, 'freely posited' by the mind? Is the colour of a rose as objectively 'there' as its geometrical shape? Is its beauty as real as its colour? 'Could' Napoleon have built an enduring empire by following a wiser policy after his great victories? Has this question a meaning at all? Does history represent, by and large, the unfolding of a moral drama? Is it, perhaps, readable in terms of conflicting group interests spun of the thread of our everyday material concerns? What, again, matters in life, or 'should' matter to *me*? To such and similar questions, no answers of the type of a mathematical theorem or of that of a plain statement of fact are given. Yet it would appear that, if we discarded such questions altogether, we could only lead a maimed and palsied mental life. It would so appear, I say, for in fact, given the complexity of human nature and the interdependence of its components, such an impoverishment of our being would render our bodily life itself impossible.

Hence the various subjectivistic counsels of despair, in one form or another, tempered, as it were, by this or that obvious but arbitrarily chosen link with recognized objective truth: the intellect will do well to adopt such a 'system' of philosophy or at any rate to espouse such convictions as are best suited to its subjective 'conditioning' according to space and time, emotional 'needs', individuality or habits of mind particular to the social environment of the subject, and so on. In reply to the protests or arguments of those who cling to the old-fashioned concept of objective truth, the subjectivists of various shades—naturalists and idealists, pragmatists and vitalists, psychologists and existentialists, evolutionists and relativists—point out that *everyone's* thought, that of their opponents as much as their own, depends on the particular character and situation of the subject, the difference between them and their opponents being merely that they are aware of this dependence whereas the latter are not. Oddly enough, then, subjectivism seems to emerge with a surplus of objectivity to its credit. For if I know that I believe a thing owing, for example, to my glandular constitution or to a certain factor in my up-bringing, I not only know more but possess a knowledge *more independent of my subjective circumstances* than if I simply cherish that belief on its merits—that is to say, in the mistaken belief that it is true. The trouble is merely that, having thus 'seen through' the real determination of my belief, I shall no longer hold it, or shall hold it in the improper sense of 'professing' it while in fact I am convinced of its untruth or at best of its objective irrelevance. I now believe to have true knowledge, not of the object of what was hitherto my belief, but, say, of my glandular constitution and its effects on my intellectual leanings. But, according to supposition, this newly won knowledge must also be subjectively conditioned, and therefore invalid. Hence the apparent victory of the subjectivist turns out to be his own undoing. In order to be able to apply consistently his 'unmasking' principle of explanation to some particular belief, naively and uncritically held by a given subject, the subjectivist is obliged to concede the basic presupposition of objectivism, the ordainment of thought to Truth as measured by its conformity to the Object. Thus his accidental discoveries are so many witnesses to his essential error.

Thought no longer aiming at objective truth is no longer, properly speaking, thought at all, but the mere vital manifestation of a nature bereft of rationality, which usurps the reason-made apparatus of signs and counters, the concept-language of thought. It is the dying outcry of thought on the point of committing suicide. To put it differently, subjectivistic thought, as contrasted with a merely 'prejudiced' or 'biased' one, is strictly and explicitly self-defeating. It is comparable to the veterinary student who is said to have believed that a horse consisted only of the diseases which seemed to compose it in the schematic drawing on the title-page of his textbook. In reality, all thought proper, even though biased, unilateral and subject-conditioned, is directed to the object. 'Intentional' object-reference is its nerve and backbone, its prime constituent, the distinctive feature that makes it thought. In its findings, therefore, however lopsided and defective they may be, truth is mingled with error. If they are in need of correction they are also capable of correction. That is why the divergence of tastes and tempers stimulates rather than stops argument. Discussion goes on *because* in his heart of hearts everybody knows that it may not be fruitless. Nor is this all. Even before all formal discussion with philosophical opponents, in our rational operations—the gathering of observations, the comparing of data, the drawing of inferences, the building of a conceptual framework for new sets of observations, the critical examination (in the light of experience) of our emotionally tinged 'intuitions'—we *do* continually overcome our subjective biases and predeterminations, surmount our subjectivity, deliver up the kingdom of our intellect to its lawful Sovereign, the Object; briefly, in a sense give the lie to the dictum that 'nobody can leap over his shadow'.

The passage from ordinary ('mathematical' and 'sensual' or 'historical') to 'philosophical' knowledge, then, involves no absolute breach of continuity, no unbridgeable abyss and no rank chaos or incurable anarchy taking the place of certitude, order and receptive openness to the Object. It means, rather, the rising from an essentially *easy* to an essentially *difficult* plane of science, where we require new helps, methods and tests; new checks and restraints, cautions and guarantees—in a word, habits of thought adapted to the purpose. In addition to the basic experience of the philosophical 'wonder' itself, with the new dimensions of intellectual sharpness, reflectiveness and conscientiousness it may call into play and keep in being, what are these 'helps' to which we must turn in order to be able to 'surmount our subjectivity' and install, in the field of our thought, the sovereignty of the Object? For brevity's sake, I may as well propose a fourfold division of these indispensable supports of valid thought.

(1) He who philosophizes must keep in as close as possible touch with the world of his ordinary experience—simple and complex, particular and general, outward and inward, speculative and effective. Roughly, this corresponds to what the Scholastics have called *resolutio ad sensum*. Truth must be linked to truth, and all thought be responsible before what is already established with absolute or at any rate with greater certitude. The professional philosopher, then, must be humble rather than haughty towards his humdrum everyday self. Otherwise the greater heights in which his thought is soaring will collapse in a mirage of irrelevant imagination, or prove to be a mere flatland of technical routine, irrelevant and deceptive. For this reason, also, the professional philosopher should from time to time train himself, notwithstanding his need for a special terminology, in the art of expressing essential parts of his speculation or knowledge in the terms of ordinary—literary or conversational—language. He will find,

perhaps to his discomfort, that such an exercise, far from slackening or soiling his thought, is calculated to make him more alive to his task of intellectual honesty, and to spur him to keener precision and even penetration.

(2) The philosopher, professional or not, must keep in reverent contact with that secular experience of the race, decisively out-ranging the ken of his personal science in however foreshortened a form it may fall within his reach, which is embodied in 'common sense', in the rules of 'good sense' and in the standards of 'tradi-tion'. Never mind the comparative vagueness, inconsistency and mutability of these things, nor that his drawing from these sources may also add to, or confirm, the thinker's personal subjectivity. What matters is their primary role in transcending it, setting it, as it were, against a background of provisional Truth independent of its particular and self-contained determination: confronting the thinker with the Object grasped in a state of solidity it could not otherwise present. To be sure, I can only think with *my* mind. But unless my mind is set to think in tune with the thought of Mankind (which is not, of course, the noisiest 'ideology' that happens to fill my environment at the moment, nor even the particular tradition in which I happen to be reared), my thought is worthless and to no purpose.

(3) Again, the philosopher needs teachers. He needs masters, forebears in a more explicit sense also. In a word, he needs Author-ity to guide, to instruct and to inform him. Here is one more duty of humility issuing from the claim of the Object to sovereignty. In fact, we bow to authority in matters of everyday experience and 'scientific' hallmarking, not to speak of historical documentation. None of us will say that a drug is of no avail to him because it is not the fruit of his own 'creative' invention, that he disbelieves Napoleon's defeat at Waterloo because he did not see it happen, or that any ordinary truth he has learned from others is not really 'his truth' but merely a 'dead formula' as far as *he* is concerned because it has been 'handed' to him like a parcel instead of spring-ing from the 'living depth' of his own mind. Yet truth—inasmuch as it is truth—is truth even though it is philosophical, and can be communicated as such. The swallowing of a hundred such truths does not make me a philosopher, and it may even be harmful inso-far as it may breed an illusion to that effect. Still, it can play a useful part in keeping out errors for a while and in setting the stage for philosophical reflection. The point is that if only I grasp a truth, be it in ever so vague a fashion, within its bounds Truth and not Falsehood will hold sway over my mind. It is infinitely better to know a truth obscurely, imperfectly, not to say verbally, with

little awareness of its backgrounds and implications, without having it connected with one's vital experience and spontaneous thought, than to cling to a falsehood howsoever ingeniously and brilliantly conceived, and howsoever 'stimulating' to one's mental processes. No less preferable is it to owe one's knowledge of truth to its being proposed by competent authority than to glory in self-made sophistry or to stick to any kind of untested and half-baked theory because one has made it up, under the impact of stirring experiences, out of one's own head. But what are the marks of 'competent authority'? It must be a philosophy that has proved its capacity to last; that is, self-consistent; that is, more than the outgrowth of one individual turn of mind or the 'product' of one historical situation; that is, based itself on a manifold transcendence and tempering of subjectivities, thoroughly and expressly objectivistic in spirit, fully alive to the multiplicity of objects and of modes of cognition, responsive to Reality and Value, in close keeping with everyday experience and common sense, and finally, on the supposition that we are examining the matter as Catholics, a philosophy well in accord and intimately consonant with the Catholic faith. To this aspect I will presently return. But let it be noted directly that this final requirement is not so much an arbitrary addition to the foregoing ones as a crowning and a condensation of them. For Catholicism, being the true religion and the all-embracing rule for the good life of Man, in its turn breathes the spirit of objectivism and realism as well as of a hearty intercourse with common sense, and demands a philosophy *intrinsically* sounder than any type of thought disconnected from Revealed Truth—a philosophy, that is, capable of holding its own, nay, of asserting its greater excellence, in a purely 'natural' field of discussion where no appeal to Revealed Truth as such is permitted.

(4) Lastly, seeing that the 'sovereignty of the Object' can only repose on an overcoming and in no wise on a *brushing aside* of subjectivities—can only be exercised, in other words, over a Subject that has been brought up to full receptivity towards it, not over a Subject that has vanished—the philosophizing mind cannot know truth except as set against a background of error. It can only grasp the contours of the object in a groping fashion, by sifting, filtering, pondering the data of its perception, by a method of trial and error, in a suppositious sense at least. It cannot know adequately what the thing is unless it knows what it might be but is not. Hence the philosopher must be conversant with the history of philosophy, and in particular, with the 'classic' errors that punctuate the course of modern philosophy. Hence, again, he must look for guidance, not only to one established philosophical authority derived from a

world anterior to most of these errors and surviving as it were on the margin of this modern world of errors, but also to those 'modern' philosophies, in the chronological and genetic sense of the term, which represent *specific reactions against the errors* from whose midst they have emerged. If no latter-day doctrine, however sound its primary impulse and however significant its discoveries, can *replace* the perennial authority of Catholic objectivism as embodied chiefly in Thomism, on the other hand the various forms of *modern objectivism and realism*, from Reid to von Hildebrand, will equip the student with weapons forged specifically for the purpose in point, with annealed steel from the armoury of minds inured to battle against the most pernicious and tempting subjectivist heresies that confront him, in a word, with guidance and support no less irreplaceable. To put it differently—the neo-objectivist tradition which, let it be stressed, has itself borrowed its main inspirations from Aristotelian and Scholastic sources and has in its turn piloted many a straying mind into the safe harbour of Catholic truth, but which has grown on modern soil and in response to the problems besetting the modern mind and inherent in the texture of modern life, may in my view justly claim to be adopted into the canonic body of recognized philosophical authority along with the Scholastic tradition which is equally but even more formally built upon a groundwork of secular and non-Christian thought.

But in this context, I believe not to be guilty of any exaggeration in maintaining that few modern thinkers, if any, have a title to consideration that might equal Dietrich von Hildebrand's: a title validly established not only on the strength of his Catholic credentials, which need hardly be emphasized, but in virtue of his peculiar and unparalleled merits in laying bare the errors of modern subjectivism especially in the field where they are most plausible, most difficult to cope with, and at the same time most corruptive— Ethics and the Philosophy of Values. The man in whose honour these pages are written (as a poor attempt to repay some of the spiritual debt one among his many disciples owes to him), is not a scholastic, but the greatest living representative of the 'school' named Phenomenology, and thus, in one sense, is highly 'modern'. At the same time he is the living epitome of the intellectual principles, habits and attitudes that *stand most opposed* to the deleterious philosophical errors specifically listed in the Encyclical *Humani generis* as poisons infiltrating at various points the thought of Catholic believers responsive to their specious appeal rather than to the solid but difficult truths Thomism has to offer. The simple alternative 'Either "Thomist" or "Modern" ' is obviously inadequate, invalid and misleading. To uphold it is to reject the co-operation of precious auxiliaries in the fight for objective Truth, and thus to betray—out of a narrow and prideful spirit of sectarian fanaticism, not unmingled with intellectual sloth—the essential cause which Thomism itself is destined to subserve.

2. THE PREROGATIVE OF THOMISM

The Church would give up her own identity, were she to part with what she commends as the *Philosophia perennis*. We know that the cause of the Church and the cause of Truth are one. In the strict interpretation of 'The Thomists', taken in the sectarian sense of the term, this implies a formal identification, we might also say an equipollence, between the Thomist system (given, of course, its 'authentic' content, on which full agreement is far from obtaining among the prominent Thomists), and 'philosophical truth' pure and simple. Together with many others, I no less strictly differ from this 'strict interpretation' and hold that the Church, as is right and reasonable, imposes nothing like an implicit belief in all Thomist assertions or in the exclusive legitimacy of Thomist methods and formulations in matters of philosophy, but a primary, thorough and reverent study of Thomist doctrine as the time-proven, the classic, the most comprehensive deposit of deep philosophical truths and enduring formulations, as the widest framework in which to approach the universal manifold of objects, and as the firmest and most elaborate safeguard against the subjectivistic suicide of thought.

Thus interpreted—as privilege, that is, not a monopoly, as a prerogative, not an arbitrary and fetishistic totality—the *ab ovo* pre-eminence accorded to Thomism is wholly consonant with the 'sovereignty of the Object' and the corresponding principle of intellectual humility. It is, indeed, not an easy and automatic business for the mind to 'lay itself open' to the Object and to receive its likeness, but a highly difficult task for which it must be properly trained. In order that it may grasp the universal and hidden aspects of Truth it needs more than an 'unprejudiced' resolution to do so. It will have to be taught, disciplined, provided with a stock of certitudes and probabilities already established and with an armature of concepts ready for use. 'Initial doubt', far from being a magic key to knowledge, is the best means of blinding the intellect from the outset and of cutting it off from the Object—thrusting it, as it were, in the midst of a chaotic welter of impressions, presenting it with a preconception of the world as a whirlwind of undistinguishable particles deprived of quality. Truth is not a thing on which the intellect will finally alight out of a state of dis-oriented flutter. On the contrary, in order even to develop an imaginative and tentative mode of approach supposed to lead it somewhere, it needs prime principles, initial certitudes, a heritage of truths and a loan of beliefs, a borrowed treasury of concepts and categories: briefly, a good deal of anticipated results which it has to take on trust and a set of implements which it can only obtain from the stores of 'Authority' and not from its own untutored vision of the Object. Thomist doctrine has the first claim to such an office of 'magisterial' authority, owing to its exquisitely objectivistic and realistic cast, to its glorious roots in the objectivistic tradition of Pagan antiquity and its remarkable enrichments by the great Commentators, to its average preferability to other trends of Scholastic thought, and to the fact of its being explicitly commended by the wisdom of the living Church.

It is one thing, it might be countered, to study a given body of philosophical doctrine with an historical intent and another to 'believe' it. In 'science' proper, these two lines of pursuits are neatly separated. For example, we generally study mathematics with scarcely any reference to its history, or to one mathematical 'school' which we should prefer to its rivals. We study, say, Euclid as a good textbook of geometry—much as we may study Hall and Knight as a good textbook of elementary algebra.[a] But philosophical thought, though equally ordained to truth and equally bound to the laws of rational argument, is an incomparably more difficult, fragile and delicate affair, fraught with much greater temptations to error, essentially steeped in obscurity and liable to confusion, stricken with the curse of dissension even on what would seem to be 'elementary' matters. It is not independent of man's conception of himself and of life as a whole, and therefore it is specifically in need of qualified guides towards the Object. Its most essential aspects, those sought for in this mode of inquiry, are at the same time most elusive as regards scientific elaboration and a sustained sense of direct and communicable evidence even though they readily enough yield certain primary certitudes. Thus it is that we find, outside the pales of Thomism and of Scholastic tradition, not plain common-sense knowledge but a witches' sabbath of 'schools' bitterly or even fundamentally at loggerheads with one another, with scant title to authority but often bristling with a sectarian and provincial authoritarianism, and mostly bearing in them the seeds, or openly displaying the flags of an arbitrary subjectivism. To withdraw from this landscape of the Modern Mind to the tidy yet richly furnished and by no means easily penetrable halls of Thomism conveys an experience much like leaving a lunatic asylum to enter a *real* high school and a habitable abode for the mentally sound, though with all the obvious defects one may expect both on the teachers' and the pupils' part. To be sure, the study of Thomist doctrine cannot be tantamount to philosophical inquiry *simpliciter*. But it is justly conceived of as a study not merely historical but properly philosophical, as a most apposite means to the philosophical *formation* of the mind.

That this study is sometimes apt to degenerate into a kind of parrot-like learning by rote of texts and formulae—including 'demonstrations', 'solutions of difficulties', ways of 'disposing of objections'—is not something inherent in the doctrine and is entirely contrary to the intentions of the leading and serious sponsors of Thomism, however 'strict' or fanatical. To study Thomist doctrine is, above all, to seek to *understand* it. This endeavour necessarily involves *philosophical inquiry* on a vast scale and an acquaintance with many kinds of objects. Its results, even though limited and in some ways distorted by an undue emphasis on 'keeping within the system' rather than keeping it in the subordinate role of one adit to the core of the Object, are likely to warrant the assumption that a fairly wide and balanced philosophical knowledge has been acquired by the student.

Nor does the objection hold that Thomism is a 'dead' philosophy artificially kept alive, a petrification of Greek and medieval thought out of tune with our own mode of intellectual and affective experience, irrelevant to the problems of modern life which we must willy-nilly recognize as ours, and thus only leading us away from a conscious thinking-out of our lives, an adequate mastering of its problems and a genuine contact with *the* objects that confront us. The danger is doubtless real, but there is a corresponding advantage all the more precious. Detachment from what actually and psycho-physically—not to say, 'topically' or 'existentially'—surrounds us is at least as essential to philosophical thought as attention to it. In other words, it is an all-important precondition of attending to it properly. That we are not only *these* men placed in *these* situations but also the offsprings of Christendom and scions of the Syrian-Greco-Roman civilization to which we attach the puerile label of 'antiquity'; that we are not only men of this historical lineage either but also *men*, and therewith, again, also animals and spirits; that in order to see a thing in its all-round perspective we must first set ourselves at a distance from it; that in order to submit to the sovereignty of the Object we must first of all renounce our allegiance to fashionable opinion and extricate ourselves from the web of the Moment; that present-day 'science' is not a pinnacle of human wisdom but a path towards the Object abounding in thinly overlaid pitfalls; that the vital 'stimuli' of our thought need nothing so much as being balanced by our becoming domiciled also in models of human thought remote from our immediate experience; that our fluid impressions and flashes of intuition, so as to be raised to the status of objective knowledge, need not only the corrective of our spontaneous reflection confronting them with one another but also a setting of rigorous thought, not of our own making, comparatively timeless the more as it derives from types of civilization more instinct than ours with contemplative habits—these considerations, as weighty as they are elementary, are what the railer against Thomism as a 'dead' body of doctrine and enthusiast of 'living' thought is only too prone to neglect. Yet in reality, the fact that a type of philosophy is 'living' —that is to say, in vogue just now, infectious as it were, and closely interrelated with the vital situation of this particular society at this particular moment—is, if anything, a *prima facie* evidence *against* it.[b] What *should* indeed be 'living' is a person's actual thinking as such, but this is not by any means necessarily a result of its being copied from thoughts that are 'in the air' about him. Neither is it so important as that his thought should be essentially true and aware of perennial truths. What I suggest, therefore, is not the *tour de force* of a Thomism dressed up as 'modern', and trimmed into being directly and mechanically 'applicable' to all problems of modern life, science and philosophy. Even less do I advocate a 'synthesis' of Thomism with what is 'most living' in the thought of the age. Rather, what I have in mind is a co-operation and spiritual communion between Thomism and what is most *true* in modern thought: most true, most emphatically objectivistic, most congenial to its own attitude, and therefore *most anti-modern*—as anti-modern in the *intrinsic* sense as it could not be were it not 'modern' in the *positional* sense.

3. PSEUDO-OBJECTIVITY AND FALSE HUMILITY

The same reasons that justify the prerogative of Thomism in Catholic philosophy—and hence its eminent relevancy for valid human thought as such—also disprove the possibility for Thomism, however completely digested and developed or supplemented, to be a sufficient and infallible guide to philosophical truth, let alone coincident with true philosophy. Because the philosophizing mind cannot simply and evidently learn 'the truth' and expand its knowledge of truth as can the student of mathematics or the recorder of 'facts', it must lean on a concrete doctrinal authority, on an historically established tradition of philosophical vision, affirmation, procedure and expression. And for the very same reason it must not lean on one alone but take account of several and be familiar with many. Philosophical truth cannot be attained except by the thinker's own judgement—a judgement well informed, well pondered, mature, enlightened by wisdom anterior to his own, manifoldly buttressed against errors especially such as convey a natural appeal to him, a judgement in whose tribunal all foregoing thinkers or schools, invested with ever so much authority, can appear in the capacity of witnesses, pleaders and experts only. Otherwise, the thinker is no longer a pupil whom his master has taught how to see the Object but a moon-struck sectarian whose gaze remains fixed upon the master, with the Object yielding its place, in his vision, to its mere reflection in the master's mind. Instead of being employed as a guide to the Object, Authority then comes to be substituted for the Object. The initial quasi-convictions taken on trust—legitimate, useful and indispensable as such— degenerate into foregone conclusions and final beliefs similar in nature to unquestioned prejudices. They are placed beyond rational discussion and are rendered incompatible with the proper character and aim of thought. It doubtless makes an immense difference whether a belief of this kind is materially true or materially false, seeing that thought properly aims not at its own 'genuineness', 'spontaneity', 'dignity', 'high level' nor at any other quality of its own, but at objective truth. Nevertheless, a truth thus held can never be truth in the full sense of the term, because the mind possesses it in a more or less verbal and, as it were, accidental fashion only. Philosophical truth held in this way is not rooted in a soil of intellectual integrity, that is, in a thought-life integrally aim- ing at truth. Its implications and interpretations in the subject's mind, its psychic intertwinement with other beliefs which may as well be materially false, its sovereign intangibility over and above any possible countervailing object-experience colour it with a tinge of falsehood notwithstanding its material correctness. Hence all philosophy taking its stand on the presupposition that whatever St Thomas teaches is true—that whatever is established by Thomist speculation must be true, and that whatever truth may have been discovered by any other breed of thinkers can be gleaned in a more perfect manner from Thomist texts—is a philosophy downrightly false and out of court, no matter how pre- ferable it still may be[c] to most modern 'systems' or 'currents' and no matter how many sound assertions and sharp-witted analyses it may encompass.

This view is not upset by the consideration that to 'understand' and to 'interpret' the classic texts of Thomism involves by itself a respectable amount of object-knowledge, subtle reflection and independent thought, leaving room for a good deal of controversy too. That is so indeed, and is all to the good. But it is not good enough. The principle of casting every intrinsic objection one may have to the obvious or prevalently received meaning of some piece of Thomist doctrine into the mould of a divergent 'interpretation' falsifies thought from the outset and degrades it from the level of philosophy to that of diplomacy.[1] Less original or stubborn minds will simply acquiesce in the fact—true but stretched beyond its relevant import—that St Thomas or his prominent disciples have been greater thinkers than they, and 'profess', sweetly conscious of giving thus proof of their 'humility'—which is wholly beside the point—the doctrine in question against their better insight which they think is only 'subjective'.[2] Thomists (thus understood) will apply their technical concepts to the problems they encounter in real life or in non-Thomist literature mechanically and schematically, without caring a whit about the inherent *logos* of the matter in hand or of the alien attitude they have to gauge, unable not only to be enlightened by what truth it may represent, but also to criticize it pertinently and to plumb the depth of the pernicious errors it may stand for. Again, therefore, the distance between the concept-world of Thomism and the reality of modern life, with its fabric of moods and conceptual patterns, will often work out unfavourably rather than fruitfully. Instead of setting up an enlivening tension between the mind and the outer world, and of providing the Thomist thinker with a higher state of critical consciousness in regard to modernity, it will blunt the edge of his thought and deaden his sense of intellectual responsibility in the context of all everyday realities and actually obtrusive problems, which he will treat in the same spirit of tame conformance and snug platitude according to modern patterns as he is wont to apply, in his 'formal' or 'abstract' philosophy, to Thomist patterns. This sort of double consciousness, as it were—a complacent, smooth and even smart allegiance to modernity on the one hand, Thomism as an alibi on the other—can be borne with an amazing ease. The sense of thought-sparing comfort it supplies may well explain, to my mind,

[1] The same Thomist—or shall we better say Pseudo-Thomist—who, supposing that he reads any modern author, will jubilantly point out a 'contradiction' in him and perhaps think to have thus 'disposed of him' altogether, may as exultantly revel in the 'obscurities' and the 'ambiguous use of terms' to be found in Thomist texts, as an occasion for subtle interpretation and indeed a sign of the superior quality and inexhaustible depth of Thomist thought.

[2] A widespread 'rationalistic' or pseudo-scientific error will have it that impressions are all 'merely subjective', while an elaborate formal construction of concepts and 'demonstrations' is a pledge of 'objectivity'. Husserl's Phenomenology has greatly contributed towards dislodging this gross equivocation.

part of the popularity Thomism enjoys today, especially in the American world. To be a Thomist out of pragmatism, to conform good-naturedly and profitably to the laws of an atheist universe with the calm conscience derived from a fringe of intellectual 'certitudes' sanctioned by Church authority—here is one ingenious way, rather in favour nowadays, of eating one's cake and having it too. It is a profanation of religion as well as a degrading misuse of philosophy for purposes diametrically opposed to its very meaning; the utmost antithesis of what von Hildebrand has called 'true consciousness' and 'confronting things with one another by confronting them with Christ'.

If this is only a caricature of the Thomist attitude as such, it is yet calculated to throw light upon the hidden strain of pride and subjectivism which warps the nature of all *'ideological Thomism'*, even though practised on a 'high level' and with great personal acumen. By that term, in contradistinction to 'Thomist doctrine', I refer to what I have already labelled as 'sectarian Thomism' and might also call Thomism of 'second intention' or 'raised to the second power'. It is Thomism considered as a magical and exclusive key to all problems within the competence of reason; Thomism as an 'open sesame' commanding access to whatever chambers the human intellect should be, but scarcely is, able to penetrate; Thomism as a religious quasi-obligation whose source is supernatural authority but whose subject is reason in its most specific character as reason, 'reasoning reason' entirely this side of Faith—that self-contradictory freak, then, that *lucus a non lucendo*, which has nothing to do intrinsically with the *contents* of Thomist doctrine and of which St Thomas might well have said, anticipating the famous and brilliant dictum of Marx, *Quant à moi, je ne suis pas thomiste.*

Here is what I mean by 'pride'. The individual mind bowing to one concrete authority—in this case, a genuine and high authority inflated by its overzealous votaries into an idol—and humbly bending its own reason to such an unnatural dictate, forcibly renounces due humility before all other authorities which it ought to consider in the order they deserve: Catholic and non-Catholic, 'scientific' and 'literary' or 'vulgar', personal and impersonal (tradition and common-sense in their manifold crystallizations, and as coming to be formulated in the individual's own 'cogitative sense'). Such a disciple would pridefully believe that, in performing the concept-ritual derivable from the one body of authority he recognizes, he will infallibly 'think rightly' and 'attain Truth'[3] through the means

[3] Of 'Truth' he may have a very material and magical, an 'objectified' rather than an objective, conception: as though it were a kind of 'philosopher's stone'

and at the level of his *reason*—reason not as such subject to and informed by Faith but miraculously and 'providentially' fortified *qua* reason by a short-cut trick whose secret he imagines to have borrowed in an underhand manner from Faith. Even the truths he may really 'possess' and the valid arguments he may have mastered will be tainted with the illusory state of consciousness in which his thinking as a whole is immersed. His illegitimate, short-circuited sense of 'certitude' may well be described as pride wrapped in an illusory sense of humility. Yet true intellectual humility is humility before the *Object* alone, and before proven authorities in so far only as they offer channels of communication (incomplete and subject to correction in the light of other adits and vistas) with the Object; it is incompatible with the pride taken in 'belonging' to a privileged circle of intellectual 'initiates' and indeed with any concept of an esoteric 'science'.

Again, as to 'subjectivism', Thomist doctrine, no doubt, is an eminent type of objectivistic thought. But no sooner do you raise the paragon above the Object itself than *your* thought takes on a basic character of subjectivism. For you have thus ceased to recognize the Object as the ultimate test, the 'measure' of your thought, and would have the Object 'measured' by the system. In other words, you have come to subordinate your global experience and vision of the Object to your allegiance to the system, that is, to one particular subjective circumstance of yours which you happen to overvalue and which lacks all direct or essential reference to the Object. The intrinsic quality of the system is, indeed, in this case, such as to preserve you from many subjectivistic aberrations. The fact, however, is not altered that once you take to *jurare in verba magistri*—no matter whether that *magister* be Aristotle or St Thomas, St Augustine, Duns Scotus or Ockham, Descartes or Spinoza, Kant or Hegel, Nietzsche or Marx, Husserl or von Hildebrand—you have revolted from the sovereignty of the Object and stripped yourself from the spirit of that absolute surrender to Truth which is really a primordial (though by no means the only) mode of our surrender to God of Whose sovereignty over us the majestic 'givenness' and independence of the Object over against our intellect constitute one dimension. Yet without that unconditional loyalty to Truth, that pursuit of truth for truth's sake (not governed by your concern about 'saving the system' or proving your so-called 'fidelity' to any human authority, even though wisely chosen and legitimately sponsored by the Church herself),

---

or a collection of precious stones, or at any rate a set of very definite secrets relating to certain precise facts; a 'thing' one may 'come by' and 'possess'.

without that perspective ordained to the vision of the Object (a
discursive, 'dialogic' medium of approach illumined by several
lights of 'authority', which is not to say by any kinds of it whatever,
gathered at random), you will not be able to grasp fully, to read
correctly and to possess fruitfully even the authentic truths *your*
chosen master really *has* to offer. For who could ever 'know' St
Thomas 'sufficiently' without being acquainted with the modern
contrasts to St Thomas' wisdom (which, whether he likes it or not,
but more likely without his being aware of it, fill the very air he
breathes, and colour the blood that flows through his veins) and
without keeping in touch with the modern *critics* of modernity,
akin to St Thomas as regards his objectivism and many essentials
centred around it? Not only do we not know the Object by knowing
merely what the Master propounds to us. We cannot even know
well what the Master tells us about the Object unless we know
something more about it. And this requires a great deal of personal
experience and reflection as well as a consulting of other 'masters'
too. Sectarian enthusiasm and the subaltern cramming of textbooks
or charting of texts are not 'intellectual humility'. Nor is the un-
avowedly and falsely religious belief in an extant '*depositum
rationis*', from which one has only to 'mine' a ready-made objective
truth, anything like 'objectivism'. Be it a paradox or not, the fact
remains that in matters 'philosophical'—that is to say, universal,
hidden, obscure, abstruse, not strictly proportionate nor immediately accessible to the human intellect, implying an 'outlook' on
manifold but interdependent single things and a 'conspectus' of
the fields of objects that surround us—'possession' ineliminably
and everlastingly connotes 'research' (though possession and not
research itself is the aim and *raison d'être* of research) and truth
cannot be truly 'handed' by any master or commentator except to
him who seeks for it, and who seeks for *it*, not for the deliverance
of authority *as such*. Be it tragic or not, outside the realm of Faith
proper—of dogmas and verities derived from express Divine
Revelation—every human formulation of truth remains, in various
ways and degrees, somehow open to question, criticism, interpretation, revision and correction. I must think with my own reason,
though it be patently inferior to alien human reason (individual
and corporate), and in need of a thousand props of information,
instruction and authority, yet in its ineluctable and *ad hoc* sovereignty *quoad me*,[4] representative of the sovereignty of the Object,
which itself stands for that of God, over *all* mere human reason.

[4] As far as I am a Thomist, I *also* claim such sovereignty for my reason, since
it is my reason that judges Thomism to be the best of philosophies and warrants
my acceptance of it. If, on the other hand, I embrace Thomism merely because

In this sense, which only fools will mistake for pride or self-conceit (or indeed, for any kind of self-appreciation), 'I' cannot inhabit securely the royal palace built with consummate mastery by somebody else, but must patch up somehow 'my' philosophical hovel, in the poet's words, 'on the wreck of a palace such as a King had built'. Only thus shall it be objectively worthy at least of being, in its turn, 'the spoil of a King who shall build'. Only thus may 'I', perhaps—and perhaps not but on no account otherwise—'cut on the timber' and 'carve on the stone': 'After me cometh a Builder. Tell him, I too have known!'

Even the greatest thinkers were disciples of their elders, scholars who had sat at the feet of *their* masters. Surely we need not be ashamed to *learn* philosophy from St Thomas. But 'we' are not worth being taught by St Thomas unless we are thinkers of a sort, which we cannot be unless we are something else besides being 'Thomists' only, and unless we are seekers for truth above all, rather than aspirants to 'faithful discipleship'. In order even to be able to carry the load St Thomas has bequeathed to us—more still, in order to fight St Thomas's battle against the Modern Mind— we must measure his doctrines in the light of our total vision of the Object as well as derive part of that vision from him. As Jacques de Bainville says, *On ne s'appuie que sur ce qui résiste.* But is not St Thomas a definitely greater mind than I am? Assuredly he is. And so are Plato and Scotus, Hume and Russell, Nietzsche and Heidegger, to omit a few others. Yet I cannot help rejecting some of their opinions, if only because they are not always consistent with one another.

But is what *the* Philosopher of the Church teaches not true philosophy pure and simple? Certainly not. For Philosophy, according to its Catholic and Thomist conception, is not a set of truths proposed for belief by ecclesiastical authority, but a work of human reason, though its findings cannot be true if they contradict a revealed dogma of the Faith[5] and though the Church is eminently qualified to advise her children on their choice of masters

---

the Church commends it I derive 'my philosophical truth' from Faith, which renders philosophical truths irrelevant as such. Moreover, the Faith too governs my acts because I accept it. Again, if I keep 'faithful' to Thomism because I have been reared in its tradition, a man with, say, a Marxian training is equally justified in sticking to Marxism. Nothing except 'my reason', frail as it is, can direct me towards Truth; every other 'conditioning' of my intellectual position means subjectivism of one kind or another.

[5] There is no such thing as a 'double truth': what is false theologically is also false philosophically. To be sure, it may nevertheless be historically linked to some relevant point in philosophy, which might still be developed fruitfully in another direction.

to preside over their study of philosophy. [6] In any other sense, there can be no such thing as a 'Philosopher of the Church'. And if Philosophy shall be a handmaid of Theology, the handmaid must be sound in life and limb, that is, the philosophy must be true and truthful *qua* philosophy, and be able to cope with that of the infidels on the fencing-ground of natural reason, outside the Seminary walls, without deriving its principles (in however disguised a fashion) from revealed Faith or injunctions by Church authority. Whoever would stretch the purport of the Papal recommendations about the teaching of a Thomist philosophy in ecclesiastical seats of learning to the point of involving a rigorous and exclusive obligation to 'believe' Thomism down to every detail, swallowing hook, line and sinker, is apt to disserve the cause of Catholicism, and in particular of Thomism, by preaching what is essentially a pietistic mysticism flatly contrary to its intrinsic spirit and closely akin to the Fideism condemned by the Church. It may repose, partly, on a confusion of self-complacent, decreed 'certitude' with objectivity, and partly, again, on a secret conviction of the superiority, in terms of plain reason, of the naturalistic and anthropotheistic Modern Mind—a conviction I, for one, refuse to share. Anyhow, the concept of a Sacred Philosophy (a system, that is, of philosophy which it were a religious duty for us to profess) implies—on the Thomist view itself, as in mine—a blatant self-contradiction, 'sacred truth' being incompatible with the primal and inalienable mode of the human intellect's quest for truth, and thus with the concept of Philosophy. On the other hand, in some respects we may not unreasonably wish for a philosophy more Christian as to its *contents* than is 'strict' Thomism, which in its purely 'philosophical' or 'natural' sector is one-sidedly anchored to a Pagan (that is, Greek) world of experience and consciousness and too far aloof from that of Christian humanity—the variant of 'natural' humanity that we know most intimately, whose mental idiom we speak and whose problems (more than those particular to any other humanity) we are called to think out. This consideration applies chiefly, though not exclusively, to Ethics. To the modern Catholic student, this branch of philosophy too often means purely and simply Aristotle's 'Ethics': a fundamental work rich in thought and abounding in significant problems, but bearing the imprint of one special civilization not ours, in some ways bordering on Naturalism and definitely

[6] Above all, she is justified in pointing out false paths in philosophy, and warning us of them with the stern voice of authority. But neither do I call in question the excellence of Thomism as a comprehensive body of philosophical tradition over any possible rival 'school', though I would not dream of accepting it *as a 'system'*, or of recognizing any 'obligation' to do so.

falling short of the 'natural' moral sense of the average man, be it a Christian or an unbeliever, of Christendom. [7] Moral theology—a splendid treasury of Christian ethics, a storehouse of introspective philosophy among other things, which to a large extent we owe to St Thomas—may not make up for this deficiency, seeing that the lay student is mostly left with a very scanty catechistic knowledge of it, but above all, because Moral Theology by its essence aims at codifying and supplementing the rules of pastoral jurisdiction rather than at the philosophical elucidation of moral judgements or of the forms of moral behaviour. No genuine study of our actual moral consciousness and no pertinent criticism of the popular naturalistic, formalistic and subjectivistic errors in ethics is possible, in particular, without a knowledge of the great British moralists of the eighteenth century and of modern phenomenological and intuitionist ethics. [8]

This need not place us in opposition to Aristotle and much less induce us to disregard him. For the truth is that in his more concrete ethical disquisitions, Aristotle the master and spokesman of *experience* proceeds from the standard moral judgements—'blame and praise'—prevailing among people, wherefore, along with Socrates but in contrast to other types of Greek thought, he may himself be called the founder of a phenomenological and intuitionist method in ethics. Nor am I prepared to say that he was wrong in trying to build his ethics into a 'physical' or 'metaphysical' framework, that is, to connect the concept of moral good with that of good in a wider sense, and thus realistically ground virtue in the perfection of human nature. But the pioneer work he performed with this end in view is anything but satisfactory; it raises a problem of paramount importance rather than providing its solution; it is apt to give rise to naturalistic misconceptions (about the moral good as a 'means to happiness' or evil as a mere underdevelopment) not truly cured by the purely extrinsic adjunction of a 'supernatural'

[7] The standard naturalistic fallacy of assimilating our moral sense, our prevalent modes of approval and disapproval, to the stock of our mere subjective and ingrained 'likes and dislikes' is sometimes echoed by such Catholic ideologists as would reduce all morality to pietistic and obediential motives. Aristotle himself (see text below) is by no means guilty of that fallacy; nor do true Thomists usually display it. But they often tend to confine all points of view 'not supernatural' to those that can be found in Aristotle.

[8] Nothing could be farther remote from the concept of ethics I am urging here than any suggestion of conferring a 'Christian' sanction upon the whole or any set of the subversive social *ideologies*, post-Christian and anti-Christian, which have been in vogue throughout the centuries of modernity (notably, the 'Enlightenment', Utilitarianism and Marxism) and which, even in a man whose mental and emotional life is thickly overlaid by their poison, are sharply distinct from his *moral consciousness* proper.

level of references. Now this 'systematic' aspect of Aristotle's achievement is much more condensable in a set of apparent 'results', more 'teachable' and 'learnable' than his method of analysing men's moral consciousness, just as the dogmatic points in his philosophy of nature are easier to 'catch' than his habit of looking about him, observing things and reflecting upon them in turn. The more express and more specialized students (in the eighteenth and twentieth centuries) of the meaning of moral 'good' are our best helpers in following up Aristotle's methodical suggestion, though the contribution of Thomistic ethics in its formally 'theological' part is no less invaluable.

Thomist philosophy embodies a world of thought of whose wealth even the least mediocre of its countless handy textbooks can but convey a very faint and inadequate idea. Very likely, most important motifs in modern objectivistic speculation can in some fashion be traced back to one or the other of its elements (often hidden or forgotten, unemphasized or unexploited) or at any rate find their place in its vast framework. The central concept of 'intentionality'—the 'reference to an object' which characterizes every act of mind—was borrowed by Brentano from Scholastic psychology. The objectivistic version of the concept of 'value', though not thus borrowed, links up rather closely with Aristotle's *bonum honestum*, of which traditional philosophy has, I think, made too little. Husserl's marvellously deep and suggestive analysis of our primary world-experience[9] appears to me very much more Aristotelian and very much less Cartesian than it would appear either to himself or to the Thomists who distrust him. A thorough discussion, in such a perspective, of this and similar basic enquiries should be a tempting task for the Thomists—not few in number, I trust—who really mean it when they say that the easy way of cheap, catchy and showy ready-made formulae is a thing they despise and that Objective Truth is all they care for.

[9] *Erfahrung und Urteil*, Hamburg 1948, 7–10. No more destructive criticism of Descartes's fallacy of a 'clear and distinct' knowledge of allegedly 'simple' isolated things could be imagined; nor any more convincing restatement of the Aristotelian position—that the only possible basis of our 'scientific' knowledge of objects is the confused and virtual world-knowledge implicit in our 'common experience'.

3

Deliberation is of Ends

I

To attack Aristotle's famous proposition *'Deliberation is of means'* may perhaps amount to flogging a dead horse, but the horse in question may after all not be quite dead and may deserve another course of flogging in order to be securely put out of harm's way or possibly to be proved immortal in some sense. Aristotle's argument for his thesis lies in the apparent constancy and indisputability of certain ends, the pursuit of which may give rise to deliberation: a deliberation by which the respective foregiven ends are not called in question. The relevant passage (*Eth. Nic.*, Book III, 1112b) runs thus:

> We deliberate not about Ends, but Means to Ends. No physician, e.g. deliberates whether he will cure, nor orator whether he will persuade, nor statesman whether he will produce a good constitution, nor in fact any man in any other function about his particular end; but having set before them a certain end they look how and through what means it may be accomplished ... And plainly not every search is deliberation, those in mathematics to wit, but every deliberation is a search ...

It might well be asked whether 'to have set before them a certain end' did not already involve deliberation.

The three examples—the physician, the orator, the statesman— are all of a different logical status; the last obviously sounds least convincing, while the first is the most plausible (and has therefore most often been quoted). Whereas to cure and to persuade can at first sight easily be conceived of as pre-established ends requiring only the appropriate means to be attained, a 'good constitution' has no definite meaning by virtue of which to function as a logical premiss; before the question of means can be gone into, it requires a definition or, rather, a determination of its content. Conservative liberals, radical democrats, communist totalitarians and fascist totalitarians might at the very best be said to pursue the selfsame end of human happiness (or of the thriving of their respective countries) by different means, but they certainly do not aim at bringing about the selfsame 'good constitution' by different means: what they differ about is the *conception* of a 'good constitution'.

Whoever denies that their *ends* are different and conflicting actually denies that there can be such a thing as different and conflicting ends. Apart from its being blatantly absurd, this is hardly Aristotle's own opinion: witness the *Politics* with its emphasis on class quarrels. As regards orators, we may certainly distinguish between the invariable formal 'end' of persuasion and the manifold and contingent 'means' preferred in different techniques of eloquence. But, as the 'ends' are necessarily controversial and persuading must be persuading of *something*, from which a rival orator is intent on *dissuading* the same hearers, it is here again less clear than in the physician's case that the deliberation preceding the performance seems to be underlain and governed by one strictly preconceived end. The doctor we *may* presume to be always out to cure his patient: is he, then, in doubt only as regards the means conducive to such a result, and does he deliberate, if at all, about means?

The answer, I submit, is No. So far as the physician confines himself to the determination of suitable curative means—often followed, in simple cases, by their application there and then—he does not deliberate but performs the theoretical activities of recalling to mind his relevant knowledge, looking up textbooks for more information, considering the peculiarities of the case in hand, weighing probabilities, comparing the average efficacy of various methods in similar cases and so forth. He does what a consulting physician, not responsible for any *decision*, might do just as well for him. The knowledge he brings to his practical task is ampler and more exact but not of a logically different nature than my wholly unpractical knowledge of the probability that, if streptomycin and some other recent therapies had been known in the middle of the last century or at least in the beginning of ours, Chopin or at least James Elroy Flecker would not have died so early of consumption. Aristotle says himself that enquiry or research is not deliberation; but he seems disposed to think that research about practically relevant matters is inseparable from deliberation, and in particular that because indeed practice necessarily bears upon 'singulars', all knowledge of and research about singulars must be intimately bound up with a practical intent and thus intertwined with deliberation. That is plainly not so, although it may be worth while to note that our thinking about such historical matters as vividly interest us will often entice us into bouts of 'quasi-' or 'phantasy' deliberation: Should I reject Parmenio's counsel of moderation if I were Alexander the Great? What should I have done in Sir Edward Grey's place in the fateful July days of 1914? However, physicians do have to deliberate a great deal, not because of the imperfection of their medical knowledge in general or owing to the incertitude of its application to the singular case, but because the *end* their decisions are ordained to, 'the cure of the patient', is not unequivocal except in a *prima facie* schematic sense, while in fact it is largely ambiguous, admitting of different interpretations, and requiring to be more closely determined according to the peculiar features of the situation in all but the simplest cases. Thus, the most effective cure here and now might appear harmful to the patient's health considered in a wider perspective, or possibly prejudicial from the point of view of public health; a radical operation or the use of some potent drug may imperiously commend itself yet at the same time entail grave risks; perhaps the doctor cannot fully devote his time and energies to the effective treatment of one case of middling gravity without unduly neglecting others, and many similar 'doctor's dilemmas'. In all of them, conflicting ends are involved (i.e. a choice between alternative goods is imposed); whether or not these ends can be regarded as 'means' to some higher ends and comparable with one another in terms of such an instrumentality, they cannot be construed as means to the one fixed and unproblematic end of 'curing the patient'. Their emergence bursts the bonds of that unique and isolated teleological constant, though of course the theme of curing the patient is in no wise invalidated thereby. Deliberation, then, arises not in virtue of the multiplicity of conceivable and available means but in virtue of the multiplicity of *other ends* as affected by the envisaged use of means in the service of *one given end*, and partly at least as implicit in the *conception* of that one end here and now endowed with a thematic primacy.

In the very passage quoted, Aristotle all but reveals this fairly simple truth, only to miss it owing to his utilitarian-rationalistic outlook. The paragraph is concluded by this sentence:

And if in the course of their search [*scil.* for appropriate means to an end] men come upon an impossibility, they give it up: if money, for instance, is necessary, but cannot be got; but if the thing appears possible then they attempt to do it.

No doubt, these clear-cut situations occur: 'the cure' for some dreadful (and some rather innocuous) diseases has not so far been found and thus the cases, to put it somewhat crudely, are 'given up', but if research should some day find the cure for one or the other of them it will be applied; I might fancy owning a well-staffed palatial house but as I literally couldn't get the money necessary to achieve this end, I utterly abstain from pursuing it. But this description is out of touch with the way things usually happen in life, and misses the real point. Money *is* in one sense a pure means, more so than Aristotle (unacquainted, I suppose, with our fiat money, lacking all intrinsic usefulness or beauty) could possibly have known; yet precisely for that reason, by virtue of its quite indeterminate and neutral convertibility, it actually stands for an indefinite manifoldness of *ends*. If I buy this dress, I cannot buy that encyclopaedia; if I make this trip to the South, I shall have to live on porridge and cigarettes alone for two months. I 'have got' the necessary money for any one or several of a hundred purchases I desire to make, but not for all of them or many of them. Economy does not mean not spending the money one hasn't got, it means not spending the money one has got—or spending it in awareness of having to face the consequences. It is a question, not of possessing or not possessing the means to an end, but of having to choose between goods, i.e. of renouncing the pursuit of one end for the sake of another.

2

It has been implicitly accorded above that the search for suitable means and the finding of such may sometimes quasi-automatically lead up to action, i.e. to the (attempted) realization of a preconceived end. Theoretical observation and calculation as such do not issue in action; hence, compared with these, the quest for means to a given end may look as if it amounted in itself to deliberation. Moreover, to contemplate almost any kind of means may involve a weighing of ends against ends (an analgesic tablet would relieve my neuralgic pain but might upset my stomach), so much so that any reference to possible means may give our practical thought a deliberative turn. Enquiry about facts or data and their numerical and causal connections is not deliberation, whether or no it happens to subserve directly or indirectly a practical object, and whether or no it is prompted or commandeered by a concrete end in view. Any purely theoretical piece of thinking may unexpectedly be turned to some practical use in a later situation, without retroactively changing its non-deliberative intrinsic nature; and the doing of a sum is no more an act of deliberation if it refers to bits of a debt I owe to somebody and intend to discharge forthwith than if it occurs just in the context of an algebraic problem.

That the technical preamble to action—the quest for means as such—is intrinsically different from deliberation is expressed in the fact that the former does not, whereas the latter does, constitute a field for the exercise of free-will. In finding out what I *can* do with a view to obtaining some effect, any intervention of my free choice cannot but falsify and invalidate the result of my quest: if I have to add, say, 33, 19 and 7, any sum other than 59 will represent an error, and it is pointless to say that I can reduce the total to 53 if I so will. I can, of course, *write* the false sum 53 underneath the column of addends if I so will. Supposing them to be items of a debt, I may do so with the object of cheating my creditor for example, having *deliberated* about whether I prefer saving 6 units of currency to keeping honest, and attach more weight to the chance of succeeding than to the risk of being caught in a disgraceful act; and having arrived at a morally objectionable and, very likely, a practically foolish decision. Whereas, then, the discovery or invention of means and the ascertaining of their foreseeable efficacy is meant to establish something *a limine* independent of my will, deliberation is the sounding-out and ordering of my preferences which *a limine* brings into play acts of choice not settled beforehand but formed *ad hoc* and thus the exercise of my free-will beyond its mere preliminary information. Aristotle was not unaware of this, for in Book VII he argues that prudent judgement, i.e. correct thinking about singular *agibilia* (preparatory to concrete decision and action, that is), presupposes right willing, i.e. 'virtue'. Deliberation is in fact an exercise of freedom in some sense aiming at the *restriction* of freedom, namely at producing not simply action but action as it reasonably ought to be, should be or must be, analogously as it were to the correct solution of a theoretical problem. But Aristotle stretches the analogy: to paraphrase Hume's words, his own reason is still a slave to the Socratic-Platonic passion for installing reason as the master rather than the mere counsellor and interpreter of the will; that is why he transposes deliberation, i.e. the genesis of 'considered' or 'reasoned' willing, into the domain of means by reference to an unquestioned end, where reason is indeed sovereign and where free choice between alternative goods or mutually incompatible satisfactions is beside the point.

3

The position 'Deliberation is of means purely and simply and *not* of ends', as exemplified above, might however be dismissed as an extravaganza to which Aristotle is not committed by his general doctrine of practice. It reveals the dominant rationalistic trend of his thought rather than his outlook as a whole. He is, at any rate, on stronger ground if we take him to mean that deliberation is of means *and* ends; ends, that is to say, considered in their means-like aspect, or in other words, in their instrumental capacity or causal connection. Suppose I set up tentatively A as a particular end for its own sake; but either A itself or some means M which I could not help using to secure it is incompatible with another end of mine, *B*, which I cherish equally or even more; now on further reflection I find that *A* not only attracts me in itself but would also act as an effective means towards securing a further end, *C*, which ranks pretty high among my preoccupations. This sounds like a possible description of what happens when we deliberate, and it certainly refers to means; to be sure, means as they affect different established or provisional ends, not means to one end seen in isolation and taken for granted without reserve. On the contrary, when a man just makes a straightforward choice according to his preference he is not deliberating. Shall we then simply meet Aristotle half-way and conclude that deliberation is of means and ends jointly? This I am reluctant to do, mainly, on the face of it, for two reasons. First, Aristotle (Book I, 1097a, b), while admitting that 'ends are plainly many',[1] is apt to object that any rational choice between two antithetic ends can only take place by reference to some higher end and that, thus, all particular ends directly or indirectly depend upon and are appraised as means to, a 'supreme good' the attainment of which constitutes the one 'ultimate end' (imposed by nature rather than freely chosen): consequently, that deliberation, even if apparently of ends, is essentially of means. Secondly, I on my part deny that the interrelationship of ends analyses without a remainder into simple, ultimate emotive preferences (stronger and weaker likes and dislikes) on the one hand and instrumental utilities in the service of some higher ends or a highest end on the other hand, and therefore deny that the weighing of ends against one another (when it's not a matter of straightforward non-deliberative choices) is reducible to a comparative assessment of means. I accordingly maintain that, quite apart from the un-reflected choice of that which unequivocally attracts more or repels less, what stands in the thematic focus of deliberative choice are convergent and divergent ends, i.e. autonomous goods, values or satisfactions with their mutual *pro* and *con* accents and implications, whereas the apprehension of means and calculation of their effects play the part of a technical auxiliary. In the following Section, I shall argue in support of this concept of non-instrumental connections, and that will issue directly in a criticism of Aristotle's mediatization of particular ends.

[1] 'Honour, pleasure, intellect, in fact every excellence we choose for their own sake.' What Aristotle has in mind here are standard and (all but) permanent categories of 'ends', i.e. concerns or interests, rather than purposes proper such as 'to win this prize' or 'to get in at the next election'; in C. L. Stevenson's terminology, 'focal aims' rather than 'ends in view'. However, concrete here-and-now 'ends in view' are logically on a par with 'healing this patient', which Aristotle does state to be the physician's end (Bk I, 1097a).

4

The frequent and indeed predominant multivalence of means is alone sufficient to confer upon them a character of relative or partial ends, while on the other hand any end may also be regarded as a means to various other ends;[2] but if the end-means pattern thus appears to slip into a mode of ambiguity and to exhibit one aspect of our practical approach to 'goods' (in the widest sense) rather than a permanent division of them into two classes (*bona delectabilia* and *honesta* and *bona utilia*), then it may more conveniently be said that in deliberating we confront mutually conspiring and mutually competitive ends with one another than that in deliberating we seek out the available and efficacious means to one determinate end. For the latter activity is a subsidiary requirement of the former, whereas the converse is not true.

But the relation between ends is by no means only causal, expressible, that is, in terms of conducive or harmful effects; it is also intrinsic. Some ends appear to be in keeping or consonance with each other; some are mutually jarring, unsuited, discordant, exhibiting a relation of contrariety up to the point of logical inconsistency. In actually setting up his ends (as distinct from unsanctioned desires, leanings or tentative visions), the agent is compelled to choose, on pain of behaving ineffectually and self-defeatingly; and of course in his choices such ends are more strongly weighted as display, in addition to their worth considered in itself, a particular 'fittingness' in respect of important other ends already established and as it were axiomatic. Thus, a man with dominant spiritual interests may control his penchant for gluttony not merely because in a consequential sense it is apt to interfere with his studies but because he is pained by a sense of essential incompatibility between these two passions; again, a traditional textbook example I think, an eminently sociable person will all the more tend to deliberately cultivate his taste for wine as a temperate enjoyment of good drinks not only promotes the forming of social ties but to some extent enriches and ennobles companionship. In view of the active, sanctioned pursuit and sustained cherishing of certain goods we may not unnaturally, if somewhat loosely, speak

[2] Cf. Stevenson, 'Reflections on John Dewey's Ethics', *P.A.S.* (December 1961): The 'large ends recommended in traditional ethics', such as 'the greatest happiness of the greatest number', are desired *partly but not alone for their own sake.* For 'focal aims' and their compatibility, nay consonance, with the *pluralism* of particular ends, see the most remarkable footnote on p. 203 in Stevenson, *Ethics and Language*, paperbound ed. 1960.

of 'ends' here, but the language of 'ends *and means*' is plainly inadequate.

Another line of argument leads in a similar direction. It has more than once been pointed out, by none so aptly and forcefully as by Sir David Ross,[3] that to set up an aim (be it even provisionally) and then to look about for the proper means to attain it is far from constituting the one universal model of practice. Often enough and quite normally, the machinery of tentative purposing and of deliberation is set in motion by occasions, finds, discoveries, offers, stimuli, temptations, suggestions, proposals and so forth. We come in possession, actual or virtual, of a good which may or may not awaken our desire to enjoy it, or a possible 'means' which starts us wondering whether we shall or shall not avail ourself of it, or to what use we might best put it. We ask ourself whether any of our 'ends' is served by this thing (would not, rather, our using it disserve one general end of ours, that of saving effort and time and perhaps money?); we look round for 'ends' to be achieved by the 'means' at our disposal. We deliberate whether we should adopt a suggested purpose—e.g. that of visiting a city, having received an invitation—or in the variant case, deliberate about possible ends for a given mean. Of course we do not form purposes out of nothing, without any conditioning elements whatever in our pre-existing emotive structure and horizon of knowledge. However, for all the constants in our mental and affective outlook which make us receptive to some kinds of stimuli and unresponsible to others, our actual purpose-formation is largely contingent on occasions and suggestive influences which happen to cross our path. Our ends are not all ready-made, awaiting their fulfilment when the proper means should have been found; they may come to life and harden into shape in fairly unexpected contexts; and their fixation involves to some extent, at times it may be a considerable extent, a revision, modification and reorientation of our pre-established structure of permanent or comparatively lasting ends

---

[3] Ross, *Foundations of Ethics*, pp. 195–9. It looks as if Ross were less willing than I am 'to give up Aristotle's doctrine, that choice is not of ends but only of means'. According to him, we do not decide whether to *desire* but only whether to *seek* an end, and the latter means 'to take means to an end'. With this I must disagree. What we decide is whether to approve or to disapprove a desire of ours (absolutely and permanently, or relatively and temporarily); our 'taking (or not taking) means to an end' *presupposes* our decision to pursue (or not to pursue) that *end* as such. In an indirect and limited sense, we even choose our desires. It becomes, anyhow, apparent especially on p. 199 how 'widely' Ross himself, in his own words, 'departs from the Aristotelian model'. [The author appears to have had doubts about the views expressed in this footnote. This is indicated by a query written into the margin. Eds.]

—I would rather say, our *concerns*—itself.[4] It is the choices, confrontations, inner dialogues, hesitations and new engagements implied in this process that *primo loco* constitute the field of deliberation.

Because the end-means relation is the simplest and the most evident of the different types of relations between the manifold single elements, phases, aspects and objects which make up the articulation of '*an action*' (or a course of action, or a project unfolding while carried into execution), there arises an intellectual temptation to extend the end-means model far beyond its true range. In proportion as a thing is means-like we know what it is for, i.e. what is its *raison d'être*:[5] a pencil-sharpener is incomparably more intelligible than, say, literature. Thus, objects of enjoyment and, worse, of reverent appreciation have been misinterpreted as means to the states of mind they or their presence or possession may evoke. It is a distorted way of speaking to call the *object* of an enjoyment a *means* to pleasure. The instrumentality implied in the *procuring* of the object (buying it in the market, etc.) is fallaciously transferred here to the object itself. Again, the components of a whole have been misnamed means to the end it is supposed to embody.[6] The earlier phases of a coherent unit of action and experience have sometimes been uncritically regarded as means to its terminal or culminating point, as if the courses of a festive dinner were means to the crowning delight of coffee, liqueur and Havana. And diverse kinds of subordination have boldly been equated to an end-means relation between the higher and the lower ranks of the hierarchy, as if (the conception is Aristotelian) slaves stood to masters as means to ends and the beef-steak was the entelechy of the cow. Similarly, there is a tendency to mistake for a mere matter of means-finding the *specification* or closer determination of an

[4] Clearly our concerns (or 'enduring interests', or 'focal aims') do not constitute a denumerable set of distinct entities, making up all together our definitive 'self'. They can be described and classified in widely different ways; they mutually overlap and are also mutually at tension. Yet they form the matrix out of which our particular choices of ends emerge, and these in their turn react upon them and may in part modify or, to borrow another term from Stevenson, 'redirect' them. As Ricoeur puts it (*Philosophie de la volonté ii, Finitude et culpabilité*, 1960, p. 171): 'Le surgissement du choix est finalement, sous sa forme la plus authentique, une discontinuité au sein même de la motivation, parfois même un renversement de valeurs, une révolution dans l'évaluation.'

[5] According to K. R. Popper ('Three Views concerning Human Knowledge', in *Contemporary British Philosophy*, iii, p. 369n.), it is man-made things such as clocks, etc. that have an unequivocal and knowable *purpose*, and thus a definable 'essence'.

[6] This traditional fallacy is exploded with peculiar vigour by Moore (*Principia Ethica*, §§20–1).

end, project or intention once conceived. To be sure, if I have to reach a given destination as soon as possible I shall take the shortest path or look for the most rapid *means* of communication; yet if I decide to go for a walk my choice of a direction—if at all a reflected choice—will not be, properly speaking, the choice of the most efficacious means but, although bearing on a very puny matter, a true deliberative choice which renders my purpose realizable by completing it and setting it in clearer outline.

5

If, to put it crudely, in deliberating we compare ends with the view of choosing between them, what are the criteria of the comparison and on what grounds do we choose or mean to choose in one sense as opposed to another? Here is a puzzle quite alien to the mere search for appropriate means, including even the cases when our knowledge of the efficacy of different means to an end is not certain but only probable. If you have decided to spend a few weeks at some southern place where you want to enjoy the warm climate but avoid the torrid summer heat, by all means go there in May or in September, though there just might be a heat-wave in either of these months and a spell of cool weather in June or in August. But whether it is more worth while, say, to make this trip or to re-furnish some of your rooms instead (supposing you cannot afford to do both) I am unable to tell you, and you may find it very awk-ward to '*decide*' which of the two you want more badly and what accessory advantages and drawbacks are implied on either side. ('Deciding' has its characteristic ambiguous sense here: it unites a quasi-theoretical act of examining and ascertaining what one most wants to a quasi-practical act, an inchoate act of willing.) Except in cases where we have a clear preference for one good over an alternative good and there is no reason why we should not follow it straightforwardly without any deliberation, we compare ends with ends *in the light of further ends* they are likely to promote or to hamper respectively, either in a causal sense or at any rate in the sense of concordance and disordance: do we then, after all, con-sider the ends between which we have to choose as if they were means to something else? No, for we feel inclined to pursue them for their own sake, without any logically necessary or previously given reference to further ends; again, these further ends or some of them may not be at all 'higher' or more important; again, some of the preferences that may ultimately play a part in our choice will perhaps only come to light, develop, mature and get more or less firmly established in the process of our deliberation. However enlightened by reason and based on or rather supported by reasons, choice is shot through with arbitrariness: that is why it centrally reveals the affirmation and exercise of our free-will, which is only marginally present in our theoretical thinking and conclusions.

The view here propounded is not wholly at variance with Aristotle's. His doctrine of the specificity of 'practical reason', open to serious objections to be sure, indicates his awareness of the gulf between theoretical elucidation and deliberative choice, including prudent or wise choice. His postulate (Book I) of a single and paramount 'final' end which is pursued for its own sake *alone* is exposed in a wary and rambling fashion revealing a common-sensical moderation of his utilitarian and metaphysical emphasis. Aristotle admits here (1) that there are at least certain general categories of particular ends—concerns, I would say; Stevenson's 'focal aims' appear to express the same concept—such as know-ledge, pleasure and honour, or some qualified forms thereof, which are desired, as it befits true ends, for their own sake, though also as 'means to happiness', i.e. subject to the arbitrament of an 'absolutely final end'.[a] He admits (2) that 'to call happiness the chief good' sounds like 'a mere truism', some 'clearer account of its real nature' being required. He explains (3) that happiness means a state of the soul and an ordering of conduct 'in accordance with Reason', a 'good life' and a 'complete life', which conveys the idea of a *comprehensive* condition of excellence rather than an isolated single 'end' from which all other ends were derivable as 'means'. And he concedes (4) that happiness thus understood, while it 'has no need of pleasure as an additional advantage but involves pleasure in itself', yet also 'requires the addition of external goods'.

Withal, the *problem* still remains whether it is not logically neces-sary to appeal to the arbitrament of an ulterior and unchallengeably valid end in order to choose *meaningfully* between competitive ends; in other words, whether the fact of deliberation does not *eo ipso* imply recourse to some practical ultimate or at any event, per-haps, to one of several—not intrinsically incompatible—axioms of this kind. One such ultimate standard of orientation would, I sup-pose, be provided by hedonic and biological utility, in direct con-tinuity with the claims of nature; another, by deontic morality; yet another, by the aspiration for a unified meaning and dedication of life which points to the religious concept of salvation or holiness; and to these might be added the sense of a personal meaning and plan of life, centred in a specifically chosen set of values. Be that as it may, the Aristotelian notion of a 'chief good' or 'final end' is undoubtedly warped to some extent by an uncritical extension of the end-means model to a field of relationships of a more complex and reciprocal type.

At a second remove, Aristotle, obviously unsatisfied with the vague synthetic ideal of the 'complete life', distorts the blanket concept of 'happiness' into the more singularized and determinate supreme value of 'intellectual contemplation' as expanded in Book X, the last. This arbitrary reinterpretation appears to introduce an 'ideal state of mind' out of contact with action and its problems, and suggesting a negation of practice rather than any directive for the ordering of it. Again, the 'complete life' is not so much sub-served by particular goods in an instrumental capacity as constitu-ted by them in the sense in which an ensemble is made up by its component parts. Any one of our particular ends may indeed be subordinate to the *conspectus* of our concerns, but unless the par-ticular ends existed in their own right the conspectus would mean nothing at all. Even assuming that there is such a thing as a superior experience of all-round happiness, somehow separable from any explicit reference to particular dimensions of good, it *presupposes* particular ends and their fulfilment; the management of special concerns may at some points decisively depend on the endeavour to attain or maintain it, but the dependence is mutual. It is not enough to say, with Aristotle, that some particular ends of high standing are 'also' desired for their own sake and not 'merely' as a means to happiness. So far as happiness is conceived of as an all-embracing ideal, necessarily relevant to any definite and concrete provinces of fulfilment, it actually *consists* in these, and possibly in the feeling of their concordance; whereas so far as it is seen as seated in a supreme mode of fulfilment set apart from others, e.g. spirituality (taking the hint of the second Aristotelian version), it is no longer all-embracing and its nexus with other autonomous ends becomes contingent and open to vastly different interpretations. In either case, the *derivation* of single ends, including humble and highly particularized ones, from a superordinate and final end is doomed to failure as a merely imaginary construction, and signifi-cant choice is shown to take place not between different means to one end but between different ends. This, it is true, still implies various kinds of hierarchic and reciprocal relations between ends so as to account for the possibility of argument and the necessity of deliberation.

6

I can but touch in passing on the *ethical* side of the matter. With his doctrine of a marked-out final end and of choice bearing upon the proper means to an end, Aristotle lays himself open to the charge of debasing practical wisdom or 'prudence', and with it 'moral decision'—since he, like many other philosophers, fails to distinguish between the moral Ought and the practical 'I had better . . .'—to the level of expediency: morality would then consist in the agent's finding the immanently right, i.e. effective, means to attain what he is ultimately striving for. But, though somehow in accord with his outlook, this is not the position he really, let alone consistently, holds. In Book I, without realizing to be sure the altogether open field of the possible autonomous ends and special predilections of men, he notes that the blank of the abstract concept of 'the chief good' has been filled by different schools of thought with different kinds of more determinate things; i.e. he allows for different interpretations or specifications of the end as distinct from different views about the proper means to attain it. And in Book VI (1144a), he expressly sets apart practical wisdom from 'cleverness', i.e. the skilful choice of means to any kinds of end whatsoever: only the virtuous person, who has opted for *the right end*, can reason properly about problems of practice, for he alone possesses the right premise for practical syllogisms. Aristotle appears to be trying to deal here with a basic ethical objection to his general doctrine of practice and morality; perhaps in so doing he lapses into self-contradiction, but anyhow he shows his aversion to sacrificing ethical intuition altogether to the exigencies of his metaphysical system, and is hinting at what is, if not a contradiction, at any rate a tension within our very experience of practice. The agent's own primary concerns are the only possible principles of his practice, for he cannot succeed or fail except in what *is* his endeavour, nor adopt objective principles except by reference to things he actually wants already. Nevertheless, can his practice in no way be wise or unwise, correct or false, *eupractic* or *dyspractic* apart from mere technical correction or miscalculation?

The following sentence by St Augustine (*De libero arbitrio*, Book I) brings out more clearly and forcefully the fundamental insight that morality turns on cherishing one sovereign right end, not on applying the right means to another end; that, however closely related to happiness at least in the eternal or salvational sense, it can neither be derived from the concept of happiness nor take the place of happiness, and itself supply the sole comprehensive final end of man:

The wicked [i.e. the lost souls] are not unhappy because they did not desire happiness, for they desired that no less than the virtuous did; but the latter also desired to lead a life of justice, which the former did not.

Particular ends, including even permanent and life-shaping personal concerns, cannot be unequivocally deduced from any pre-established conceptual scheme or ideal, be it ever so fervently adopted; deliberation cannot be replaced by a mere technical 'application' of overall principles. If the concern of morality and the imperative of honesty cannot be conjured, except fictitiously, out of any conceptual apparatus of 'pleasure-and-pain economy', on the other hand even a man endowed with the keenest sense of honesty does not as a rule make business transactions from the motive of practising the virtue of honesty, and the rules of honesty tell him no more in what business transactions he should engage than the rules of chess tell the player what moves he should make in order to win the game.

Moreover, ideals are not only in need of being implemented by personal acts of choice but are themselves chosen, not imposed by nature or rational self-evidence;[b] and however defensible, commendable and extensive in scope they may be, they inevitably fall short of representing the totality of the worthy purposes of man. Whoever identifies the ideal of his choice with the 'ultimate end' of the universe or history or God in a sense exclusive of other points of view or experiences of value, is a prey to fictitious judgement and cramped pretension. This truth finds a masterly expression in Tennyson's verses:

> And God fulfils Himself in many ways,
> Lest one good custom should corrupt the world.

If not of Tennyson's, Plato and Aristotle and their system-happy followers might have taken heed of Heraclitus' warning:

> Better is invisible than visible harmony.

7

I fear I must wind up by a dismaying anticlimax: the concept of deliberation I have tried to outline seems ineluctably to involve what I would venture to call somewhat pompously the fundamental paradoxy of Practice. If deliberation was not of ends but of means, i.e. if it were reducible to rational computation—which in my view merely belongs to its forecourt, as a technical auxiliary—no such paradoxy would arise; there is nothing paradoxical about the possibility of inaccurate knowledge or miscalculation. But again, if choice was a purely gratuitous affair, a display of the freedom of indifference, a wilful act of 'engagement' no matter for which cause or in what course; if significant choice bore on questions like 'Which boot shall I put on first when dressing?' then too we should be baffled by no paradoxy. Straightforward preferences are self-justifying and random hits stand in no need and do not admit of justification. But neither would deliberation then exist at all. In fact, it is not so. Placed before significant choices, man cannot but deliberate, weighing ends as if they were means, comparing them as if they were fixed data accessive to theoretical measurement, whereas their weight depends on the seesaw of his own tentative willing and on his emergent *parti-pris* as well as the other way round. In some sense, it is an inherently deceptive, not to say deceitful operation, with loaded dice as it were; the agent cannot help weighting what he is weighing, though neither can he do the weighting without a vague but imperative reliance on the results of his weighing, some would say the illusion of his manipulating objectively fixed weights. This circular and puzzling character of deliberation arises, not from plain irrationality as present in our spontaneous preferences and emotive whims, but from the interplay between an ineliminable irrationality (the fact that free-will alone, not reason, can choose and sanction) and an equally ineliminable rationality in the genesis of choice: a rationality whose primary habitat and starting-point is indeed, so far Aristotle's dictum remains valid, the consideration of means in view of ends. In other words, the paradoxy is rooted in the twofold fact that man cannot but choose freely, that, to give Sartre his due, he cannot abdicate his somehow gratuitous and groundless freedom, and that on the other hand he can only will goods and not the exercise of his freedom as such, and therefore *in choosing cannot but try to choose wisely*, i.e. to make a choice that *is* supported by grounds.

Wise or *eupractic* or correct (as opposed to false) choice is not a concept invented and foisted upon man by prigs or preachers; it is what man of necessity desires and hopes against hope to contrive. Nor is the concept as I here mean it and as men mean it confined to that of a well-informed and pondered choice, made in awareness of the factual circumstances and on the basis of a correct reasoning about foreseeable effects, as opposed to ignorance, error and precipitancy. Nor again, of course, is wise choice identified with one that actually happens to lead to success and beneficial results—the lucky hit as it were. Theoretical judgement also is largely conjectural; it may be as sound as possible and yet objectively wrong by accident, and inversely. But action may be sagaciously planned and carried out with complete success in the immanent or technical sense, and yet end up in a consciousness of practical failure. The fulfilment, secured at a high cost perhaps, of his purpose may leave the agent with a bitter tang of disappointment or worse in his mouth, and the definite feeling that he ought to have known this in advance and that he was a blundering fool or misguided by a perverse mood when taking his decision—not just ill informed or guilty of rashness or levity or miscalculation of probable effects, nor even just a different kind of man than he now is. (It is worth noting here that hesitancy and over-deliberation as well as thoughtless haste and audacity may adversely affect practice.)

If elaborate and pedantic rules of felicific practice, *Maximen der Lebensweisheit* as the Germans put it, are sometimes utterly fictitious or irrelevant and nearly always fallible, if it is derisory and often dangerous—a sure sign of unwisdom—to follow them slavishly, not to mention the contradictions between their respective emphases, it may nevertheless be useful to know and occasionally to consult some of them; and above all, they testify to man's *craving* for practical wisdom. An incurable but not really a morbid craving, for it is an absurd misuse of language to call our very being and constitution a disease (*une passion inutile*), whatever the incongruities and paradoxies inherent in it; yet it pertains to our constitution to deliberate with a view to arriving, not just 'to a decision' but to 'a wise' or to 'the right' decision, I do not mean to 'a wise decision or none'[7] but to a decision which shall be a wise decision. More briefly, it is part of our constitution *to deliberate*, since 'to deliberate' *is* to confront, compare, forecast and argue in view of a happy choice. By the same paradoxy, our free-will has to be exercised and can only be exercised in a self-restrictive fashion, for the ends we set up and stamp with the *fiat* of the 'sanctioning' imperative power of decision subject us to so many commitments and objectivizations, which are henceforth to circumscribe and govern our will though engendered by its ruling. We cannot want this to happen at random; we cannot help wanting that it should happen in a way attuned to what we most urgently, most perdurably, most evidently and most appreciatively want, and even that the emphasis of our wanting should be so ordered as to make this possible. Hence we cannot prescind from wishing to choose, not indeed 'from' reason or at the dictate of reason, but with reason, as if the ends we choose were underwritten by a pellucid will, unmarred by incertitude and tottering, which we do not actually possess; as if they bore the guarantee of rational evidence and the seal of objective truth.

Self-restrictive willing, the only mode of effective willing we can conceive of, is not for that reason self-destructive (though so many

---

[7] Practical decisions are not on the same logical footing with theoretical problems. Phrases conceived in the mode of doubt or a divided mind, such as 'We have no means of knowing . . .', 'More likely, it is so . . .', 'Partly this, partly that . . .', etc., are possible final answers to theoretical questions but not to practical alternatives. I cannot, e.g., for ever probably accept or probably turn down a concrete unique offer, nor in general partly accept and partly reject it.

of our actions inevitably are); and the paradoxy of choice is not exactly a contradiction. Deliberation cannot be cleansed from an ingredient of sham rationality, but it does not follow that the problem of wise and unwise choice is itself a sham problem. It would be more difficult to construct paradigms of wise and unwise than of moral and immoral or, what is even easier, of technically prudent and imprudent action, mainly because the sorting-out of 'irrelevant circumstances' which conditions the force and applicability of hypothetical models and general criteria is more open to logical objections in the field of *eupractic* than in the fields of moral and of expediential judgement; and yet most of us, I suggest, could point at least to some sparse instances of arguably, if not demonstrably, wise and unwise choice in our own life-experience. The very fact of disbelieving altogether in the possibility of a wise choice would impair a man's deliberation and make him choose all the more unwisely; and so would an uncritical belief in rationality and disregard for the fact that all choice connotes and requires arbitrariness and entails risks. A choice that would on the face of it be deemed 'wise' on conventional grounds is likely to be wiser than an act of romantic irresponsibility; again, an apparently eccentric choice which expresses the 'authentic' bent of a fearless and passionate but reflective soul might be wiser than the obviously 'reasonable' choice in its place would be on that agent's part. It would always be ill-advised to act automatically on the principle expressed in William the Silent's motto '*Nul n'est besoin d'espérer pour entreprendre ni de réussir pour persévérer*', but it may be wise to act so in selected cases.

Aristotle's general concept of practical wisdom reveals the defects of an all too self-confident and short-circuited rationalism, ill compensated for by his rejection of all general criteria of wise choosing in the concrete case and his mystical idol of a postulated 'virtue of prudence' untestably operating on singulars. That is no reason, however, for turning a blind eye on the problem which this great pioneer of the theory of practice has bequeathed us. It may be elusive and bemusing but is not, I think, barren or nonsensical.

*   *   *   *   *

The thesis argued against in this paper, 'Deliberation is of Means not of Ends', is linked up with the following six Aristotelian positions, all of which except the last are touched upon in the text but which cannot be *in extenso* discussed here.

(1) That, as Practice necessarily bears upon singulars (Book I, 1097a), so also singulars constitute the object of practical knowledge only, Science proper being about universals. Thus all thinking

about the particular circumstances of a concrete case, especially about means, is practical not theoretical thinking, and amounts to deliberation. (2) That, since Practice (as Plato decrees) has to be governed by Reason, yet (against Plato) demands a specific attention to singulars and cannot be determined by the 'scientific' or 'sapiential' knowledge of universals, there must be such an entity as Practical Reason or Prudence (Book VI, 1141b). This confusing hybrid concept is, then, introduced so as both to safeguard Platonic rationalism and to tone it down as a concession to common sense. A valid insight into the *non-rigorous use of reason* is implied therein, though in fact non-rigorous rationality plays an immense part also in theoretical thought. (3) That *eupractic* and morally good conduct and *dyspractic* and morally bad conduct are respectively identical: an apparently self-evident presupposition for Aristotle and countless others ever since. The roots of this confusion are partly sham-scientific, partly naturalistic and utilitarian, and partly moral-pedagogical; but it also arises, I suggest, from a misconception of the really arguable *consonance* between virtuous and *eupractic*, evil and *dyspractic* conduct. In the so-called Franciscan tradition (as contrasted with Thomism) in Christian-Scholastic thought, the distinction between (prudential) Practice and Morality is vigorously upheld, and a particular '*moral* practical reason' as well as a 'supernatural *moral* end of man' in discontinuity with the natural striving for 'happiness' (the latter necessarily present in all men, the former not) are asserted. See Jean Rohmer, *La finalité morale chez les théologiens de saint Augustin à Duns Scot*, especially the chapters on St Anselm of Canterbury and Duns Scotus. Evidently if moral valuations and norms were not autonomous but were just prudential rules, that would add to the plausibility of deliberation being 'of means'. (4) That Practical *Reason*, not the Will, takes the initiative for, and finally 'commands', action (Book VI, 1143a). Cf. about this odd and much-disputed doctrine, G. E. M. Anscombe, *Intention*, §35 and pp. 74, 75 nn. If it were so, that again would displace the central emphasis of deliberation from ends to means. See P. Ricoeur's excellent criticism (*Philosophie de la volonté*, i, p. 161) of 'the intellectualist theory of choice', all the more significant as Ricoeur also justly rejects (p. 166) the voluntarist theory of choice as advanced by the existentialists, as apt to blur the experience of values and engulf valuation in decision. (5) That the higher a being ranks in the Universe or in the State the more it must be ordained to one determinate 'end', e.g. 'Man *qua* Man' more so than Man in his capacity as a craftsman (Book I, 1097b). This fantastic notion is obviously rooted in Aristotle's cosmology and originates from the Eleatic (monistic and geometrical) concept of 'perfection'. For a devastating criticism of the 'cosmological theory of the will', the idea of 'particular goods as means to an end', and the alleged 'universal desire for a *bonum generale* from which anything might be derived by way of syllogisms', see Ricoeur, op. cit., pp. 180–6. (6) That, finally, the objects pursued by an unjust or vicious will are not real goods (wrongly coveted or unsuitable in the circumstances or even chosen in preference to *greater* goods) but '*apparent* goods' (Book III, 1113a, b). Thus, immoral conduct and *a fortiori*, *dyspractic* conduct in general, though undoubtedly bound up with affective misdirection, would rest on a mistaken judgement and a consecutive choice of immanently improper 'means' to the unequivocal 'final end' we all invariably pursue by metaphysical necessity.

4

Morality and Practice I:
The Ambiguity of Good

According to some people, including some writers on Ethics such
as Kant, the fundamental problem of Morality could be condensed
in the succinct query by Man, 'What shall I do?'. The amazing
unnaturalness of the suggestion, which nevertheless does not attain
to complete absurdity, at once opens up the vista of the relations
between Morality and Practice, which I propose to examine in
these pages. Perhaps our insight into the equivocal character of the
concept of Good will offer a more essential line of approach, but
'What shall I do?' appears to me to provide a livelier beginning.

It is hardly a widespread habit of men to ask the question 'What
shall I do?' in regard to their *general* conduct of life—for example,
on entering 'the age of reason', whenever that may be. The closest
approximation to such a use of the phrase may be found in the
words a young man will possibly utter when pondering on the
choice of a career, though they might rather take the form 'What
shall I do for a living?' or 'What shall I do with myself?'. That is
clearly not a request for *moral* guidance except in an accidental and
marginal sense. (A friend to whom the young man turns for advice
may perhaps dissuade him from engaging in the liquor trade or in
armament manufacturing as morally objectionable, or commend a
doctor's or a teacher's profession as morally preferable to purely
commercial pursuits; but such points of view may not enter at all.)
Mostly one will ask 'What shall I do?' in regard to a concrete here-
and-now situation, with some well-defined end or ends in view,
and faced with a particular dilemma. The practical problem on
hand may be wholly or principally moral; it may have little or nothing to do with any moral consideration; or again it may represent
a conflict between the suasion of conscience, i.e. a moral demand
(whose validity is not perhaps wholly above doubt) and some non-
moral, but urgent and in itself legitimate, interest of the agent.
The well-dressed but pathetic young lady of a once flourishing
advertisement poster who addresses an equally elegant and dis-
creetly smiling railway porter in the words:

Oh, Mr Porter,
What shall I do?
I was reading *Everybody's*
And went on to Crewe!

obviously is not asking for moral guidance; what she has in mind
is hardly some noble action she feels impelled and half-way obliged
to perform or some crime she feels tempted to perpetrate. She is
grappling not with a moral but with one kind of a practical—an
eminently 'technical'—kind of problem. We might provisionally
establish that, whereas everything moral is also practical, seeing
that morality necessarily bears on conduct (action, decision, willing, etc.), the converse does not hold: everything practical is by no
means moral, such themes of practice as success, 'coming out on
top', tactical skill, etc., being plainly non-moral in nature, moral
adiaphora as it were; morality would then appear to constitute one
department, perhaps the 'highest' and most important, of practice.
Against this, however, some would set the 'ultimate' moral relevance of all practice; and again it might also be objected that
morality is something specifically different from practice altogether
for practice is concerned with the agent's attainment or non-
attainment of his purposes, whatever they are, whereas morality
is concerned precisely with the quality of his purposes regardless
of his skill in securing them. Be that as it may, the question 'What
shall I do?' cannot but be practical in *some* sense. Suppose he who
asks it means it morally, being really anxious to find out what
would be the *right* thing for him to do, what indeed would be his
duty, in the given situation: even so, he is indicating that he feels
committed to *doing* the right thing and resolved to adjust his practice to the moral demand. But no less certainly, the question can
be practical in a closer, more directly self-regarding and 'technical'
and, *except for* the possible moral meaning of *all* practice, definitely
non-moral sense. (It will then stand for 'How can I most easily,
promptly and cheaply extricate myself from this quandary?', 'How
can I most effectively secure that advantage?' etc., or again, a less
technical type of problem, 'Which of the two promises greater
satisfaction?'—and so forth.)

'What ought I to do?' is perhaps likelier to connote a moral
meaning, 'What can I do?' undoubtedly likelier to be meant in a
technical sense than 'What shall I do?'. But, rather than dig into
the grammar, partly of course peculiar to English, of Shall, Should,
Ought and similar auxiliaries or kindred phrasings, I would point
to another possible shade of meaning attaching to the original
question. 'What shall I do?' may be so used, and is perhaps most
naturally or straightforwardly so used, as to invite neither a moral

direction or counsel nor a properly practical advice but a command
or 'instruction', or at any rate the expression of the interlocutor's
own wish as such. One would thus address a military or administrative superior, or again simply a friend or other person to whom one
has undertaken to do some service. The appropriate answer is not,
here, 'You ought to . . .', 'You had better . . .', 'You should . . .'
or an equivalent phrase, but 'You shall . . .' or a plain imperative
or a definite request couched in more polite terms. The agent is
not here being helped or guided in his own pursuit (including or
not his concern about morality) but, subject of course to his own
will in some sense, and within certain limits, is acting on another's
behalf—without any thematic reference to what the aims subserved
may intrinsically mean to him (in terms of pleasure, interests, moral
aspirations or any of his own concerns). Here too we have a standard practical model, which does not *per se* involve any moral
point of view, but which, it might be argued, is somehow relevant
to the formal structure of morality as a whole. For there is something 'imperative' about morality: it presupposes our capacity to
'obey a command', to act independently of our directly felt desires
or impulses and even our considered interests and enduring
concerns.

2. THE PURSUIT OF 'THE GOOD'

Good in the widest sense is that which, again in the widest sense,
is desired, wished for, wanted, intended, moved towards, pursued,
loved, liked, approved (desired to exist), appreciated, by an agent,
that is to say, a conative, estimative and active subject. In the
Aristotelian phrasing, *omne intendens ad bonum operatur*; in modern
parlance, 'good' is the most general and comprehensive of '*pro-
words*'. According to the kinds of things and of qualities inherent
in certain things as also to the various respects in which they may
appear to be desirable, satisfying and valuable, there are many
specialized uses of 'good', very often perfectly understood in the
context of utterance but sometimes apt to give rise to misconceptions and pointless or confused and fallacious arguments. I may
call good what here and now pleases me or attracts me, what I am
conscious of needing in a constant manner by virtue of certain invariable or habitual effects of it, what I hold in high esteem, what
I think to be appropriate to a definite particular purpose, what is
known to be desired by or useful for people in general or a category
of people, or what is established as good by certain received public
standards, and so forth. Equivocal usage extending over so wide a
scale is not gravely harmful, since there is a fairly general awareness of it and a great variety of more differentiated and precise

value-terms exists and is resorted to in all civilized languages and at all levels of discourse. It is no doubt in some ways a good thing to keep alive this short, plain, dignified and warm-blooded word, with its suggestion of a faint but deep consonance of all things joyous, helpful and noble, instead of relying exclusively on its thinner and more artificial substitutes, many of them stretching into the regions either of clumsy technicality or of vulgarism, and not all of them free from ambiguity. Yet all the more keenly must we guard against the danger of allowing sham-scientific sophistry to benumb, whether with an edifying or a debasing intent or simply from intellectual pretension, our sense of distinctions perfectly familiar to the minds of ordinary men (including our own) and mostly well discernible in their use of ordinary language. When we speak of the good the agent is pursuing (perhaps efficiently, with the appropriate means, and successfully) or of 'the good of man', and when we speak of the goodness of conduct or of a 'good man', we mean by 'good' sharply different things whatever relations we may on closer enquiry discover between them; and to force them into a conceptual frame of short-circuited unity cannot but result in a distorted vision both of morality and of human wanting, 'happiness', and practice.

The Aristotelian equivocation, as it might be called, does not of course altogether dominate and falsify Aristotle's ethical thought; nor did it begin with Aristotle or survive through the mere accident of Aristotle's authority. To *blur* the distinction between 'the good' pursued and the moral goodness of conduct (of the will, of the agent) is as much an ineradicable tendency in man's mind as to *make* that distinction expresses an ineluctable finding of his consciousness. But Aristotle typifies it in a particularly interesting, classic fashion because, unlike the straightforward hedonist-utilitarians, he does not clearly identify 'good' with pleasure or with the object of desire whatever it may be but from the outset invests it with a kind of metaphysical status and autonomous validity over and above the brute fact of subjective appetite, thus presenting the naturalistic confusion between the moral and the non-moral 'good'—or again, between morality and practice—in a more respectable guise and in bolder logical outline. It is, so to speak, more pleasant to deny that I always desire 'pleasure' or that whatever is desired is *ipso facto* 'desirable' than that my pursuit of *my* 'true' good is what makes *me* good, and yet the fallaciousness of the latter assertion is far easier to see and of more basic significance. Ethical thinkers of the 'deontological' type from Duns Scotus to Prichard have of course seen it, and the insight is present in other forms of religious or axiological ethics as well (from St

Augustine and St Bonaventure to Brentano, Moore, von Hildebrand, etc.) though in a less unequivocal form; to my knowledge,
however, the confusion I mean has only once been laid bare in a
fully explicit and thematic fashion: namely, by Professor E. F.
Carritt, a philosopher mostly mentioned together with Sir David
Ross and Prichard, in his paper *An Ambiguity of the Word 'Good'*
(Proceedings of the British Academy, 1937, pp. 51–80). Strangely
enough, I cannot remember having ever noticed in recent British
ethical literature a reference to this short but rich and penetrating
study, although to me, in spite of its less sweeping title, it appears
to be more fundamental and less open to criticism than Prichard's
famous *Does Moral Philosophy Rest on a Mistake?* (*Mind*, 1912).

Having thus emphasized Carritt's priority and, in my opinion,
outstanding merit, I shall now try to re-state the distinction between these two principal meanings of good—which however may
not be exhaustive, or incapable of further differentiation—in my
own words. A person, say John, in shaping his conduct is necessarily pursuing 'his good', or seeking after something that is 'good
for him'. This necessarily implies a positive nexus with his
appetite, desire, impulse, or wanting, and with a feeling of satisfaction or pleasure so far as he attains or is near to attaining his object;
but the configuration of such relations may be extremely complex
and may vary greatly in different circumstances. John may now
follow the trend of his impulsive and intense desire directly, now
on the contrary obey his *preference* for 'a good' not immediately desired or promising anything like 'pleasure' proper at all, though
still necessarily connected with some of his more constant appetites
and established aims; the satisfaction he derives from the 'good'
obtained may fall short of, or outrun, his expectations; he may
choose one good as against another according to a quantitative calculus, from a pre-established 'axiomatic' preference, or without any
clear 'justification'; the part played by insight, comparison, reflection, principle, etc., may be very different in kind, degree and
structure. It is even possible that, acting under the sway of an
overwhelming sensuous passion or a possibly quixotic 'high principle', John should have the definite feeling of behaving in a manner *contrary* to 'his good'; but 'good' has here acquired the
narrower, standardized sense of 'interests', disregard for which
does not alter the fact that he is still acting for the sake of 'a good',
or more exactly, of what he here and now experiences (though not
putting it in those words) as 'his good' above all others. On the
other hand, he is likely to have a clear concept of a vast multitude
of 'goods' (goods-of-his, things good-for-him) that he is not and
presumably never will be actually pursuing at all, for example

because they are utterly out of his reach for financial or other reasons. How do we, now, get from this conceptual framework of 'John's good' or 'Good-for-John' to the notion of John, or John's conduct, will or desires being or not being 'good', i.e. morally good? That, I submit, demands a relinquishment of the 'John's good' point of view, a decisive step beyond the John-centric system of co-ordinates, a radical change of perspective. Good, for John, is that which John finds pleasant, sweet, comforting, etc.; that which John covets, pursues, tends towards; that which John enjoys and benefits from. But it is not *John* that John finds pleasant, pursues, enjoys and the rest; reflexive appraisal and self-judgement doubtless exist but are higher-order acts which presuppose *other*-valuation, self-detachment and a conceptual apparatus of great complexity: they are alien to the primary mode of discerning and pursuing one's good. It is *other* people—parents, relatives, neighbours, friends, 'society'—that will develop a primary awareness of John's being good *in a sense analogous* to *John's* experience of what is good *for him*, finding (so we suppose) John to be kind, co-operative, affectionate, obliging, reliable, cheerful, pleasant to deal with, good at useful jobs, and so on. If all good in an elementary sense is a 'good-for', then John's being thus good is *not* a being good 'for' John but a being good for others in whose world John occurs, just as the objects John registers as good occur in *his* world including his social environment.

None of the obvious objections, only too vividly present to my mind, are relevant to the argument. Moral goodness in a person is not adequately defined in terms of what is 'pleasing to others': surely not, but more so than in terms of what is pleasing to the agent himself; the former, not the latter, perspective is that in which the agent naturally, *in continuity with the primary non-moral meaning of good*, figures as an object instead of as a subject of valuation. If 'others' are neither incorruptibly morality-minded nor infallible nor necessarily unanimous in their appraisal of John and his ways, let us say that the good conduct we attribute to John is a conduct that is pleasing to God; but 'pleasing to God' is all the less identical with 'pleasing to John'. Perhaps moral goodness often, or predominantly, or ultimately always, earns its 'reward' in terms of happiness, thus being conducive to the agent's own maximum good; but even if that is so, that circuitous and tangled connection (the very word 'reward' hints at a type of consequence more arbitrary and extrinsic than anything like essential implication or natural causation) supplies no evident passage, as does the agent's appreciation by others, from the idea of good-for-oneself to that of objectively or morally good. At a certain level of moral virtue, i.e. if he is really 'good', John will be *concerned* about being virtuous, develop a sensitive conscience, and suffer whenever he has failed to follow its suasion, and thus the goodness of his will has indeed become a precious part of 'his good'; but this means a *reception* into the structure of his wanting of a *claim on him* as contrasted to the autonomous unfolding and pursuing of *his desires* as such and a readiness to renounce frequently, at the cost of pain and effort if necessary, 'his good' in the direct, perhaps fully experienced and often even very comprehensive sense of the word, and to check his pursuit of it. The common-sense consciousness of men has indeed always keenly distinguished between a man clever at securing 'his good' or even a man prudently mindful of his interests, and a good man, although at the same time it has again and again revealed its yearning for a 'higher justice' which should ultimately recompense unselfish virtue and bring the unscrupulous to fall; philosophers' perversity alone could call in doubt or feign to ignore the distinction and undertake to conjure the agent's moral goodness out of his pursuit of his good.

3. GOODS, 'THE GOOD' AND MORAL GOODNESS

To re-state the basic distinction, in its crudest form, once more—the agent's primary pursuit of 'his good' is a tautological, necessary and non-divisive datum, seeing that *omne intendens ad bonum operatur* and whatever I seek for *is* my good; whereas the agent's willing, striving, intention, direction and conduct may or may not be good just as a certain food, air, sight or state of affairs may or may not be good for him and constitute his good, and this radically different concept of *his being good* links up with the primary concept of *his good* through the perspective of *other* subjects of valuation and pursuit in which *he* takes the place of an object among other objects, now attractive now repulsive, good or bad. But for that radical distinction, nothing could be good or bad except things in the agent's world, considered from his subjective point of view; his own appetite and striving, always directed to good, could only be called invariably good or else the standard of Good which is not itself judgeable under the category of Good-and-Bad; the theme of *moral* Good and Bad would not emerge. The argument, it is true, needs one modification. It would still make a difference whether the agent is pursuing 'his good' impulsively, irrationally and blunderingly, or 'intelligently', i.e. reflectively, prudently, in a well-ordered manner, and thus efficaciously and successfully (subject only to unforeseeable chance factors in his environment). So far, then, a man *could* be called good or bad in proportion as he pursues his good ably and to his satisfaction or ineffectively and self-defeatingly. This is indeed in keeping with strict utilitarianism and largely, though by no means wholly, with the doctrine of Aristotle, a subtle and tortuous thinker given to tempering his *bel-esprit* Platonism and biological naturalism with an irrenounceable, if not always sustained, regard for common sense. And common sense itself has on the whole, though not unambiguously, inclined to credit prudence and will-power with a positive moral value; yet it is not in these qualities but in a self-detached and other-regarding *intrinsic direction* of the agent's will, and his submission to objective standards, that it would see the root and centre of moral goodness. That goodness, in other words, is in no way a function or expression of the agent's able management of his interests and ample attainment of 'his good'; it is anything but a result or index of his sating himself with '*goods*'.

By the plural noun 'goods', language—English, German and Dutch perhaps more conspicuously than other languages—has come to denote objects or classes of objects of recognized utility, standardizable means of satisfaction, commodities, wares, quantified objects of economic behaviour, things produced, priced and bought and sold. In the singular, the same use of the noun 'good' is possible (fountain-pens are goods; a fountain-pen is a good) though much less frequent, and suggests a back-formation; in the Teutonic languages, the singular noun is written and pronounced the same as the adjective, and is therefore less apt to carry the special 'commercialized' meaning. It is rather, for example, health or an untarnished reputation—any particular kind of 'precious possessions'—that we would ordinarily call 'a good'. In English, though not in German, it is also the same word 'good' that constitutes the expressions 'a good' and the highly philosophical or indeed ethical 'the Good' (*ein Gut—das Gute*). In contrast with material articles, performances and accomplishments, even if marketable, are hardly ever called goods: hence the economic term 'goods and services'.

It is well to think of 'goods' and meanings of 'good' in the neighbourhood thereof in order to appreciate the distance that separates the agent's good from his goodness or that of his conduct: to illustrate the ambiguity of Good. An astute professional fraud who secures a lavish income, taking ingenious and elaborate precautions against being found out, operates splendidly 'well' by reference to his possession of disposable goods yet not so at all by reference to the goodness of his conduct; he is definitely not an asset to Society; that in spite of the ample satisfactions he gains he in some significant sense is not effectively pursuing his own good is, outside special religious beliefs at any rate, at best an arguable but a highly debatable assertion. To derive the coruscating evidence of our moral judgement in this matter from so dubious a construction of non-moral data would amount to a desperately forced and topsy-turvy conceptual venture. To be sure, even if we did believe firmly that his immoral practices *must* tend to plunge a man in sore un-happiness we could not in terms of such a connection account for the peculiar contents and tint of moral as contrasted to prudential experience. Reckless temerity and neglect of his safety, more mani-festly and very likely gravely harmful to the agent, earns him no moral disapprobation except of a much milder and more peri-pherical kind; whereas the practical foolishness we may attribute to an evildoer however calculating and cautious largely *presupposes*, rather than begets or explains, the moral evil his actions represent: it is apt to be dangerous to make oneself liable to moral condemn-ation by one's fellow-men, and a suppressed conscience may come alive one day and visit the depraved man with the torments of self-contempt.

But this picture, somewhat overdrawn in the intuitionist sense, is not meant to be definitive; it demands an immediate correction. I may best put it in the form that 'good' has not simply two distinct and extreme meanings, one straightforwardly moral and one prim-ary and subjective, entirely contingent on appetite and pleasure as such, but unfolds into a scale of distinguishable shades of meaning which might roughly be adumbrated by a trial scheme. (The 'ambiguity of Good' is ambiguity in the philosophic sense of an equivocal, i.e. a non-univocal concept which nevertheless retains some significant unity of meaning, not in the trivial sense of a mere 'mistake' on which traditional ethics were supposed to 'rest' or of a crude verbal confusion as, for example, between the zoological and the nautical meanings of 'cat'.) The trial division we might tenta-tively apply would comprise, in addition to the hedonic-utilitarian good of whatever is desired and pleasure-giving, such as 'goods' demanded and offered, and the moral good predicted of intention, conduct, character, etc., the further concept of an *intrinsic* but not in itself moral good which is not, then, a quality or characteristic but (along with 'goods') an *object* of the agent's pursuit yet at the same time endowed with autonomous validity and a standard or measure of the quality of that pursuit rather than a function or consequence of it. Such a concept would obviously approximate to the idea of 'the Good' in ancient and traditional philosophy (with echos in Moore and Ross) as well as to that of Value in modern philosphic style. What is the point of introducing such a, shall we say intermediary, concept of Good? Is it meant to revoke the

4

sharp distinction between hedonic-utilitarian and moral good, and to insinuate that all pursuit by the agent of his good is at bottom a 'moral' pursuit or that morality compels its realization by natural necessity? Nothing is further from my thought. The point lies in the actual manifoldness, as distinct from a sheer duality, of our valuational modes as revealed by reflection upon linguistic usage— a difficulty in approaching the third type of 'Good' concepts results from experience offering too ample rather than too scarce foundations for it—although, undoubtedly, I would also refuse to dismiss as irrelevant the concern of utilitarian and metaphysical thinkers to find for moral virtue not merely a logically possible place but an essential basis in the texture of 'natural' reality. Moral self-detachment may itself become more understandable, more credible as it were, if seen in the context of somehow analogous objectivizations than if regarded as an isolated miracle.

Forbearing from any discussion of them in detail, I will but briefly list here some of the standard concepts of Good that do not stand unequivocally for either the subjective and hedonic or the properly moral meaning of the term. (a) The concept of 'goods' itself marks an inchoate objectivization: certainly the character of anything as 'goods' depends directly on the supposition of its being 'in demand'; but a class of objects established as 'goods' would still be so designated even when no longer required by anyone and unsaleable for the time being or perhaps for ever. Moreover, it may be the offer of the goods that awakens the demand for them. Goods are not simply 'means' for the fulfilment of a purpose that would necessarily exist in the same form if *they* were not in sight and accessible. On the other hand, there are many kinds of desires and pursuits to which no category of 'goods' corresponds. (b) The 'goodness' of a thing is not always an exact equivalent of its being-desired or its enjoyability according to its express or usual function. It may connote its wholeness as opposed to defectiveness, a property closely relevant to but entirely independent of fitness for use; again, it may connote the property of having been skilfully made or done. (c) Welfare and whatever is conducive to welfare, i.e. 'wholesome', typify a meaning of 'good' intimately connected with but clearly detachable from its primary definition as the object of appetite. A man may care more for some excessive or vicious pleasure than for his welfare; he may also care for knowledge of some kind, for his moral integrity, or for some morally significant special purpose, more than for his (or some other persons') welfare. Health and certain other staple 'interests' do not constitute the global world of our 'good', yet both our practical thought as a whole and our moral thought necessarily refer to them

as ineliminable constants of man's good and of practical orientation. (d) Human virtue in the original sense of the word (ἀρετή,
virtus, virtù; ability, training, skill, prowess, accomplishment, high
quality) is certainly not identical with moral goodness (being 'virtuous', in modern usage) yet at the same time is appreciated as an
autonomous modality of goodness, not as purely instrumental or
wish-dependent. A good craftsman is something 'good' (admirable,
pleasing and praiseworthy) besides being a convenient source of
certain goods we may need; and even the epithet 'a good man' we
may not apply always in an exclusively and unequivocally moral
sense. (e) Knowledge or understanding (according to Brentano,
even *Vorstellen*, i.e. consciousness or mental representation) claims
to be recognized as good *per se*; however it may tie in with one
dimension of pleasure and one aspect of morality. A similar claim
appears at least to be arguable as regards beauty and special
aesthetic qualities perhaps not exactly interpretable as constituents
of beauty. Unlike commodities or any objects of appetite *as such*,
'values'—*bona honesta*—are 'respected', appreciated by the valuer
as above himself and prior to his concerns in a peculiar and well
characterized fashion; yet this experience does not in itself imply
any reference to the moral law or moral virtue; and insight or
erudition, while they 'adorn' a person, lie closer to the category of
'his good' or indeed 'his possessions' than does moral excellence.
The landscape of Good, then, is more variegated than the dicho-
tomy between good for ... and good absolutely, or John's good
and John's goodness, or the non-moral and the moral good, would
suggest.

4. ARISTOTLE'S METAPHYSICS OF GOOD

If good is that which is desired and pursued (*appetitur*), how can
desire nevertheless go wrong, and behaviour be objectionable? And
does a man's goodness consist in his being desired? Or if not—for
to Aristotle's *Ethics*, this approach is alien; the 'desirable man' is
for him not the 'good man' but the 'good citizen', a concept that
finds its place in the *political* perspective—is a man's goodness
constituted by his effective pursuit, acquisition, experience, possession, absorption, etc., of goods and forms of good? (If I have a
good steak but the dog eats it instead of I, that does not make him
necessarily more comestible, while pig-swill and mere grass go to
the making of bacon and beef; if I eat it myself I may not thereby
become more virtuous. Yet appropriate food tends to increase
strength; study to increase wisdom and learning; and the contemplation of virtue, virtue ...) Aristotle, tempted by the mirage

of a unitary Good but not unaware of its ambiguity, makes some contributions to the subject which are worth a critical recording.

His point of departure lies in the conception of good as *'perfective'* of the thing whose good and, basically, the object of whose striving it is. Good is inconceivable without a reference to its power of attraction; but that attraction is thought of as consequent upon the objective *need* on the part of the attracted thing for having its being 'perfected'—sustained, accomplished, enhanced—by 'its good'. Pleasure is thus regarded as a sign of the attainment of the good, rather than as its stuff or definiens proper. That the appetite 'tends towards' the good is not a mere tautology but rather a universal fact of nature, a metaphysical law (in non-Aristotelian language). Good thus becomes a concept subordinate to that of perfection of being according to its essential nature—*qua* the kind of being it is: man, of course, *qua* man—and this first principle may present us with a key to the solution of both puzzles.

If appetite though necessarily directed to the good, does not strictly speaking define the good, a cleavage between its virtual or essential and its actual *nisus* is thinkable without contradiction. It can be misdirected and faulty in its operation, not only in the trivial sense of the ineffectual and frustrated striving but in the sense of intrinsic aberrancy. It is of its nature good-bound and therefore actually groping towards some good and some aspect of 'the good' but may adhere to something not actually perfective in the given conditions and in proportion with the pull it exercises. And the signal of pleasure (or pain) may accordingly be misleading. This may, not exclusively perhaps but especially, occur in man, as the ransom of his metaphysical excellence, i.e. his privilege among animals of being endowed with reason. In virtue of its quasi-divine universality, its overture to an infinitude of objects, man's Mind enables him to turn to all kinds of things and by judgement and intelligent choice reach for the good that suits him best. However, if man is an image of God he is also an embodied animal and his soul partly a machinery of sensuous urges; his reason both controls and ennobles his sensuality but at the same time is subject to its pressure and vulnerable to its warping influences. For the somehow god-like height and wealth of his mode of life, for his perfection unique in the physical world, he pays with the possibility of erroneous judgement and vicious choice, nay, an innate inclination to misuse his powers, allow his unbridled desires to stray into ways of degradation, and fall short of his essential stature. While always of *a priori* necessity pursuing a conceptual semblance (*species*) of good, he may pursue a merely *apparent* and disregard the *true* good. To avoid this and ascend to his 'natural' perfection, he needs education, i.e. instruction in philosophical (scientific) knowledge including that of ethical principles and moral training: for theoretical knowledge even of the human good and moral virtues in general is compatible with practical error, that is to say a misjudgement by the agent of what is 'his good here and now', and thus with moral lapse and vice. Man needs to acquire, then, the intellectual virtue of correct 'practical judgement', *prudence*, and *moral virtues* proper such as temperance and justice, habits intrinsically guiding desire, passion, ambition and behaviour in the right direction—towards the agent's true good. Prudent judgement requires theoretical knowledge including general moral insights but is not guaranteed thereby; it is also conditioned by moral virtues although it informs and presides over their operation and actually 'commands' each single right choice. The dependence between prudence and right willing is reciprocal; and moral virtue in fact begins with, though it does not consist in, the enforced habit-forming practising of right acts not as yet inspired by the agent's own prudential judgement and thus not so far genuinely moral. In sum, Aristotle's key idea here appears to me to be the distinction between true and apparent good; seeing the objectivity of good which implies a certain disjunction of it from appetite and pleasure, he is not committed to the absurdity of calling a misdirected will too a 'merely apparent' will, or contending that an un-virtuous pleasure is not really a pleasure.

As to the second problem: the relation between man's pursuit of his good and his own goodness resides in the perfective action of the (*true*) good. Every being in pursuing its good is building its own perfection *qua* that being, which means its own goodness (again perfective in certain ways for certain other beings); but man can only do so by displaying his right knowledge and habit of right choice, i.e. moral virtue. To be sure, the ultimate emphasis lies, not on moral virtue, i.e. man's goodness as commonly understood —although so understood in the Christian more than in the Greek world—but on man's perfection as specific to man, which means his being securely centred in 'reason', dedicated to theoretical thought and wisdom, and the supreme happiness which in Aristotle's view that state constitutes for him; yet this perfection presupposes and includes moral virtue, and plainly also connotes goodness in the sense of being perfective of other men through justice, teaching, example and friendship. It is the easier for Aristotle to paint a conspectus of good desired and moral goodness as it never even occurs to him to pay any attention to the deontic concept of morality, the concept of Moral Law or Duty as the concept of right action regardless of the agent's own weal or woe, more familiar to us but by no means unknown to the Greeks of his time and earlier[a] including even some philosophers: δέον, from which 'duty' derives, can be found in Democritus. The Greeks, as Hannah Arendt acutely observes, were neither ignorant of the theme of Right and Wrong nor simply set it at naught, but they were prone to accord keener attention to some other dimensions of value. (The store we set by technological power and material comfort might well surprise *them*.) Aristotle's own interest is obviously and self-evidently hedonic-utilitarian (appetite, pleasure, ends and means, and largely prudence and reason in the sense of a rational conduct of life belong in this context), but in a hardly less central though less fundamental manner it is also directed to morality; witness his zestful rather than merely derivative discussion of the moral virtues seen in their intrinsic contents, and his occasional appeal to the test of *consensus* ('praise and blame'). But all this is overarched by the metaphysical dominant of 'perfection': good is a token of what is conducive to the elaboration of being (and therefore needed and coveted by it) as well as a mark of its proper exercise or 'act' (and therefore characterizing it as 'virtue'). At its accomplished height, man's mode of being approximates to the 'purely intellectual'—this fancy largely accounts for the solemn and pompous features in Aristotle's vision of the 'ideal man', his notion of virtue as connatural to a kind of cultured gentleman's existence, his doctrine of 'natural slaves', etc.—but in its central reality, Aristotle is well aware of it, man's mode of being is ineluctably *practical*, i.e. choice and action prepared, enlightened and ordained by thought interwoven with behaviour and adapted to its emergent concrete problems. Right practice, the art of the 'good life', appears to rise both above mere wish-gratification and hedonic calculus on the one hand, and above deontic or 'intuitive' absolute morality on the other: the 'true' good of the agent, selected by his 'prudence', already implies a reference to his goodness, and his goodness remains embedded in his pursuit of *his* 'true' good.

This tangled conceptual scheme is obviously open to the charges of circularity, arbitrariness, and contortion; it is not free from contradiction and verbal jugglery; inspired by a unifying endeavour, it may well appear to complicate matters beyond their inherent complexity; its author may be accused of trying to explain *obscurum per obscurius*. I am nevertheless inclined to think that it represents a great (and lonely) piece of pioneer work in the philosophy of Practice. Credit is due to Aristotle for having raised the *problem* of a vitally important meaning of Good neither properly moral nor purely conative or hedonic though connected with both these meanings, a meaning dependent on subjective concerns but

connoting objective appreciability; for having raised the problem of
'*right*' or '*wise*' *practice* not identical either with moral conduct as
such or with an efficient technique of securing determinate aims as
such, though he would confuse it now with the one now with the
other; and for having raised the problem of the *relation* between
the agent's 'pursuit of the good' in his object-directed actions and
intentions and his 'shaping of himself', a principally moral theme.

Aristotle's perfectional reading of 'the good' and of moral goodness manifests on the one hand the naturalist's mind one-sidedly
and obsessively focused on vital growth, unfolding and wealth, on
the other hand the preponderant Greek emphasis—less conspicuous in Socrates, and much more in Plato—on the production of
works of art and craftsmanship. The high-bred, admirable type of
man, 'wise' (the universal Greek magic-word) in the substantive
sense of being entirely centred in Reason, the highest and hegemo-
nic 'faculty of the soul', which is installed in secure command over
the rest; the fine product of education but also of self-education
through rational practice which at the same time means the exercise
of virtue—to the elucidation of this supreme shape of embodied
nature, rather than to an analysis of right and wrong ways of acting
or good and evil intentions, Aristotle's ethical thought is ordained.
But, in reality, notwithstanding the sidelights thus thrown on
various aspects and possible relations of 'good', its meaning or
scale of meanings hardly becomes more intelligible by being arbitrarily bent into the service of such a special endeavour. Whatever
meaning 'perfection' may have, it is *per se* a highly nebulous and
indeterminate one, which requires the filling-in of more directly
comprehensible and evident concepts of value and desirability.
There may be a natural *nisus* towards perfection, but even in order
to ascertain this we must have a standard of perfection, only to be
filtered from intuitive consensual valuations, independent of our
observation of the bent of nature itself. Being is (in various senses)
good and bad alike; an essentially positive relation between being
and good may plausibly be suggested, but the initial postulate of
their identity hinders rather than helps us to understand what
'good' means. It may well be morally good to promote the 'perfection' of self and of others in any meaningful sense of personal
perfections, but neither does this in any way define or comprise
morality nor is it true that a man is morally better for being more
perfect in any, however basic and desirable, non-moral sense.
Man's being distinctively human or fully developed *qua* man cannot be the criterion of his morality, for what distinguishes man
from the 'brutes' is his being morally *accountable* (though brutishness in man may be evil)—in *Politics* I, 1, Aristotle justly notes

that man in virtue of his intellect, indeed of his 'virtues', may become the most dangerous of beasts unless bridled by civic order—
and moral goodness and wickedness, by standards similar to ours,
are quite conceivable in non-human beings behaving in the mode
of judgement and free choice.

Again, good in the primary sense of 'good for . . .', though it
may contribute to the agent's perfection in some non-moral or
moral respect, is essentially correlative not with the agent's quality
or value but with the agent's desires, wishes, wants, aims, concerns, interests or needs. Aristotle's distinction between 'true good'
and 'apparent good' is largely specious and misleading. So far as a
certain object is 'good for me', it is no less of a true good if I obtain
it by theft or fraud than if I obtain it by honest means. A really
'apparent' good for me would be a thing which, on having been
coveted and obtained by me, turns out to be something different
from what I assumed it to be, or descriptively the same but failing
to yield the satisfaction I expected from it. No doubt, I may
(ignorantly, foolishly, perversely, or perhaps only in somebody
else's opinion) pursue a *lesser* 'true good' in preference to what
would be a *greater* good for me; but, apart from the extreme complexity of the comparison in many if not in most cases, this is
wholly different from pursuing what is merely an apparent not an
actual good. Again, I may immorally pursue a true good for me
which in the circumstances, or even absolutely, I *ought not* to pursue; and this also might be interpreted as the sacrifice of a 'more
precious possession', namely my moral integrity. And I may
obsessively pursue some good to the detriment of my welfare, i.e.
a conjunction of my more constant interests; though lack of prudence in the schematic and easily testable sense may sometimes—
it is not now the time to argue the point—justify itself, on a higher
plane of consideration, as a form of practical wisdom, linked perhaps to the suasion of a delicate conscience. If all striving is directed
to something good yet not necessarily in a way conducive to the
agent's deep or enduring satisfaction, or likely to promote his all-
round well-being, or indicative of his goodness, the reason is not
that he illusively mistakes for good what is bad or indifferent—a
trivial, extrinsic accident beneath the level of the problem—but that
all striving is by no means necessarily directed to comprehensive,
many-sided, highly objectivized and widely proven good, or again,
to moral good.

5 . BAD AND EVIL

Notwithstanding the obvious dangers of word-fetishism, the study

of linguistic usage—at any rate, where it is stable and extends over
several language areas—is seldom unrewarding from a philosophic
point of view. It is the philologist's, perhaps the cultural or racial
psychologist's, business to pry into the finer points and the history
of German *soll* with its almost exclusively imperative, Dutch *zal*
with its exclusively temporal (future-indicating) and English *shall*
with its delicately balanced twofold function; or again, to muse
over the curious affinities between English and Spanish: the English continuous present and Spanish *estar* used with the gerund,
the English and Spanish use of the composite perfect, the absence
in English and Spanish of an exact equivalent of *volo, voglio, je
veux, ich will*, etc. But a comparative glance cast upon the Teutonic
auxiliary shall-soll-zal-skall will at any rate tell us something about
the possible interfusion of the notional forms of command and
futurity, with some confirmation to be gained from the emphatic
Decalogue imperatives in French (*tu ne tueras point*) and Spanish
(*no matarás*); again, English *I will* directs our attention to willing
as emergent doing, English *I want* to willing as consequent upon
lacking, needing and desiring, Spanish *quiero* to willing as a collateral of loving (and, by etymology, as germane to seeking). Surely,
however, there can be no more fascinating revelation of language
than the asymmetry, so far at least as the world of modern European languages extends, between the unitary basic *pro*-word Good
and the plurality—more essentially, duality—of the corresponding
basic *con*-words such as Bad and Evil, along with Ill, in English.

We have perhaps more than a hint in a similar sense in Latin
malus and *pravus*; true, I dare not rely much on Romance pairs
like *mauvais, méchant* and *malo, malvado*, nor would I trespass on
Greek territory. But Bad and Evil have their fairly exact counterparts not only in German *schlecht* and *böse*, Dutch *slecht* and
kwaad but also in Russian *plokhóy* and *zloy*, nay, in Hungarian
rossz and *gonosz*. Yet the majestic *pro*-word *good, goed, gut*, etc.,
stands unfractured and in unchallenged uniqueness everywhere.
This is not to deny that there are manifold secondary variations in
its use: thus, in some languages more than in others 'good' itself or
some derivative of it (*goodly, bonito*) is or may be used to designate
'beautiful'; again, *ein guter Mensch* is not an exact equivalent of
a good man (even apart from the fact that *man* means both *Mensch*
and *Mann*), the German expression connoting kindness or a well-
meaning disposition more and firmness of character less emphatically than the English. Nor would I deny or forget that all
languages contain a host of differentiated, including composite and
technical, words expressing various shades and aspects of goodness
and badness according to the speaker's need or purpose: words like

virtuous, fine, worthy, praiseworthy, wretched, depraved, dastardly, etc., or phrases like 'morally good' or 'physical evil'. In English, we even have another short antithetic formula with a powerful and substantive ring: Right and Wrong (not entirely matched by *Recht und Unrecht*).ᵇ But none of these considerations can impair the significance of the basic distinctness of Bad and Evil, lacking a counterpart on the side of Good.

If language is logic-crazy and the fertile womb of all notional subtlety, it is also notoriously illogical and exasperatingly heedless of the crop of confusions its whims may breed. Confining ourself to English and German, let us confront the triads *bad, ill, evil* and *schlecht, übel, böse*. Unless I am sorely mistaken, whatever divergence of meaning may obtain between *bad* and *schlecht* is so slight as to be negligible ('A bad tooth' can be rendered literally in German; not so, 'a bad finger' or 'a bad ear', and even less 'a bad headache' or 'I want it badly . . .'). The position of the other four words concerned is more confusing. *Evil* and *übel* are materially the same word, but their 'behaviour' is only partly the same. Their meaning as *nouns* (an evil, *ein Übel*), non-moral or rather comprehensive like that of 'good' or 'bad', is wholly, or almost so, identical. 'Good' and *gut* make nouns, but 'bad' and *schlecht* do not; in both tongues we must speak of bad things, something bad, bad traits, vices (a slighter vice in a person, an unvirtuous trait, is *eine Untugend* in German); but a bad state of affairs or anything bad considered as an undesirable fact, a 'disvalue', may also be called 'an evil' and analogously in German, as in the famous verses of Schiller:

> Das Leben ist der Güter höchstes nicht,
> Der Übel größtes aber ist die Schuld.

(Life is not the highest of goods, yet Guilt *is* the greatest of evils.) However, the *adjective* 'evil' is much more frequently used than *übel* in German, and with a stronger moral emphasis roughly on a par with German *böse*, though very occasionally it takes on a non-moral tint as in the phrase 'evil-reeking'. Illiteracy is an evil, but an illiterate person is not for that reason evil. The German adjective *übel*, perhaps a more literary word, has a less unequivocally moral meaning, and tends to connote moral contempt rather than violent moral condemnation. English 'ill' is a tricky word, today at any rate nearly always used idiomatically in non-moral contexts (ill-timed, ill-bred, ill-starred, ill-written; I feel ill, he fell ill, illness; 'ills' as a synonym for 'evils'; though 'ill-disposed', 'ill-will', 'ill-feeling' denote malignant or inimical attitudes not weakness or faulty functioning). I propose to set aside 'ill' and *übel* and to tackle once more 'evil', *böse*.

The equivalence, needless to say, is not complete. 'Evil' and *böse* are very stern words, but 'evil' preserves a closer vicinity to 'bad', 'ill', and its own German variant *übel*—cf. 'an evil', 'evils'—whereas *böse* refers more strictly to active moral evilness and, moreover, has a significant collateral (not properly moral) meaning of its own, to be presently stated, which is quite alien to the English word. In some sense, *böse* is better translated by *wicked*; but, seeing that 'wicked' in modern language is more often used nowadays with a twinkle of jocose quasi-condemnation—in the sense of 'naughty' or 'wittily malicious'—rather than as a term of true moral opprobrium and that no antithetic pair 'Good and Wicked' can be joined to Good and Bad, Good and Ill, Good and Evil, I propose to dismiss 'wicked' here and fall back on 'evil' as the classic moral antipole to 'good'. Now, by consulting the German for 'evil', *böse*, a ray of light may be shed on the distinctive nature of the moral sphere. As denoting not a quality but a condition, comparable to 'I feel bad', 'he is worse today', or Spanish *está bueno* in contrast with *es bueno*, in current idiom *böse* means 'angry', 'irked' or 'vexed'. Thus *er ist sehr böse* he is very angry (but *eine böse Tat* an evil deed, *er ist ein böser Mensch* he is a bad or wicked man); *ich war auf ihn böse* I was angry with him; *wir sind (mit einander) böse* we are on bad terms (with each other). This leads us to recognize enmity, aggression, malice, malevolence, malignancy as a note at least virtually attaching to the meaning of moral evil, wholly absent from the meaning of 'bad' as such but directly expressed in the three Latin derivations, just listed, from the root *mal*. The same hint is conveyed by English 'fiend', devil, compared with its German form *Feind*, enemy; indeed, in old-fashioned religious language the Devil is sometimes called in German *der böse Feind* 'the evil enemy', or *der Widersacher* 'the Antagonist'. (It may be mentioned in passing that *Bosheit* may mean both the quality of being wicked in the serious sense and a malicious insinuation, while *boshaft* always means 'maliciously aggressive', mostly with a connotation of wit.)

In contradistinction from 'bad' pure and simple, 'evil' (wicked, evil-intentioned) thus seems to emphasize the note of enmity, malevolence, and something like 'deciding *against* . . .' or 'siding with the enemy camp'. It may obviously be objected (*a*) that the frequently observable habit of confusing what is hostile or harmful to oneself with what is morally evil is itself immoral and embodies a falsification of moral experience; (*b*) that malevolence is only *one* dimension of moral evil, and has hardly anything to do with, e.g. untruthfulness, and less with unchastity or intemperance; (*c*) that immorality as 'taking the enemy side' has no meaning except in a religious, especially a Christian and perhaps even more in a Mazdaistic, perspective.

In reply to objection (*a*), with whose content I of course whole-heartedly concur, suffice it to say that the egotistic confusion is beside the point; even the speaker committing it in moral discourse means, not that friendliness towards his particular self defines morality but that friendliness and the reverse towards one's neigh-bour is *per se* a test of moral good and evil *and* that when *he*, who is supremely important to himself, is that neighbour the clause *per se* may evidently be omitted, i.e. that for any behaviour directed against *his* wish or interest the possibility of justification does not arise.

Objection (*b*) is also correct in so far as the concept of evil is not generally reducible to that of malevolence to others; but this is not what I was suggesting. My point is, rather, that the concept of moral evil essentially and characteristically refers, not so much to a deficient degree of certain required qualities, which is what 'bad' primarily means, as to a decision or sustained decision, a *direction* of the will, *contra* as opposed to *pro* in regard to certain privileged ends, values or principles of which the 'good of' human and (to a lesser degree) sentient beings in general constitutes one prominent type. 'Rebellion' against an accepted order, law or standard is in this respect on all fours with malevolence; in any case, an aspect of wilful oppugnancy, a central feature of 'contrary' choice appears to be inherent in moral evil as distinct from the unsatisfactory or inferior quality, or even the factually thwarting, repellent or painful effect of that which is just 'bad'.

Hereby, objection (*c*) also has largely been answered. Ethical analysis certainly cannot be conducted on particular religious sup-positions or even on those of an assumed 'natural' theology; for just as it would be meaningless to attribute strength or power to God unless we had some idea of strength or power drawn from our experience of the physical and social world, so also if we had no intrinsic concept of good we could not meaningfully call God good or say that what is commanded by God or pleasing to God is good. It might still be true that a believer can penetrate more deeply the meaning of good and evil than an atheist, or again that our moral consciousness is historically underlain by a (broadly speaking) Christian conception of the world and that men's awareness of good and evil in general could not have come into being without a collateral set of beliefs in Godhead and in spirits at harmony or at discord with it. On the other hand, the formal model '*pro* or *contra*' (good as 'loyalty', and evil as 'siding with the enemy') may not necessarily, and even on the religious view need not exclusively, refer to the transcendental duel between the Lord of the Hosts and the Prince of Darkness. It might refer to antagonistic prototypes of willing at work in each of us or as 'social forces' whose conflict were one of the dominants of history. It is sufficient to retain here so much: unlike the distinction Good-Bad, the disjunction Good-Evil seems to imply a conceptual mode of antithetic attitudes, a category of *Assent and Dissent*, as it were a free act of acceptance on the one hand and a gesture of *non serviam* on the other.

Acceptance of what, however? And given some metaphysical or more narrowly naturalistic answer, 'Being' or 'the Order of Nature', how to account for the *mysterium iniquitatis* of a will rebellious to it, since such a will must itself be part of what is and spring from the entrails of nature? But the point I have tried to make may be registered without our straying further on the path of speculative construction, as a descriptive datum of moral experience. In some broad and loose sense, being in its manifoldness and coherence and the functioning of nature *must* be 'good', for it is only in that frame of reference, against that background, that we come to contrast good and bad at all, and it is things conducive to the undisturbed processes of life, to security, unfolding, etc., that we call good, and destruction, obstruction, deformation, etc., bad. We are not thereby committed to interpret all dimensions of good and bad in such terms, or committed to an interpretation in such terms of all standard meanings of good and bad, and notably to any rash explanation of the morally good and bad in terms of biological concerns or their rational governance, but we may vaguely assume some sort of congruity between the natural and the moral good rather than a relation of strict mutual irrelevance: is not, say, human life or bodily and mental integrity somehow morally entitled to respect, and is it implausible to assume that the flourishing of a society depends in some manner and to some extent on the prevalence of moral principles and habits? Nor are we committed by that initial concept of an ontological or natural 'good' to the fanciful view that being, life, nature or the universe constitutes a kind of undivided unity with its unequivocal and identifiable 'interests' as a whole, it being the glorious 'good of' the antelope to be eaten by the lion and so forth. But suppose we admit that, at least within an area of possible understanding and co-operation, concord and orderly procedures are in some very fundamental sense to the 'good of' all concerned and a good thing in itself, e.g. a breeding-soil for particular desirable things; pleasant to look at; bearing in it a promise of continuity and durability. Disruption, disintegration, dislocation, destruction, shrinking, a welter of fleeting and evanescent existences would accordingly seem bad. This canvas of values and disvalues has nothing primarily *moral* about it; we may easily keep it free from the stark hues of moral approval and condemnation. But neither is it rigorously exclusive of, or even unrelated to, what we know as moral experience and its categories. When we think of, be it so called, a 'well-ordered ensemble of human realities' (or more generally, of sentient and intelligent beings and their works), we have something non-moral and *also* something moral in mind, without feeling any stringent need or great eagerness to nicely distinguish between the two aspects and to keep them carefully asunder. And similarly, for the dissonant and unfit, the unadapted and the poorly contributing. We may speak here of bad things, bad influences, bad elements and bad human material, of failures and of irritating presences, etc. Our dissatisfaction is not meant in a sense anxiously confined to a mode of non-moral evaluation, but the sharp tinge of moral condemnation proper has not so far flared up, though an innuendo of it may be discernible, a virtuality of it may lurk in the background.

The moral theme, however, will enter with its full weight with what we experience as a 'wilful' negation of the indistinctly (non-morally and morally) 'good' order, a challenge and rebellion to it. *Evil* in this sense may be particularly conspicuous and, as it were, primordial in the shape of treason and murder, though I would not insist on the point; organized banditry or dogmatic anarchism, though graphically suggestive of the idea of the 'enemy side', are perhaps somewhat over-explicit illustrations of the distinctive meaning of moral evil, and foreign conflict or the clash of hostile tribes and civilizations offer a rather misleading example for reasons I cannot go into at the present stage. (Moral evil is not reducible at all to alienness nor detachable from the concept of badness seen in terms of descriptive qualities; of course, the foreign enemy *may* be regarded as evil and in part actually detested from *that* motive, and a tendency to magnify his bad traits abusively is rarely absent in situations of conflict. But this is parasitic on the genuine concept of moral evil, not prototypal of it.) At *what* points—what neuralgic points, one might say—of life, of constitutive human forms of activity and inter-personal relations, or of a network of conscious existences as such, that experience of a wilfully challenging and subverting intention arises would again not profitably be discussed at this moment. So much appears certain to me that in it lies the essential origin of the concept of moral evil with its characteristic contents and its distinct status, evoking in turn a more explicit differential experience of the moral good which finds its expression in formalized standards and codes. And hence, again, a more precisely workable formal concept of evil as 'transgression' results—'the Law creates Sin', in St Paul's words, although of course the Law does not create intrinsic Evil but answers a need created by it. It will be noted that in the conceptual schema here sketched, howsoever naturalistic and Aristotelian it might appear to some, no attempt is implied to equate good to being (or nature), to deny the plain reality of evil, or to account for the possibility of evil by the concept of a shaky and diluted being 'mixed' with 'non-being' or, more particularly, of a soul 'fettered' to the body and 'reason' paralysed or overgrown by 'sensuality'. Rather, the possibility of evil—but therewith of moral good as well—is seen here to reside in the imperfect, problematic and vulnerable attunement of 'being' to 'being', or to put it differently, in the mobile equilibrium of plural centres of consciousness and will, susceptible of divergent slants in their strivings and of manifold lines of competition and linkage, within a field of ordered co-existence and co-operation. Evil is seen, then, briefly, as active unruliness of some basic kind, not so far determined, in relation to a pre-moral order bearing a general sign of good, and further defined and characterized by the reaction of moral pressure from the part of that order and the loyalties it commands. What matters in the present context is the *secondariness* of evil by reference to a framework of life somehow *presumed 'good'* (not an epitome of moral virtue and splendour but a matrix of satisfactions, mutual sustenance and things and modes of being worthy of appreciation; an order inviting assent), and attached to it the *thematic primacy* of evil by reference to a distinct *moral* consciousness, to moral legislation and to conscience, though this again sets the concept of evil into higher relief and, while repressing evil in part, in part also calls it forth in a more decidedly conscious form.

What may thus be called the ontological primacy of Good and the thematic primacy of Evil will of course have to be discussed at greater length. It is relevant to the distinction between Morality proper and Practice proper, for in the perspective of Practice the agent's ends are *per se* taken for granted as if they self-evidently embodied 'the good', whereas in the perspective of Morality they are subject to the check of conscience, the 'voice' that warns of the actual or threatening presence of evil, and judged by tests established outside them. The point I have been urging here is the comparative unity in our experience of the non-moral and the moral good and the more manifest cleavage between our experience of the non-morally bad and that of the morally evil. That fundamental asymmetry is impressively reflected in the classic and broadly based constant of language I have started from in this section, the indistinct use of 'good' as contrasted with the duality of 'bad' and 'evil' (though complicated by interfusions of usage and further complicated yet also confirmed by other basic words such as, in English, 'ill' and 'wicked'). What is 'well done' may be either a project ably carried out or a praiseworthy action representing a virtuous intention, as if language testified to men's desire to see practice embody a union of both kinds of excellence; greater care, however, is taken to prevent confusion between a thing badly done or bungled, a target missed, an ill executed project and an evil deed (though also described as a 'bad action'), the expression of an evil will. Linguistic usage, to be sure, is not always rigorous or uniform. When, in a war broadcast early in 1941, the British Prime Minister called his German and Italian counterparts 'these two bad men', he was clearly referring to their moral quality; 'evil men' might sound unidiomatic or archaic or too excited, 'wicked men' might carry an uncalled-for tinge of banter if not of endearment, while 'a bad man' is seldom if ever used to designate an incompetent and feeble-willed person. But Maria Theresa's preferred style for Frederick the Great, *der böse Mensch*, was equally idiomatic and philosophically more precise (if less justified intrinsically); for in German *ein schlechter Mensch*, although like 'bad man' a term of moral discourse, could not be predicated of a nightmare tyrant or even an unscrupulous aggressor and *Machtpolitiker* but would be applied to a hard-hearted creditor or a man who neglects his duties to his family and spends his money on drink and women. The ambiguity of 'good', then, is also proper to 'bad' though perhaps not quite to the same extent, but for 'morally bad' there have arisen other, specialized and yet basic—short and original—adjectives, the principal one being 'evil', whereas no analogous split exists on the side of 'good'.

It might be contended that our evaluative consciousness tends on the whole to satisfy itself more easily with attesting order, well-being or 'integrity' *as such* than with denouncing disorder, disturbance or deformation as such; in regard to something bad, it tends to be more *immediately* interested in the particular mode of the disvalue in question. We say 'all right', but 'something is wrong'. When a person is said to be in good health, it would (unless some special reason, such as a recent or suspected illness, motivates it) appear redundant, irrelevant and altogether odd to enumerate his various organs or their functions, assuring the hearer that each of them is up to standard; it can likewise be stated that a person is ill or in poor health, without going into details, but it is not unnatural to say instead, or as an addition, that the person referred to has indigestion or leprosy, or perhaps (naming a basic mode of disturbance) that he suffers from an acute fever or a chronic ailment, or is not right in his mind. In fact, the plurality of 'bad'-words ('bad', 'ill', 'evil', 'wicked', sometimes 'poor'; *schlecht, übel, böse, schlimm*) suggests that the tendency to differentiation is not entirely confined to the distinction between non-moral and moral evil.

6. CONVERGENCE AND CONFUSION

Language is a precision instrument which can. and often is, used with a view to careful distinction; it is also a living thing given to sloppiness and confusion, of which the speaker may be a deluded victim or an artful manipulator, or perhaps a vaguely conscious beneficiary. The philosopher should above all guard against the temptation to consolidate falsehood, suggested or made plausible by the accidental or not-so-accidental pitfalls of language, into a whited sepulchre of formal precision. But, subject to that prime duty, beyond the critical piercing of muddled obscurity he should also probe sympathetically into the motives that may have under-lain its genesis or its persistence, for they are likely to reveal some hidden and elusive truth which it *is* his business to bring into arti-culate shape. To show up the ambiguity of 'good' and, closely tied up therewith, the confusion of practice and morality, is necessary in the first place; to salvage the valid insight overemphasized and mis-stated in that illegitimate conceptual game, to analyse the essential interwovenness or convergence (for want of a better term) of practice and morality is a less elementary duty but a no less necessary and obviously the more fruitful task.

When Plato argues that 'to suffer wrong is better than to inflict it' and that 'the just man is happy'—he was not the first and by no means the last dealer in such edifying stock in trade—I feel im-pressed with the mass of intellectual distortion, *bel-esprit* ungenu-ineness and cheap preaching packed into a concise aphoristic form. In the plain natural sense in which it is better to win than to lose a battle, or better to be the rider than the horse or an eater of beef than food for a beast of prey, it is patently better to inflict wrong (that one gets away with it is presumed) than to suffer it; and in an equally plain moral sense, he who does not inflict wrong (but rather, so far as that may be the alternative, endures it) is evidently *a better man* than he who does. To inflict wrong is evil, although to suffer wrong is not in itself either good or bad morally, and as a voluntary act *may* indeed be evil inasmuch as it may be a mani-festation of cowardice and an encouragement to evildoers. I ought to abstain from wrongdoing because it is evil, not because it is, truly or allegedly, bad for me. Justice is good, whether it brings happiness or unhappiness, or neither, to him who practises it. If, practising justice, I find that 'nevertheless'—nevertheless, for my living up to a standard to which I attach great value *must* indeed offer me *one* kind of gratification—I feel unhappy, either because of the disadvantages I suffer for justice's sake or for other reasons, I must not try to persuade myself or allow myself to be persuaded by oily-tongued sophists that 'in truth' I *am* happy although I may evince some discomfort. How shaky the ground is on which Plato stands here is astoundingly demonstrated by the fact that, although starting from the laudable endeavour to confound the more primitive and outspoken sophists according to whom morality was an irrelevant fancy only heeded by fools (or a self-protective invention of 'the weak'), in the course of his argument he comes to distort the concept of justice out of recognition, defining it as the order of a well balanced soul and travestying it, of all things, into a principle of totalitarian tyranny. (On this path at least his great pupil, court tutor and social snob that he might be but not a fascist aesthete, did not—be it said to his honour—follow him at all.)

And yet, is Plato and are the many moralists who indulge in more or less similar speculations wholly wrong, or let us say merely wrong? Is the age-old human worry, which they voice and which they would fain appease, about the tension between the self-regarding or natural and hedonical, possessive, etc., pursuits of man and his equally irremovable subjectness to moral judgement nothing but *une passion inutile*? Can the weight of oughtness be made valid in actual reality—and that is its inherent claim—but more, can a serious meaning be attached to its 'ideal validity', unless it is seen as aligned with what *is* the constitutive endeavour of man (or of thinking and willing finite souls)? Is there not something touchingly absurd, nay, an air of false sublimity reminiscent of Plato, about Kant's definition of morality by 'purity of motive', i.e. 'reverence for the concept of Law' as the only motive for action irrespective of anything else, seasoned with the pathetic remark that the validity of the moral demand is independent of whether anybody has ever really performed a moral action? Especially so if one considers Kant's admission 'by the back-door', at the later stage of religious reflection, of the 'postulate' of happiness as a reward for goodness, brutally but not inappositely described in a chapter-title of the utilitarian Friedrich Jodl's *Ethik* as *Der Einbruch des Eudämonismus in Kants Ethik*. And, passing from Kant's idealistic formalism—not to forget his identification of the good will with the will *of* the entity labelled 'intelligible ego' or 'true self', which has brought down even on him Moore's anathema for 'naturalism', though of the 'suprasensible' brand—passing, then, to straightforward intuitionism, how many are those who accept

Prichard's peremptory decree that an obligation is just an obligation directly recognized as such and there's an end to it as a fully
convincing revelation and the last word on the matter? Are we on
the horns of a dilemma? Man's striving must be judgeable as morally good *or* bad: it cannot be the test and standard of morality; on
the contrary, it is tested by the standards of Good and Evil which
do not express *it* but represent something else, rather as the goodness or badness of a foodstuff is tested not by the immanent vital
tendency of the plant or animal it comes from but by our taste and
want. But food *meant* by producers, processers, retailers, cooks and
servers for consumption should, so we would at any rate candidly
imagine and expect presumably be good rather than bad, not un-
predictably either good or bad as if it was *a priori* anybody's guess
which of the two it would turn out to be. If striving is morally
indifferent and the turn it takes in choice, will or action only *happens* to be now good now evil, it would seem that we cannot expect
it to be prevalently, intrinsically or consistently good even in a
comparative and imperfect sense. Moreover, in contrast with the
example of food and its estimation, the principles of moral judgement must involve the quality of the appraiser's own striving as
viewed in the same terms and the goodness of striving must involve
principles held by the agent himself. The moral *demand* declares
not what the agent *is* but what he *ought* to be, granted; but its inherent claim to be effective compels it to take on the form of the
moral *appeal*, which no less essentially is directed not to what the
agent *ought* to be but to what the agent *is*. In other words, so far as
the agent does not recognize that for him to do what is good is in
some way to pursue his good he will not do it, for that would mean
that another is doing his actions in his place, not to say in his skin.
Similarly, the author of moral judgement cannot be, as such, simply another person than the person he is. Taking the word 'life' in
a broad sense encompassing natural constitution, primary pursuits,
self-regarding ends and the concerns developing from and round
these, etc., we may say that morality seen in isolation from life is
powerless, and that for this reason but also for the more basic reason that it can not only not act upon life but not even raise a claim
on life, i.e. not even come to be conceived and formulated, without
in some essential way relating to life, morality seen in isolation
from life is meaningless. That, more particularly, morality can only
be thought of in the context of *practice* is even more evident, for,
while spontaneous natural life as underlying practice concerns
morality no more than in part indirectly and in part extrinsically
(as one of the object-areas of its references), all practice and nothing but practice is directly subject to moral judgement, and choice

is the focal seat of both the moral and the practical perspective. Only consider that what is sometimes drastically called 'the choice between Good and Evil' is in reality some salient instance of the practical choice *between two goods* where the choosing of one of these carries an emphatic note of assent and submission to the moral demand while choosing the other amounts to an act of defiant disobedience to it, though the first good may indeed be chiefly or perhaps wholly constituted by the agent's concern about duty or his own goodness itself and the attraction of the second perhaps be fused with an explicit delight in moral perversion itself.

On no account should this insight into the essential relationship between good *sans plus* and the moral good, between Practice as implying or not implying Morality and Morality as a particular set of standards imposed on Practice, be distorted into a confusion between the two orders. The sterile and unhelpful doctrines of a dry dogmatic intuitionism, which at any rate have the defensive merit of casting light and placing stress on the peculiar tonality and the paramount dignity of the moral demand, are still vastly preferable to every kind of reductionism and naturalism, i.e. the attempts to define the moral good as the greater or greatest good *of* the agent or in terms of welfare or the thriving and unfolding of life, or to define conscious personal morality in terms of prudence or a well-planned, ably managed and felicitous practice. That naturalism, largely inspired by the sham-scientific relish in reduction to the material, mechanical and calculable, linked to impatience with moral restraints, may also (or at the same time) repose on a 'moralistic' and paedagogical intent is illustrated by the example not only of the Platonic-Aristotelian and the Stoical currents but, less manifestly, also by modern Utilitarianism with its puritanical subsoil. That moral nihilism in its turn may also strut about in a putatively or partially anti-naturalistic guise will be touched upon later. I now propose to wind up this discussion[e] by looking into a question-phrase in some way complementary to the one with which I have introduced it.

7. 'WHY SHOULD I BE MORAL?'

This queer-sounding question, which we may meet with either between inverted commas, in ethical texts of non-naturalistic but not exactly Prichardian inspiration or, entirely without inverted commas, in actual discourse with a person who feels like disregarding some moral norm too little in accord with his convenience in a given case, represents one terse way of formulating the problem of morality in the context of practice. It would not be asked by the deontic intuitionist for whom moral obligation is a matter of all but logical self-evidence which needs or indeed tolerates no further justification, nor by the thoroughly moral and securely virtuous person to whom the idea of sacrificing moral duty to a non-moral interest would appear revolting to the point of being practically unimaginable. But neither is the question likely to be asked by a utilitarian or any kind of reductionist, or again by anyone set in an attitude of moral nihilism, unless, in either case, 'moral' be meant ironically in the sense of one particular code or tenet of 'conventional' morality, a here-and-now prevailing datum of social exigence or preference comparable, say, to fashion. For the naturalistic type of thinker, what I 'should' do is unequivocally determined or determinable by my own wishes or well-being ('my good', that which is 'good for me') or by ends or commands imposed on me from outside (the trends of evolution or history, the will of an all-powerful authority, etc.), and what I am thus *made* to do—if not infallibly, at any rate with no alternative but extinction, misery or frustration or self-stultification—is *eo ipso* the *moral* thing to do. Again, for the amoralist there is no point in asking why he 'should' be moral, since he is not annoyed at the moral claim but fails to accord any meaning to it; the question for him can only be how far he 'should' or 'shouldn't', in the purely practical sense of 'should', take account of the machinery of the police and the courts of justice, of the wishes of certain people whose attitude to him affects his interest, or of the possible unpleasant consequences of some pleasures that tempt him. He who asks the question 'Why should I be moral?' also means 'should' in a non-moral practical sense—unlike the ambiguous 'shall' in 'What shall I do?'—but he, on the contrary, ascribes to morality an autonomous meaning and weight. As a theorist, he is precisely *puzzled* by the experience of moral obligation and *in doubt* as to the cogency of naturalistic explanations (Is the social good I promote by my moral actions really conducive to my own good? What if a methodical pursuit of my own happiness makes me feel particularly unhappy?); he would like to discover *what* makes moral obligation 'valid' even when it implies a painful sacrifice. And the person who so asks in a crucial practical situation does not *believe* that morality is a mere delusion but *doubts* that (or perhaps only doubts *whether*) in this case or in similar standard cases its weight is really great enough to countervail against *other* practical weights which stand in opposition to it.

I may be mistaken in so far as 'should' perhaps does connote a meaning of moral oughtness itself in this type of query, less in an alternative 'either-or' fashion than 'shall' in 'What shall I do?' and more in a mode of ambiguity that suggests an amalgam of the non-moral and the moral meaning. Suppose, the anti-naturalistic inquirer may say, that a moral (i.e. morally right) conduct *is* always likely to profit me in due course or 'ultimately': but why *should* I seek for what is profitable to me? Suppose there *is* an infallibly victorious power or trend: but why *should* I conform to it? This of course would express doubt as to the morality of such conformance, which seems to discard the question 'Why should I be moral?'; but the former objection can be put in the form 'Granted that moral conduct invariably benefits the agent, but this empirical fact or even this law of the universe cannot define the meaning or constitute the criterion of morality, for I see no reason why he ought to seek to be benefited; I recognize moral standards and appreciate moral conduct and also believe that it is good for me to behave morally but still fail to see on what grounds I not only 'had better' do so but *ought* to do so, what *makes* moral conduct obligatory'. Again, the vacillating person may say 'I know that for me to do x would be moral, and that matters a good deal to me, but why should it matter *more* than y which I *want* to do and which is not moral and not compatible with x? I prefer to be moral, but why should this be my principal and sovereign preference? The moral point of view admittedly has pith; but is it as compulsive, as important, or shall I say as moral as all that?' Moral appreciation is recognized here as authentic and descriptively true so far as it goes, without any polemical use of the word 'conventional' suggesting that moral qualities are merely a decorative mask for what is beneficial to some non-moral alien interests or moral categories a mere persuasive sham; but the agent is wondering what their compelling force or evidence may consist in, why he must incorporate them as a privileged concern above his other—more spontaneous and intensely felt—concerns.

'But moral *means* obligatory' he will be told, and perhaps thus *ex contrario* be pushed towards moral nihilism. 'All right, then; suppose I said "A fig for morality!"' Or else he might retort 'Very well, then I no longer agree that what you call moral is really so; what you commend would be a handsome or correct thing to do but not exactly *moral* in the full sense of the word!' Now this same critical model can be transferred to the practical, extra-moral realm of 'hypothetical imperatives' itself, in which case it may or may not assume again a positively moral tinge. Whether with a moral intent (perhaps in the course of the foregoing discussion) or not, the adviser convincingly explains to the recalcitrant person where his true interest or good or happiness lies. 'But why *should* I follow my true good, etc.?[d] Even if it is convertible into a manifest excess of pleasure over pain, is that an aim at all worth pursuing? Bother the balance of pleasure and pain!' 'Ah, but you simply *cannot* disregard your good!' 'Can't I? Why not?' 'Because you *are* pursuing your good anyhow; you are so made.' 'But if I am pursuing my good whatever I do, it is a matter of indifference *what* I do: why should I then do *x* rather than *y*?' 'No, no: I meant your true, your fundamental good; you are in fact pursuing *that* anyhow, but you may do so in an unwise fashion, and fall short of it.' 'Indeed? But I, aware of all the circumstances you have been arraying, prefer the pleasure of doing *y* to all the host of pleasures attaching to and resulting from *x*. No matter what you say and how plausible it sounds, having weighed all the *pros* and *cons* I decide for *y* against *x* and thereby prove to you that *x* is *not* my true good!' The lame answer is likely to follow, 'Well, I have warned you; at any rate I must disapprove of your course'. The adviser may be right intrinsically, or is thus right by supposition; but he has not been able to prove his point.

That is not necessarily a matter for regret. What has been defeated is neither the meaning and weight of morality nor the possibility of inquiring into its nature but only an extravagant intellectual pretension. A person who did not *want* to be moral could not 'be moral' anyhow, however conclusively it was shown to him that he 'should' be; that would at best persuade him to comply externally with certain moral duties, and it might sear rather than quicken whatever genuine moral motivations might be germinally present in his mind. A successful reductionist answer to the question, were it possible, would indeed amount to a fundamental uprooting of morality and its supersession by something else, though its name and many of its particular contents might remain in use. In a more modest sense of elucidation as distinct from proof, the question is certainly capable of answer; for both the deontic purport of moral valuation and its linkage with other standard modes of pursuit and appreciation are open to manifold analysis. Perhaps the elusiveness of 'Why should I be moral?' is calculated to help the moral philosopher in three ways. First, it warns him against the simplifying temptation of restricting the concept of morality to that of Duty and to sharpen his vision of its descriptive aspects and classic particular contents as well as of its consonance with *per se* non-moral but morally relevant needs, values and aspirations. Secondly, it may tend to make him aware of the peculiar difficulty of *practical* certitude, choice and judgement, i.e. of the inadequacy of utilitarian calculus even as a principle of Practice considered in itself, regardless of the moral demand. It is, as we shall see, in one sense a much easier but in another, important sense a much less easy undertaking to show a man what is to his good than to show him his duty. Finally, his failure to cope conclusively with the question 'why I should be moral' may make the philosopher sensitive to a rationalistic-naturalistic misdirection always latent in ethical speculation: the mirage, that is, of a necessary goodness of Man— or of every Will—and of evil as a mere appearance. Behind the claim of 'proving' to me that I 'should' be moral there is at work the fond hope, self-contradictory and Utopian, imbued with an atmosphere of all-goodness and all evil in its implications, of demonstrating that I *cannot but* be moral even though some of my operations are ill-conceived and harmful owing to error, inadvertence or technical disability. The practical conclusion to which this speculative schema would point is excessive mildness in dealing with immoral conduct and boundless tyranny in dealing with people, i.e. the policy of cleansing the world from evil and fashioning it in a moral mould once for all, by a comprehensive plan of coercion, need-gratification, indoctrination, training and selective elimination. Yet the real supposition underlying the query 'Why should I be moral?' is that I *should* be moral, which I *may* or *may not*, in transient and permanent senses, *be*.

5

Morality and Practice II:
The Moral Emphasis

Man (in which concept that of any possible 'similar' kind of being
may here be included) is not a constitutively moral being in the
sense that his natural perfection or full unfolding or all-round
thriving means moral goodness, but *is* a constitutively moral being
in the sense of his intentions and actions being again and again,
ineluctably, moral or immoral, i.e. good or evil; and in the closest
interconnection therewith, in the sense that he as ineluctably exercises moral appraisal of his fellows and of self. On this note the
preceding discussion[a] has concluded.

It is as important to realize and uphold the distinction as it is to
realize that nevertheless man's being and goodness do not stand to
each other in a relation of pure independence and neutrality, nor
goodness and evilness to man's being in a relation of unslanted symmetry. This follows not only from even the most elementary analysis of the content of moral sentiments as remarked previously, e.g.
the fundamental moral value of benevolence and disvalue of murder, injury and malice, but also, in a rigorously formal manner,
from the fact of moral appraisal and its inseparability from actual
moral goodness and badness. If man is divided between good and
evil, it is not in the way in which he may be divided between two
coalitions of Powers, or two antagonistic ideals, or two rival interests. It is indeed natural to him to be moral *or* immoral, but it is
equally natural to him to approve of morality and reprove immorality. The former is a term of commendation, the latter a term
of condemnation. 'Good' and 'Bad' are applied to moral and immoral conduct with the same spontaneous force of discrimination
as they are to wholesome and palatable food on the one hand, to
tainted and repugnant food on the other. Most certainly, not only
immoral conduct but also perversions of moral judgement, and
what is more to the point, atrophy of moral sensitiveness and
'cynical' indifference to moral points of view occur; but a basic and
consistent reversal of the *pro* sign attached to moral good and the *con*
sign attached to moral evil is a wholly eccentric, a merely marginal

possibility, and one which is logically—to say the least—'odd'. A man will act on the maxim 'I should like to do x but *will* do its opposite y because x is immoral and y is my duty', or inversely on the maxim 'I ought to do y but will do its opposite x because x greatly pleases me (or eminently suits my interests)'; he will hardly act on the maxim 'I should like to do y and it would be beneficial to me, but I will do its opposite x because x is thoroughly immoral'. Rather, the scoundrelly type of man, Aristotle's 'intemperate' or 'vicious' as distinct from the merely 'incontinent' or 'morally feeble' person, will tend to justify his conduct by ethical sophistry, speciously interpreting its immorality (with, e.g. a reference to patriotism, or to the ultimate interests of mankind, or to 'community', or to personal 'authenticity') as a sort of 'higher' morality. I see little point in talking either of the inherent goodness or of the inherent depravity of man and do not know how to balance his virtuous against his evil dispositions or actions; but the very phrase about the 'corruption of human nature' suggests a decomposition of something in itself good rather than bad, morally legitimate if not morally admirable. If man is to the utmost extent morally 'vulnerable', at any rate it is to the wound not to the wounded body it afflicts that we assign a primary quality of badness. We might, then, say that man is a moral animal not only in the sense of being good-and-evil or good-or-evil, i.e. subject to moral judgement, but also in the sense, not that he is 'good' but that he exercises and thus *submits to* moral judgement. Morally praiseworthy and blameworthy, the latter perhaps in the first place, he is also morally *aware*.

Having accorded as much as that to naturalism, let us now turn to the phenomenon of moral emphasis which it is the main business of naturalism to ignore or to blur. In the opening sentence of this section, I spoke, carefully choosing my words, of man's 'intentions and actions being *again and again*, ineluctably, moral or immoral, i.e. good or evil'. It would have been simpler to say, and more consonant with the stern adverb 'ineluctably', that they were *always* moral or immoral, good or evil; yet I would scruple to do so. It might not be patently and definitely incorrect, but it would have introduced a false note or at least carried an easily misleading suggestion. For one thing, are all of our *morally relevant* actions either unequivocally good or unequivocally bad? Far from it; many of them exhibit *both* virtuous and objectionable dispositions: thus, in one and the same concrete intention, the motive of curbing an evil influence and that of inflicting a grave evil on our 'enemy', or the motive of helping a person in need and an unconscionable disregard for the rights of third parties may be intimately alloyed. It might be contested that the decisive point is whether an action is or is not contrary to duty. But apart from the fact that we should hesitate to call an action 'good' merely for not constituting a breach of any duty, in the face of mutually conflicting *per se* obligations it is sometimes hardly possible *for the agent* to determine what *is* his duty or perhaps even *objectively* impossible to do so—whatever the exertions and merits of moral casuistry and whatever the excellence of the given moral code it must presuppose. Moreover, even an action objectively right and even performed with duty-consciousness may at the same time be prompted by evil motives. Secondly, and this is what I here have chiefly in mind, *are* all our actions morally relevant? And I do not mean half-conscious, involuntary or at any rate wholly unreflected actions but actions proper, nor even unimportant actions alone. *Need* it be morally relevant whether I decide to buy a new pen-knife next or to do with my old and defective one for the time being; whether I vote for party A, B or C at the next elections; nay, whether I decide to embark on this or on that of two alternative projects, the decision being for me a highly important one and either project appearing to be morally quite impeccable and even definitely calculated to promote, each in its way, the good of a wider circle of persons? Note that, in the last case, it may be objected that whichever project I choose on mature and conscientious reflection I shall have made not a morally indifferent but a morally good choice, but that, supposing this to be true—no doubt a matter for satisfaction, so far as it goes—it does not remove, rather its illustrates, the point of the question. For precisely my problem was not a moral problem: what baffled me was not which of the two alternative courses was morally obligatory or almost so, and which immoral or near to it; what I am morally credited with is not my having chosen A as against B or B as against A but merely my careful deliberation, whichever its issue; yet the choice, a weighty choice, was not about the manner of my deliberation but about the project I should pursue, i.e. between A and B; the morally creditable way in which I have chosen has presupposed an alternative quasi-indifferent from the moral point of view but of great practical importance to me and involving a not immaterial repercussion on some other people's concerns. Here is plainly a marked *disproportion* between the *moral* and the *practical* emphasis.

Nevertheless, the opponent may argue, you have acted morally not indifferently as regards morality, whereas if you had chosen with careless levity you again would have acted not in a morally indifferent but in an immoral fashion. But, I retort, observe how *unemphatic* this moral appraisal is either way, though perhaps

especially on the approbatory side. The accent of the 'choice between Good and Evil' is entirely lacking. A strange idea indeed, to
be engaged in a momentous choice and (by applying due care)
prove my moral worth *whichever way I choose*, or (by omitting due
care) reveal my moral inadequacy *whichever way I choose*. Attending with care to one's business is not an outstanding moral merit;
the contrary deficiency, supposing that no grave *moral* issue is involved, is not an archetype of moral transgression. And what if the
choice is *not* practically momentous, again supposing that each of
the alternative courses of action is morally 'all right'? Whichever I
choose I still engage in, and shall perform, an action in the strict
sense of the term, though of slight importance: can I then be said
to be acting or have acted either morally or immorally, on no
account indifferently?

To be sure, there are also complex *moral* dilemmas in regard to
which little more can be said conclusively than that the agent's
decision has been right so far as it has emerged from his thorough
conscientious reflection and wrong so far as he has irresponsibly
followed one moral impulse (perhaps aided by some non-moral
interests of his) without due regard to other *per se* obligations; here
too moral appraisal fastens on the quality of his deliberation, not on
its outcome in this or that alternative sense. But in this case intrinsic moral judgement (by the onlooker) is *difficult* rather than merely
marginal, out of place as it were, as in the former instance; it may
depend partly on personal variations of our moral beliefs; the
agent *may* have actually made a *right* or a *wrong* moral decision; at
all events, a direct reference to intrinsic moral principles occupies
a central place both in the agent's deliberation and in the appraiser's
judgement. The fact that some actions which obviously are morally
relevant cannot easily and with certainty be declared good or evil
does not by any means show that actions (including important actions) *not* on the face of it morally relevant must nevertheless be
morally relevant 'essentially' or 'ultimately' and that all conduct is
either good or evil.

The problem here discussed is not new, though it has been
accorded less than due attention in modern ethics. It constitutes
one of the salient points of controversy between St Thomas
Aquinas and Duns Scotus. Moral theologians are unanimous in
asserting that there exist intrinsically good, intrinsically evil, and
intrinsically indifferent modes of activity or *kinds of action*. (I would
not go now into the problems implied in this concept. Obviously,
much depends on the way in which we define 'kinds of action', or
the extent of specification to which we go in so doing. Thus, it is
evident that 'torturing' is intrinsically evil, while 'hurting' is not,

though neither do I admit that it is intrinsically indifferent; I would call it *per se* evil yet in certain circumstances morally justified or even obligatory. Again, 'ministering to another's need' is a kind of action intrinsically good in a much stronger sense than is 'aiding another'. The classic instance of an intrinsically indifferent kind of action is *ambulare*, taking a walk.) But according to the Angelic Doctor, a concrete *single action*, e.g. my journey to Holland and Belgium in August 1962, cannot be morally indifferent but must be good or bad, whereas according to the Subtle Doctor, it *can* be morally indifferent as well. Most moral theologians have, to my knowledge, adopted the Thomist position; my own, as the reader may have noticed, is substantially, though perhaps not unreservedly, Scotist. Both are arguable, and the antithesis may be partly verbal; partly, it is inherent in the contrasting general outlooks of these two eminent Doctors of the Church. For Aquinas, an Aristotelian naturalist salved with a drop of pantheist mysticism, whatever is practically well accomplished is according to man's true nature and thus indirectly conducive to his supernatural 'final end' (*via* the proper accomplishment of his earthly life); it therefore marks a positive conformance to the moral law, Law being 'the right ordering of things *by Reason*'. An express moral intention is not required therefor. Inversely, 'practical error' is *eo ipso* somehow contrary to the moral law. For Scotus, a voluntarist stressing the freedom of indifference and a concept of the moral law as decreed and imposed by the divine Will, an action not falling under the terms of reference of the explicit stipulations of the moral law is *eo ipso* neither moral nor immoral but indifferent. It will be seen that Aquinas's view is in some sense 'deeper', tending to enhance the moral significance of each of our voluntary acts, but liable to misuse either in an obsessively moralistic or in an optimistic and pragmatistic direction (all imperfection, mediocrity or practical failure may come to be branded as sinful, or inversely, all 'thriving' and practical achievement may raise a claim to moral approval); and that Scotus's view is more in tune with the commonsensical data of moral experience, though it may also invite the dangers of moral formalism and legalism, perhaps literalism. I would not wholly refuse to see Aquinas's point and feel inclined to grant that our conduct as a whole, and our every deliberate act— indeed, even our single spontaneous acts—carry some moral *connotation* (often hidden and, in such cases, hardly ever imputable); it is, however, obvious to me that Scotus's distinction of the properly moral from the non-moral practical relevance of human acts supplies us with a valid elementary axiom of ethical analysis (and represents a progress in it hard to overestimate): and thus, while admitting that all our acts, manifestations, dispositions, etc., may have some moral relevance, I would insist that only a selection of our pursuits, intentions, decisions and projects carry a moral *emphasis*, which is *not* a mere expression of their vital and practical import nor necessarily and invariably proportionate to it.

By 'emphasis', of course, nothing like the subjective intensity of moral emotions is meant. Emphasis in the sense here meant is not the affective condition of the (sensitive) appraiser or of the (conscientious but perhaps strongly tempted) agent; it is the peculiar, sharply characterized tone attaching to every experience of what strikes us as morally relevant, a tone of warning, urging, vetoing and commanding with an 'absolute' and 'unconditional' ring of ultimate gravity about it. There is no reason to see in the moral emphasis and its emergence an 'unanalysable mystery': a good deal more can certainly be found out about it; but that is not my present business. The point is here only that it exists and is the basic subject-matter of ethical enquiry; and that indeed, rather than pervading life and its practical management uniformly as if it were identical with interest as such or with salient or common interests as such, it 'emerges' in some—in very different—contexts and in manifold ways. It emerges 'again and again', virtually omnipresent but by no means always protruding into focus; its claim is privileged and autonomous rather than all-embracing. How, then, is the moral demand 'ineluctable'; in what sense is it the case that we cannot help behaving either morally or immorally? In many limited respects, the alternative *can* be evaded: a man may without immorality make few promises only, and thus seldom be compelled to keep a promise yet never break any; if he stays single he will not be either a faithful or an adulterous husband, and so forth. But it is impossible to live without being 'again and again' confronted by the moral demand, to evade duty and steer clear of transgression by disclaiming a special interest in morality, to renounce the merit of a positive moral intention while also escaping guilt and to plod through life in a state of neutrality between Good and Evil. Reluctance to rebellion against the moral law implies an inchoate assent to it, and refusal of assent amounts to dissent. As the Thomist poet puts it, severely but impressively, in the Third Song of *Inferno*:

> Ed egli a me: questo misero modo
> tengon l'anime triste di coloro
> che visser senza infamia e senza lodo.
>
> Mischiate sono a quel cattivo coro
> degli angeli che non furon ribelli,
> nè fur fedeli a Dio, ma per sè foro.

2. NEGATIVE AND POSITIVE MORALITY

The rise of the Moral Emphasis takes place, schematically speaking, in a non-moral practical world to which it adds a new note of a peculiar kind. Life and its manifold concerns, including aesthetical, intellectual and (in the widest sense) political interests, would be quite imaginable without the intervention of morality, whereas morality is quite inconceivable without the background of life with its confederate and competitive concerns. Yet the new note morality brings into practice is not a superadditive enrichment or optional refinement but a somehow extraneous claim to *its* regulation, supervision and—in many ways—redirection. Of course, this also carries with it a material amplification, the emergence of new contents and *motifs* and shades of valuation neither strictly moral nor conceivable without moral presuppositions. Concrete moral codes or 'tables' are new historic entities, objects of special knowledge and even material objects or generative of such; without moral references and commitment there might be no such thing as the legal machinery; although personal sympathies and aversions are not in themselves a moral phenomenon, some reference to moral character is mostly and quasi-evidently included in judgements like 'He is a nice person' or 'He is an unpleasant fellow'. There also exist branches of activity expressly concerned with moral values or the moral phenomenon as such: thus, certain reformatory and educative pursuits, or ethical speculation. But this is secondary; the true original locus of moral emphasis is the conduct of life itself in its various—essential, urgent, critical, problematic—aspects, structures and junctures. Thus, somebody does me a service in exchange for a promise of mine; each of us is actuated by the motive of his own advantage, perhaps purely material; my partner is not moved by any anxiety to succour me or exercise the virtue of charity, nor do I give my word in search of an occasion for duty-fulfilment, fretting as it were to 'observe' the rules and 'realize' the values of justice or fidelity; but suddenly a voice intervenes, reminding me that I have made a promise and ought to keep it—a voice within myself, or (if I have tarried too long) that of my partner still pursuing his own good but appealing to my conscience, or perhaps the voice of a third party, an 'impartial authority'. This is not the only model for the primary and elementary, not to say elemental, rise of the moral emphasis, but certainly one classic instance of it. Morality does not, then, constitute a realm of activities or a domain of practice comparable, say, to material production, trade, science, the fine arts, religious ritual, organized government, etc. A man may intend to devote the next morning to office or laboratory work, drilling soldiers, negotiations, contemplation, lounging in the streets, nursing his flu' in bed and countless other occupations, certainly also such as involve a great deal of duty-fulfilment or a particular moral aim, e.g. attacking a nest of public corruption; but he cannot very well plan to spend it 'being moral' or 'cultivating morality'. A few minutes or an hour may indeed regularly be set aside for 'examination of conscience', but this is definitely a second- or rather third-order activity, analogous not to painting or carving for example but to the artist's occasional pondering about whether he is on the right way in his projects and methods of painting or carving; a habit of supervising one's recent activities from the moral points of view that may apply to them.

And, if morality is not a primary, substantive domain of activity beside other such domains, neither is it the sum total of a person's activities or the comprehensive ordering of his aims and pursuits. It is not, at least not *primo loco* and characteristically, personal in *that* sense. Men's careers, plans of life, dominant projects and personal aspirations differ widely and differ legitimately, connoting of course also different tones of moral accent (as typified, e.g., by the so-called 'professional ethos'); but the basic principles of morality, even though not professed unanimously in an identical form, are universal and strictly unfit for any close adjustment to the contours of a particular—be it personal or collective—unit of practice or network of pursuits. This crucial fact is often lost sight of because, undeniably, a person's circumstances of life, commitments, temperament and tastes as a rule colour his subjective experience of the moral emphasis, making him more perceptive to some moral points of view and less so to others, increasing the points of application in his life for certain moral norms and reducing others to slighter actual relevance for him. Obviously I who am not a doctor or surgeon can neither observe nor infringe the rules of medical deontology, and similarly I cannot conform or offend against the professional standards of lawyers, preserve or betray atomic secrets, observe or break the Party discipline, and so on. But I can, and indeed on the whole *cannot but*, treat my relatives, neighbours, etc., kindly or heartlessly, keep faith or break it, speak the truth or swear falsely, be a loyal citizen or commit treason, take my duties seriously or neglect them, try to exercise some salutary influence on young people's minds or to corrupt them, and do good or evil in other ways. So far as I may have a professional conscience, it is grafted on my moral conscience proper as a mere specification of it; and I am quite vividly aware of the moral evil incarnate in the cruelty of despots though I have little natural inclination and less opportunity to imitate their deeds. Again, I am very keen on inquiring into certain problems, on expressing myself correctly in a few specified languages, on having access to certain (rather than other) more or less innocuous enjoyments, etc., but am emphatically unaware of these same concerns' constituting an obligation binding for the sons of men or for personal beings as such, and hold that they have in part only an indirect and conditional moral relevance, in part but a vague and optional one, and in part none at all. But suppose, now, that one or another of these interests, or some concrete and determinate wish affiliated to any of them, comes to assert itself imperiously yet could only be satisfied at a heavy moral cost, e.g. by means of my committing theft or fraud or arrant betrayal or at least brazen deception: *then* will moral emphasis enter in its fully fledged and concentrated form. According to the degree of my virtue or depravity and according to circumstances, it may enter, psychologically speaking, in the shape of forewarning conscience, effective at once or after some struggle only, or defeated in the end and returning in the mode of accusing conscience; or in the shape of other people's reaction and my awareness of it; or perhaps only in the shape of my fear of exposing or having exposed myself to moral contempt and to retaliation largely based on it. The sharp and peculiar tint of the moral emphasis does not depend on the psychological volume and intensity of manifestation in the given case. In a very virtuous and for opposite reasons in a very vicious person, conscience will sometimes hardly reach the threshold of consciousness at all, and grave but undetected immorality committed by the second kind of person will evoke no actual moral experience of any kind. Moral emphasis attaches to the morally relevant state of fact (*Sachverhalt*, or 'it-being-the-case-that') and, so far as actually experienced, it presents its peculiar characteristics and is what it is—just as, although a bullet that misses its aim will not kill or hurt nor perhaps even scare, and a bullet that kills instantly may cause no suffering, the nature of bullets, fire-arms and shooting is in no way altered by these possibilities.

We have no empirical experience of an *amoral* human state of perfection and bliss or utter foulness and wretchedness or total solipsistic isolation, and thus if we sketch the lineaments or retrace the unfolding of human practice and social life as a whole, morality will appear in the picture as a kind of obvious prolongation and implication of essential non-moral concerns, attitudes and requirements. Thus, from our natural attachment to life it will be explicated that we demand of the individual to respect the lives of others, that we abhor and punish murder; it is a good thing to possess information and worse to be misinformed than to be merely ignorant, wherefore we disapprove of lying and deception; a helpful, co-operative and sympathetic person promotes the good of others and therefore we call him good; an intemperate attachment to sensuous pleasures is apt to disturb the orderly process of life and thus certain restraints are generally regarded as highly desirable *ab ovo*; a community intent on surviving, flourishing and stamping its print on the world will naturally exact loyalty from its members. We may in this way, imperceptibly or surreptitiously as it were, introduce the moral theme while starting from life and practice as such. That is a possible (naturalistic and rationalistic, if not necessarily Aristotelian) method of ethics; but the frontal approach to Moral Emphasis appears to me to be greatly preferable. Moore's Butlerian motto, 'Every thing is what it is and not some other thing', needs some modification, for 'things' are not disconnected atoms or items or pictures and cannot be known otherwise than in their contexts and horizons, i.e. without a reference to 'some other things', but on the whole it is sound, and reductionism a fountain-head of blurring misconceptions and illusory explanations. The moral emphasis, in especial, if not independent of vital needs and practical concerns, is distinct with a character wholly its own, as if it could be said to trench or incide upon the business of life from outside (though it does not actually connote a hint as to 'wherefrom'): that is what Kant sensed so acutely and tried to express in his infelicitous construction of the 'categorical imperative'; Professor N. H. G. Robinson has aptly spoken of the *intrusive* quality of the moral demand. Now it is almost self-evident that, as I have stated earlier and as has been noted in various ways and from various points of view by Westermarck, Scheler, Bernard Mayo, Professor Findlay and others, the moral impact should be experienced as *primo loco* negative, that is to say, prohibitive, restrictive, and disapprobative. In the above example about my dominant concerns and the temptation, vetoed by conscience and fraught with the danger of retaliation by others, to serve them by dishonest or obnoxious means a simple and conspicuous model is provided for the 'negative' operation of that impact.

Negative morality is prior to positive, not because the practice of life is *a priori* morally bad rather than good, so that its maiming and suppression were the principle of morality, but because the practice of life is *a priori* good, and that neither in a properly moral nor in an exclusively non-moral but in a *pre-moral*, a virtually moral sense. 'Nature' and its requirements are, on the whole, 'legitimate'; they cannot as a whole be repressed and are as a whole entitled to respect and protection; they are presupposed by a positively moral, morally valuable mode of existence, and some classic types of immorality obviously embody a destructive attitude towards them, others at any rate can be interpreted in similar terms. Moreover, in fact the pursuit of primary human interests is established in such forms as already imply a positive reference to explicitly *moral* desirabilities and obligations: a man will get up in the morning, have breakfast, and then go about 'his duties' by virtue of the same routine; yet attending to one's duties is also part of one's moral duty-fulfilment, and the special endeavours it mostly involves (e.g. to do one's job 'well', or to improve on some customary pattern or some accepted norm of achievement) are likely to have a degree of positive moral significance. Even some general moral principle or ideal of comprehensive 'good', religiously and socially hall-marked, may be presupposed as '*already* present' in the texture and self-guidance of practice. So far, then, we have an interfusion of life and morality rather than an intrusion into life by morality, and a primacy of positive over negative morality rather than the inverse. But, this being taken for granted, the moral demand in its concentrated and pointed form will emerge as an intrusive, auto-nomous and uncompromising *veto* (let me quote B. Mayo's brilli-ant phrase, *Protests not precepts*) in the face of *evil*, accomplished or tentative, in its turn rooted in the soil of nature, stimulated by vital interests and strayed into by practice. The *preambles* as well as the *crowning peaks* may be unequivocally positive; its *central, deontic body* is—not unequivocally or exclusively, but primordially—negative.

To take a standard model once more—what is meant by the moral 'sanctity of property'? Property is a highly significant cat-egory of human or human-like existence, but I cannot see anything notably moral or holy in man's ability to occupy, appropriate, manufacture, use, and keep for his use, certain places, objects of value, tools and other goods. It is only as threatened by interference from the part of others that property becomes 'sacred' and *morally* significant. I am keenly aware of its being good for me to have the typewriter I am now using at my disposal, but if there is any holi-ness or moral admirableness about this fact it completely escapes me. The primary *moral* aspect of property consists in the evilness of robbery, theft, fraud, looting, etc.; more remotely, of avarice and waste, but these again point towards more general and indetermi-nate modes of moral valuation. It should be noted that when we speak of 'respecting' alien property (as also life or rights) we use that word in its weak sense of 'leaving alone', 'not touching', 'not interfering with', much as it is used in French medical language (the rash of typhus fever 'respects' the face, i.e. in the soberer style of English textbooks, the face 'escapes'), not in its strong sense of positive appreciation for something distinctively noble and respectable, e.g. a *virtuous* person or indeed the *moral law* which prohibits interference with alien property. Similarly, what of the moral value of 'truth-telling'? To tell a truth may be morally good, indifferent or bad according to circumstances; there is no moral precept of truth-telling. What is really meant by truthfulness or veracity is *not* telling *lies*. Compare, further, the moral disvalue of murder with the moral value of saving lives or perhaps with that of engendering new lives; the moral disvalue of lechery with the moral value of exemplary married life (or of the positive, 'dedicational' aspect of monastic chastity); the moral disvalue of oppression with the moral values that *may* blossom out of liberty which is their *presupposition*. On every count, a massive deontic charge appears to be proper to the negative side; whereas on the positive side, though of course the *height* or excellence of value achievement is greater than that of the value consisting in mere freedom from the corresponding disvalue, the urgency of obligation is more uncertain, more variable and more dependent on particular circumstances, and moral emphasis is far more mixed with various non-moral desirabilities. Consider, also, the asymmetry in our attribution of guilt and merit. In our judgement of every misperformance, we are normally anxious to disentangle the element of moral guilt from other factors of failure or disaster, over which—be it shortcomings of his own, or external handicaps—the agent appears to have had no control; in our judgement of fine accomplishments involving the operation of moral virtue, we are not so anxious to isolate moral merit proper from other personal qualities and abilities or even happy environmental influences: we care less about merit than in the other case about guilt, and are accordingly disposed generously to extend the concept of merit far beyond the boundaries of the morally imputable. (We say 'Poor fellow, it's not all his fault: he has been crippled by a sinister family atmosphere in his childhood, years of grinding poverty, etc. Still, he deserves stern blame at least on the score of——'. We hardly say 'His merits are great, but how far is it his merit? After all, he went to such a good school!')

But are there not *stringent positive duties* as well? The keeping of a promise (of active help), the payment of debts, serving one's country and several other emphatic duties seem definitely to consist in positive actions, not mere acts of abstention. But it may be questioned whether physical (including even mental or intellectual) performance as opposed to non-performance of the same thing, rather than a new or 'extra' decision, a change in policy as it were, is the criterion of positive action in the relevant sense. If I have decided (and perhaps promised) to write a certain letter here or now, it is not my finishing the letter that may *in the sequel* be looked upon as 'an action' but, rather, my interrupting the writing of it and sitting still or twiddling my thumbs or going out for a walk *instead*. Omission to keep a promise or to pay a debt and in general to honour an express commitment may thus be regarded as a sin of *commission*; less evidently but still to some extent, omission to obey the command of a lawful superior; less evidently again but still not wholly arbitrarily, omission (in certain conditions) to warn a man of a special danger that is threatening him without his suspecting it. There still remain such unequivocally negative immoralities as sloth, lack of patriotism and other failures to evince a normal and due loyalty, and callous indifference to the welfare (though not the rights) of others; but these are obviously toned-down and often dubious forms of immorality, while the morally valuable contrary attitudes, being highly positive, are comparatively indeterminate as to their deontic content and *necessarily* admit of a great deal of variation. On the positive side, morality tends to merge into the manifoldness of non-moral, largely 'natural' concerns—patriotism and dutiful family loyalties provide typical instances—and into the alternating, space- and time-dependent, circumstantial activities of life. It is an axiom of life that duties of omission *obligant semper et pro semper*, whereas duties of commission *obligant semper sed non pro semper* (they are always valid but not always in point: while writing this text I am 'complying with my obligation' to abstain from shop-lifting or adultery but cannot be complying with my obligation to do some other job I have undertaken to execute or with that of nursing a sick relative).

Bernard Mayo has recently argued—as Scheler did half a century ago, though with a different edge, intent on superseding 'duty ethics' by 'value ethics'—that *all* duties, whether of omission or of commission, are negative; an action that it is obligatory to *do* is an action that it is *wrong* to *omit*. In other words, to prescribe *x* is to prohibit *not* to do *x*, and positive imperatives, like prohibitions proper, are addressed to possible transgressors. Professor Findlay's distinction between *minatory* and merely *hortatory* imperatives (though one would call the latter 'appeals' rather than actual 'imperatives') points in the same direction: values are an object of commendation, whereas obligation, the main expression of the moral demand, refers to the evilness, i.e. the somehow intolerable disvalue, of doing or—as regards duties of commission—of not doing a thing. The priority of negative morality would thus appear to be established on a formal plane, in a quasi-logical sense as it were. But so far as this might be interpreted as a mere matter of the definition of duty or 'law' as contrasted with commendation, appeal or 'counsel', it would hardly be very significant; what is really significant is the underlying fact that moral emphasis does strike us in its most distinctively characteristic form as an experience of 'duty' or 'imperative' or 'ought' or 'thou shalt' *on pain of* . . .: that is to say, an experience pointing to the 'intolerable' disvalue of 'sin' or 'moral evil'. And this same fact also manifests itself in the axiom of moral valuation according to which, other things being equal, sins of commission are graver than sins of omission, another principle laid down in moral theology; again, it ties in with the general, extra-ethical fact that, other things being equal, to remedy an evil (to alleviate suffering) is a more urgent task than to create a good (to procure pleasure), wherefore it is also a greater obligation for us to help our fellow-creatures in their distress than to heap this or that kind of positive benefits upon them. Two, obviously interlinking, biological (if not 'metaphysical') facts should be remembered in this context: that pain tends greatly to surpass pleasure in intensity, and that the normal course of psychophysical life necessarily connotes a variety of pleasant sensations while pain, a sign of disturbance, is by no means necessarily always or nearly always present. Pain as such intrudes upon consciousness far more than pleasure as such; in a pleasurable or joyous state of mind, we tend to concentrate on the specific object that pleases, thrills or cheers us, as opposed to our own condition. Hence a practical priority of *urgency* on the negative side, as expressed, e.g. in the more solid and substantial status of curative medicine in comparison with hygiene, let alone eugenics; the primacy of evil in a similar sense shows up in the time-honoured maxim of medical deontology *Primum non nocere*. Again, while interpersonal relations are primordially—more naturally and more rationally, one may safely venture to say—friendly and irenic than hostile and agonistic, and of necessity very much more manifold on the former than on the latter side, the most unequivocal, momentous and definitive thing a person can do to another is to kill him (a fact that obsessed the shrewd Hobbes to the point of nearly driving him mad); and albeit we can owe untold, invaluable and exceedingly multiform benefits to one another there is no archetype of benevolent action on a par with the archetypal crime of murder.

However, if the priority of urgency proper to negative as against positive morality appears in some way to be grounded on a similar law of our pre-moral (natural or 'ontic') constitution, on the human or human-like condition as it were, the principle nevertheless applies to the moral realm in a stricter fashion. Whereas in the vital and practical perspective great sufferings and disadvantages may meaningfully and often 'wisely' be endured by one's own choice for superior benefits' and advantages' sake, no such barter between good and evil seems to be acceptable to the moral sense unless there is flagrant disproportion between their respective degrees and unless the moral sacrifice in question is slight in an absolute sense. I am not allowed to kill and despoil a rich man in order to turn his whole fortune to laudable uses, though most of us think that Kant was wrong in decreeing that I must not tell a lie to prevent an innocent man's capture by his pursuers. Roughly speaking, to trade any of the basic moral taboos against moral aspirations however lofty or benefits howsoever morally desirable seems to stultify the meaning of the moral ought, moral evil being experienced as 'intrinsically intolerable'—which 'disvalues' as such are not. Moral theology has put this in the form of the somewhat grim-sounding maxim *Bonum ex integra causa, malum ex quocumque defectu*: to be a good action, an action must be good on all counts; if it is evil in one respect it is an evil action. On the contrary, in the practical perspective we must continually renounce one good in order to obtain another, and that may again and again involve accepting a 'lesser' evil in order to secure a 'greater' good.

3. THEMATIC AND IMPLICIT MORALITY

Although the note of urgency is in no wise confined to the moral sphere and indeed originates in areas of meaning completely independent of the moral—lethal peril and severe pain; the primacy of elementary needs over luxury and refinement; elementary understanding as a precondition of deeper intellectual penetration —it is, as we have seen, proper to the moral emphasis in a peculiar fashion. The moral demand presents itself, not as one claim among others but as a claim which, by its intrinsic nature, has to be satisfied 'before' all others, *as if* it stood for something like the preservation of life, the condition of all pursuits and enjoyments *within* life: *as if* the unconcerned acceptance of immorality within a person's life or a unit of practice rendered all achievements within it null and void, all values invalid; also, transposed into a positive phrasing, *as if* 'to be a good man' mattered incommensurably more than anything else one might be or accomplish. Perhaps this datum of moral experience will be called in question as a mere dependency or reflection of the Christian or at any rate religious outlook: a paraphrase of the notion of 'mortal sin' and of 'salvation' as the 'final end' of man, with 'damnation' as its rigorous alternative. I would not deny the religious relevance or the Christian elaboration of the ethical points here in question, but merely observe that this specific priority of the moral demand is implied in the very concept of *obligation* as contrasted with human 'assets', values and accomplishments in general; adding that the unqualified attribution of 'goodness' in itself expresses a privileged and decisive valuational intent and that 'goodness' in reference to a person is always used in the sense of *moral* goodness. But of course few people, even of an extreme monastic cast of mind, would suggest that however good a man already is he ought to aim exclusively at becoming ever saintlier to the neglect of physical wants, art, science (including perhaps theology), etc. The *urgency* attaching to moral perfection still primarily centres in the negative, i.e. freedom from moral evil, although it will justly be maintained that this is inseparable from a basic reference to the positive background of morality—personal beings and the order of their lives are positive realities, not the absence of a bad reality—and likewise inseparable from positive moral aspirations or ideals. Urgency, then, is a characteristic note of morality as distinct from other lines of personal or human accomplishment, and again of negative morality, as distinct from 'supererogatory works' or special merits and perfections, within the moral sphere; but urgency is not everything, and, moreover, it implies a negative emphasis only in a certain characteristic sense but not in every sense, not invariably or exclusively. Leaving aside, here, the question how the moral goodness of a person (or the moral rightness of an action or pursuit or project of his) relates to his (or its) non-moral, general or comprehensive value, I would re-call now an expression earlier used and qualify the concept of the primacy of negative morality as a concept of *thematic* primacy.

This does not mean that the production of moral good is less extensive, less frequent or less normal, or even of slighter importance, than the avoidance of producing moral evil, but that a specific and as it were unalloyed moral emphasis adheres, and a specific and urgent attention is normally directed, to the presence or danger of moral evil more than to the presence or realization of moral good.[b] Compare, for example, the case of a generous donor with that of a conscientious person who exposes himself to considerable discomfort or to the risk of losing a precious advantage rather than committing an act of mild and practically undetectable dishonesty. The first man is as real as the second, his action is as real as the other's but of greater practical consequence, and his action is as unequivocally moral, in the sense of morally *good*, as that of the second man; perhaps even of greater moral excellence, apart from having ampler beneficial effects, if the donor is a man of means but of comparatively limited means rather than actually rich, and makes his gift at the cost of sacrificing a good deal of irreproachable but more self-regarding satisfaction. Yet, excluding the very particular and uncharacteristic case of the donor's conceiving of his gift as a kind of debt he all but strictly 'owes' to a certain institution, his act cannot be regarded as *thematically* moral in anything like the same degree as the second person's act. The latter has been motived by an exclusively and explicitly moral consideration; the giver's motives may be just as moral, again in the sense of 'noble' or morally good, but they are extremely unlikely to have been as strictly moral and nothing but moral. He is likely to be specially interested in *that* foundation (or whatever the recipient of his gift may be) and its aims, which again are 'moral', i.e. morally laudable, not however defined in terms of morality alone: they would concern the welfare of a certain category of people, or the promotion of learning or some branch of it, which in spite of their essential moral connotation are not as such primordially moral concerns. The giver *may* have in mind—to use Price's word—the 'general duty' of gratuitous beneficence, but he must have some other motive besides for making this particular gift. On the other hand, quite possibly the aims of the recipient and the motives of the giver are related to some more controversial issue or arbitrary preference which we should recognize as licit but not as evidently worthy of moral approval; yet even in this case the moral nobility of the generous act remains. (A man who loves *something* outside his own comfort and security, say horses *or* dogs *or* cats but little else, is still—other things being equal—much preferable morally to one altogether devoid of unselfish affection.) More generally—although it is inconceivable that a person who in his practice of life worries a great deal about moral problems should present a case of thorough and contemptible immorality, or that an obviously good person should hardly ever give a thought to moral points of view, there is no coincidence or necessary proportion between the degree of conscientious care about morality and that of moral accomplishment or praiseworthiness, between conscious moral reference and actual moral excellence. That a person may have morally more felicitous or more undesirable *natural dispositions*, implying as such no merit or guilt of his but highly relevant to his likely conduct of life, with emergent merit and guilt, is part of the picture. Again, from causes largely independent of his moral preoccupations, a man may come to develop great love and esteem for A or an intense infatuation for B, and the moral principles or attitudes of A may happen to be excellent and those of B unsound or objectionable in some important respects: the disciple's moral conduct will doubtless, within certain limits, be favourably or adversely influenced (soon or in the long run) by the respective moral views and character of his chosen exemplar, though he may but very incompletely be aware of the fact and though his attachment originates in personal circumstances and non-moral valuations rather than in his moral preferences as such. In these and similar ways, moral character and performance, the actual exhibition of a person's morality not only as a whole but in its significant single aspects and manifestations, depends *also* on factors other than the intrinsic rightness of his professed moral principles and the sincerity and keenness of his adhesion to them. In other words, a person's being moral in the sense of being focally aware of and keenly attentive to his moral obligations (and, more generally, moral points of view) and his being moral in the sense of morally good, i.e. deserving of moral approval and praise, are, however closely interrelated, two different things. The moral values we produce (create or represent) reflect, and spring from, our moral intentions proper, our moral convictions and the promptings of our conscience; but they also emerge as concomitants, by-products and consonant features of our non-moral, i.e. not properly, explicitly and centrally moral, concerns, pursuits, valuations and attachments. This I would put in the form that, inevitably—by no means in the sense of a regrettable moral imperfection—our morality is partly *thematic* and partly *implicit*. It is not necessarily better or higher in proportion as it is thematic (say, duty-conscious), nor in proportion as it is implicit (say, spontaneous and quasi-identical with our 'natural' being), for moral man is neither an 'intelligible self' concerned with nothing but morality and an impeccably functioning machine for duty-fulfilment devised by that self's own engineering, nor a lovely plant or the all-wise human gardener who breeds it. In neither way can man be 'all moral'; his morality and his practice cannot *be* each other; the two antithetic conceptions are equally utopian and morally subversive; and both thematic and implicit morality integrally belong to the moral being of man.

Deontic, prohibitive (negative) and thematic morality on the one hand and aspirational, prescriptive (or, rather, positive) and implicit morality on the other represent a basic ethical division, although of course no two concepts on either side are by any means identical. Regardless of the negative aspect which the very notion of strict duty analytically implies (keeping your promise is normal; *not* keeping it is a moral event or theme, i.e. evil unless specially justifiable in moral terms), strict obligations can be definitely positive (serve your country as you are required to do, or as best you can, in war-time), whereas a moral advice or counsel can be negative in content (you had better not indulge in that kind of amusement; it is not exactly immoral but it somehow ill comports with

moral earnestness and tends to conjure up moral temptations otherwise avoidable). Again, positive moral obligations and merely hortatory moral stimuli can be highly thematic (I ought to dedicate
myself to some higher purpose in life, as A does), whereas implicit
morality involves a quasi-automatic avoidance of some moral dangers and inferiorities. Nevertheless, the predominant emphasis of
thematic morality is prohibitive, whereas implicit morality means
primarily the creation and emergence of objectively valuable human
realities, such as a fine character or a well ordered and noble pattern
of interpersonal relationships or a kind of work that connotes moral
significance: in a word, the presence of something exquisitely
positive.

The Decalogue, an incomplete moral code but the best and most
classic of brief moral compendiums widely known, may aptly be
resorted to for purposes of illustration. It has often been remarked,
sometimes disparagingly, that the Ten Commandments almost
exclusively consist of taboos or 'Don'ts'; and religious people have
often retorted that the Don'ts are subordinate to, and depend
upon, the prefacing declaration 'I am thy God ...' which is
emphatically positive and which, though not put in a properly
imperative form, implies of course the fundamental commandment
'Thou shalt revere Me above everything and obey My laws'. Both
points of view are pertinent, but both are in need of closer examination and rectification. The First Commandment is of course a
Rahmengesetz (in German legal idiom), a constitutional law which
points to the positive frame or compass of all particular commandments. So far, it stands for *implicit* morality, though it also marks
the focal *theme* of the religious consciousness. That it should be
cast in a declarative not an imperative mould is by no means an
accident. 'Be moral' or 'Be good' is not a moral imperative proper
but the logical presupposition underlying all concrete moral injunctions. Even though there may be such a thing as an all-
pervading moral principle—'Love God and love thy neighbour as
thyself: this is the sum of the Law and the Prophets', Jesus will
say—there is no such thing as a 'Categorical Imperative'; the ultimate basis of all 'rules' is not a Rule but a Fact: namely, the intrinsic relevancy of rules and their content for the life of personal
beings (in the context of the human condition, we might also say),
and inseparably linked therewith, their emanation from a sovereign
Authority. God in the First Commandment does not *begin* by
'commending' something but *states* the relational framework in
which the rules decisive for men's shaping their own lives shall be
inserted. They are not evident to Mind like axioms of geometry or
like perceptual facts, nor corollaries of the concerns of life or

nature, which, as it were, *invite* a system of moral regulation but do not *produce* it, seeing that they form no self-contained and self-sufficient unity and, while 'destined' to the attainment of good, are also essentially generative of evil in their operation. The rules are, then, formally an imposition by the will of the Authority presiding over the destinies of creation. Yet neither are they arbitrary impositions lacking any intrinsic evidence: thus, while I may certainly kill and steal without being indifferent to my own life and possessions, there being no actual 'contradiction' between my protecting myself and injuring others for my own benefit, nevertheless the moral prohibitions of murder and theft somehow rationally link up with our anxiety to preserve our own integrity of life, body and ownership. Moral rules are on the whole *intelligible*; they do not possess the same kind of evidence as do sense-perceptions or analytic propositions, but neither are they opaque in the same sense as mere orders or wishes as such, which just invite obedience or compliance without conveying any *appeal*. If 'I am thy God', then 'Thou shalt not worship alien gods' follows analytically, and 'make no carven images' is implied intelligibly though not rigorously. The remaining, *moral*, commandments possess contents whose meaning and validity do not depend on the fact of their being commanded; but their specific status and paramountcy, their distinctive relief and gravity, are thrown into emphasis and even in part constituted —the point cannot be argued here—by the sanction of express Divine commandment.

But what meaning does this carry to the *non-religious* mind? It is certainly not translatable into non-religious language *without a remainder*; it is, indeed, an open question how far a 'Christian ethic'ᵉ can be upheld prescinding from Christian belief, and how far the belief in moral *obligation* is tenable at all without a reference to transcendent Authority. However, the need for a constitutional framework of single, concrete and largely prohibitive moral rules as symbolized by the structure of the Decalogue is arguable on its own merits, within the limits of the analysis and interpretation of moral experience itself, outside religious presuppositions; and, as an aspect of that framework, the fact of consensual moral valuation and its pressure on men's individual *and* joint lives as manifest in the phenomena of conscience, responsibility and the moral critique of collective behaviour. Concepts of this order may make an assentient discussion of the Decalogue meaningful to the atheist, and even as theists we cannot dispense with them in philosophical ethics. But the framework, natural and supernatural or 'supra-sensible' or 'spiritual', is something positive and is not directly to thematically moral: that is to say, it has a non-moral meaning or which its meaning *as* a framework of morality is soldered. The the-ist doctrine of 'Commandments' and, in a less pregnant fashion, also the consensual or any kind of 'prescriptive' doctrine emphasize the implicit and positive aspect of morality; the conception of mor-ality as obedience, conformance, assent or submission, be it even abstention from certain things rather than the performance of cer-tain things that is *primo loco* demanded, places the moral intention in a context of relationship with something existent and life-pervading. On the other hand, the same imperative doctrine ('im-perative' in the widest sense, embracing the hortatory or 'appeal-ing' mode) also goes to sustain the thematic and negative aspect of morality, by stamping it with the 'sacred' seal of a sharp distinction from the autonomous policies of practice as such and implanting the notion that anything immanently desired or feasible or expedi-ent *may* be tabooed from above or vetoed from outside.

With one significant exception, all properly moral command-ments of the Decalogue—imposed by divine Authority but having no reference to God in their contents—are indeed negative and thematic, i.e. expressed in the 'Thou shalt not' phrasing, and rigidly stripped of all sympathetic appeal to the subject's own extra-moral interests or happiness. The exception is the first properly moral commandment, next in order to the properly religious ones, which enjoins filial respect and piety: the prototype of the obligations of *loyalty* (in German, often called *Pflichten der Treue*, while English ethical idiom tends to reserve 'fidelity' for the faithful observance of contracts). It is, I think, no mere accident that to this command-ment, alone among the ten, should be appended an immanent utilitarian sanction: 'that thy days may be long in the land'. *Implicit* morality is stressed at this point; the preservation and con-tinuity of life is given a complementary moral emphasis; the natural fact of parental authority and the natural sense of distinctive solidarity with *one's own* kin receive a moral support and reinforce-ment; God the Lawgiver is as it were proclaiming here His identity with God the Creator. The rest of the Ten Commandments, the main body of straightforward deontic and thematic morality, is made up of five or six 'Don'ts' bearing on murder, lechery and adultery, false testimony, and disrespect for alien ownership. This material predominance of negative rules, of *Verboten* signposts, is inherent in the deontic emphasis of the Decalogue, which is neither a guide to happiness and a Hellenic recipe for 'wisdom' nor, as is largely true of New Testament doctrine, a guide to moral perfec-tion and a holy life, but a basic code of morality. If we compare the 'Thou shalt not' commandments with 'Honour thy father and mother . . .' from a logical point of view, we find a fundamental contrast between the much higher degree of determinateness on the former and a relative vagueness, an open horizon as it were, on the latter side. Filial piety and the various—by no means unequivocally determined—things it implies are themselves of the very stuff of life, an extensive part of practice; on the contrary, 'not to steal' for example, while just as directly and closely bearing on practice, is a directive for or a point of practice but not actually a province of practice. The shaping of practice can undoubtedly be guided and canalized to a degree by negative and even by positive rules (e.g. 'Love thy neighbour', 'Visit the sick', 'Execute thy work with care', or St Paul's 'Take some wine for thy stomach's sake', and so forth), but cannot be unequivocally predetermined by universal obligatory rules; whereas the mere moral *cleanness* of practice can be so predetermined, if not to the absolute exclusion of any doubt or ambiguity at least with a kind of genuine approximation to such a standard. The lives of all honest people, e.g., will be all exactly alike in that they all equally lack the element of theft, robbery, fraud, embezzlement, bribery, forgery, etc.; but take a number of persons who are all not only honest but full of other virtues as well, nay, attached to the same specific religious creed or secular canon of values, even to the same vocational ideal, and you will still descry most significant differences in their practice of life. For their tastes, predilections, constitutions, circumstances, antecedents, talents, etc., cannot but largely differ. Similarly, any two persons endowed with natural affections and equally mindful of the 'Father and Mother' commandment may exhibit marked differences between the ways in which they respectively obey that commandment, and still more as regards their family relationships as a whole. Whereas, the strict determination that pertains to the logic of the 'Thou shalt not' commandments is owing to the fact that they do not merge or blend into the operation of life concerns but only circumscribe it; that they do not partially constitute or embody but only *punctuate* practice.

Thematic morality, i.e. advertence to the moral theme as standing out against the constitutive concerns of life and the sharp impact of Conscience upon the shaping of Practice, has its locus in the middle regions rather than at the lowest and highest levels of moral achievement. The moral barriers against which the primitive, rough, morally uneducated or grossly self-seeking person comes up in following his impulses or policies are 'not yet' properly moral or thematically experienced as such: for the very young child or the asocial or the unsubtly religious kind of person, 'ought' means what superior alien force may compel him to do, and 'ought not', that for which he is liable to punishment (*poena*, 'pain'); the proverb

La peur du gendarme est le commencement de la sagesse hints at the *inchoate* genuine morality which may be implicit in the outwardly correct behaviour of the unscrupulous person who obeys the law under the suasion of a 'deterrent'. Again, the 'saint' (in the widest, including the Kantian, sense of the word) moves in a perspective in which thematic morality, though certainly present, is 'no longer' prominent, since there is little either in his actual conduct or his pre-practical inner tendencies and tentative projectings against which his conscience may rise in protest or to which it may point an accusing finger. The 'harmoniously' virtuous type of person may effectively lead a clean and exemplary life, rich in moral accomplishments, without a more than occasional intervention of moral scruples and without intense and central moral awareness; the Christian saint or the tense kind of virtuous person dedicated to morally significant tasks will, in somewhat different ways, be exercised a great deal more by moral scruples and problems, but that only in virtue of their special (perfectional, vocational, reformatory) aspirations, not in the sense of having to assert their moral character in the teeth of fundamental temptations: the moral direction of their willing is 'spontaneous' and they conform to 'the law', in a high measure, without experiencing it as such. Thematic morality is topical, rather, in cases where the moral sense is developed, vivid, and more or less firmly and deeply rooted, but is far from having integrally pervaded the texture of desires, valuations and affective or prepractical imaginations. We tend to envisage and appraise the moral behaviour of men normally, as it were generally and 'conventionally', in *this* perspective; on the one hand, men are '*supposed*' to know good from evil and to recognize moral obligation, and on the other hand, we presume the best of men to be morally fallible, as indeed 'saintly' persons have often expressly declared themselves to be.

I am only too conscious of the over-simplified character of this schematic picture even as a rough sketch of the 'levels of morality'; it is merely meant to further illustrate the distinction between thematic and implicit morality and to designate one aspect of the manifold relations between the moral and the non-moral being of man.

4. THE DIMENSIONS OF MORAL EMPHASIS

It is plain that the moral demand presents both an aspect of unity beyond the mere formal concepts of 'imperative', 'commending' or 'approval' and an aspect of far-reaching diversity. The fact that moral consciousness, quite apart from arbitrary philosophic exaggerations such as the 'oneness of Virtue' or the 'categorical imperative' or so-called Moral Principles (the utilitarian 'maximization of good' or the Scholastic 'rational nature'), has always insisted on unitary concepts like 'a good man', 'a sinner', 'guilt', 'good intentions', etc., shows that the general categories of morality are no mere accidental compositions, useful for some special purposes, of essentially disparate qualities of conduct and character but express something real about morality. Different moral qualities, say benevolence, truthfulness and modesty, do not just happen to be pleasing in men or required of them but must have something intrinsic in common to be objects of the same *kind* of evaluative and imperative emphasis; and, although some of them may exist conspicuously and others scarcely at all in the same person, some of them at any rate tend to imply others directly and others again indirectly, while the general and formal moral quality of conscientiousness or a comprehensive moral ideal or 'vision of man' tends to imply all or most of them. On the other hand, they are by no means mere modes of appearance, in different types of situation, of one and the same quality of virtue or goodness or submission to 'the' imperative or to the will of an authority; and conscience does not primarily generate or decree the standards of 'good' conduct but on the contrary, means awareness of them and presupposes them in their diversity. Again, interpretations of a particular moral rule as an 'application' of the supposed central or supreme moral rule impress us for the most part as artificial—sometimes the inverse relation may appear just as plausible—and some of them, as definitely fictitious if not fallacious. Those who have been partial to such 'deductions' have largely confused the rôle of this or that norm or virtue as a logical or technical *condition* of the agent's consciousness of other norms or his exercise of other virtues with a relation of *identity* or a necessary implication of the conditioned by its condition. Thus, if it be true that justice presupposes a primitive or basic sympathy, it does not follow that justice is merely a derivative of sympathy or a form of extended and consistently practised benevolence, and if enlightened charity in the higher sense of the term implies justice it is not therefore a manifestation of justice, nor does a high sense of justice guarantee the presence of charity; nor again is all conscious morality ultimately justice because all sense of what is *due* connotes an aspect of justice; only a rational being can conceive of morality and entertain moral intentions, but moral intention cannot be defined as 'prudence' (the application of reason to practice, that is); it is impossible to exercise virtue without a degree of courage, endurance and self-control, but the other virtues cannot be accounted for in terms of these. The intuitionists have rightly stressed that all justification of promise-keeping and other forms of

contractual fidelity (including truthfulness) in terms of their social
utility 'in the long run' hopelessly falls short of our emphatic and
unequivocal experience of this set of moral themes; and the numerous and desperate attempts to justify sexual morality on some basis
quite alien to its actual meaning (such as altruism, hygiene or the
common good, the productive use of time, or 'self-respect' which
in reality *presupposes* the unworthiness of debauch and lascivious
states of mind), attempts undertaken so as to escape the charge of
'superstition' or 'puritanism' and of libertinism alike, cannot very
well be discussed at all except in satirical fashion.

Philosophical interest will not be satisfied with a purely empirical
gathering-together of moral intuitions found at random, or a taxa-
tive enumeration of duties or virtues, injunctions and taboos, or
moral points of view contained in an historically given code or in a
collection of codes and maxims; we feel the need of some orderly
division and rational classification of particular moral principles—
many such schemes of classification have been and can be constructed, and if all are defective and some of them better adapted
to certain purposes and more misleading in other respects than
their rivals they are not for that useless. Accordingly, we are also
interested in more abstract unitary notions of morality as such, in
a 'meta-ethical' interpretation of moral experience as some would
put it, and would expect such a general concept of the moral good
and evil to yield a key to the problem of the relation between morality and practice: if the domain of practice is interspersed with
manifold moral signposts, their common significance may explain
to some extent their geography. It may tell us at what points or
along what lines of practice moral emphasis, and of what particular
kind, is *likely* to arise. The pitfall to be avoided is the assumption,
or postulate, that a unitary constructive concept of ethics may
supersede our direct apprehension of the data of moral experience
and our receptiveness to moral emphasis in its various dimensions.
The endeavour to render moral consciousness intelligible is justified so long as it does not degenerate into explaining moral intuitions away in order to get rid of their residual obscurity. I should
indeed argue that, as hinted before, a feature of resistant opacity
actually belongs to the essence of moral emphasis: the mode of
compulsive blind obedience falls beneath, but a complete rational
demonstrability of its ground would again uproot, the idea of moral
obligation.[d]

Seeing the multiplicity of the elements of practice—its staple
aims, concerns, situations, types of activity—it might seem reasonable to assume that the plurality of the dimensions of moral emphasis was simply a function of that multiplicity and reflected, as it

were, the lineaments of practice. Such a conception would tally with the Platonic assignment of the single virtues to the corresponding 'parts of the soul' (one of the virtues expressing their equilibrium as a whole) and its Aristotelian-Scholastic modifications (the virtues as inherent 'regulators' of the different kinds of activities). We might thus say that benevolence was the right attitude towards others, justice the right management of contractual or administrative relations with others, self-control the proper behaviour in regard to passions and pleasure, courage the proper way of affronting dangers and hardships, and that the respective commandments of the Decalogue similarly enjoined the proper kind of behaviour in reference to such goods as life, property, the communication of knowledge, and family ties. Again, by giving this construction a slightly new turn we might end by establishing that the manifoldness of moral emphasis meant straightforwardly its adaptation to the various departments of life: engendering an ethics of interpersonal relations in general, an ethics of the family, an ethics of property, an ethics of power, an ethics of work, an ethics of war and peace, an ethics of sex, an ethics of eating 'and' drinking, an ethics of discourse (and thought), an ethics of civil service . . . down to medical deontology, perhaps with a differential ethics of gynaecology and conceivably of dental surgery. The conception is ambiguous; it points in two possible directions. The variant of departmental ethics suggests a unitary moral principle, applied to any existing or emergent sphere of activity, or at any rate a plural code (presupposed, not analyzed or interpreted) the component rules of which are of course involved or actualized in different degrees and proportions by different sections or different modes of life: education for example involves greater and different moral points of view than agriculture, or the sanctity of life is a more prevalent theme in obstetrics than in erotic play. The traditional doctrine of an object-dependent differentiation of 'virtues' suggests, on the contrary, the notion of an essential identity of morally good conduct with the immanently good management of activities and affectivities, i.e. the naturalistic confusion of morality and practice.

It is none the less true that subordinate technical studies, such as medical deontology, may have their practical justification and even give rise to philosophically interesting questions—'sexual ethics' or 'political ethics' do perhaps constitute genuine sub-disciplines of moral science—and it is also undeniable that the dimensions of moral emphasis are inseparable from the fundamental aspects of life and the non-moral concerns and emphases of practice. Thus, benevolence would have no meaning whatsoever if life was not subject to the category of 'Good *for* . . .'; and the moral meaning of chastity essentially depends on the peculiar creative and subversive qualities of sex in the context of personal life. Although veracity is not morally good in virtue of, much less in proportion to, its social usefulness—quarrelsome non-co-operativeness can be more hurtful socially than a lying and dissembling type of character, but, though morally disvaluable, it is free from the morally disgraceful tint of the latter—it nevertheless presupposes men's interest in knowing 'the truth' about any subject that comes their way and especially in *not* being a victim to any *error*. Justice, again, owes its speciality to one fundamental, we might say institutional, aspect of interpersonal relations, namely the possibility of contractual arrangement and existence of contractual types of situation (in the widest sense, including of course non-explicit accords); and contractual arrangement is not itself a moral postulate but a tool of practice which seems to determine a prominent, perhaps the central, modality of moral emphasis. The duties of loyalty even more clearly and unequivocally confirm, as a mode of moral emphasis, a natural trend powerfully present without any necessary reference to morality. The distinctive feature of this class of obligations is that, whereas contracts are 'naturally' meant *in general* to be observed and statements to impart truth according to the speaker's genuine belief but the correct observance of such—largely onerous —rules may not suit the agent's taste unless he has the moral virtue of justice or honesty and is not plainly *continuous* with his 'natural' self-love, loyalty to his own people *is* thus continuous and is directly in keeping with his *pre*-moral inclinations. However, in the given case, to support his family, to act patriotically, etc., may also impose a burden on him and conflict with his primary inclinations, and it is here that loyalty becomes morally thematic and invested with an obligation in conscience.

I would conclude that the plurality of moral points of view does indeed depend on the manifoldness of the aspects of practice but neither merely reflects nor completely expresses that manifoldness. Moral emphasis, though by no means monistic, is selective and thus both autonomous and restricted in extension. It does not, or does not significantly, endorse all vital interests and practical desirabilities; it fastens specifically on *some* points of the practical order, such as the mutual recognition of divided interests and the high value of contractual reliability. It attaches, as we have seen, more urgently and directly to the cleanness than to the richness of life. Be it even true that 'honesty is the best policy', the moral demand will insist on honesty even in circumstances where it is *not* the best policy in any conspicuous and immanent sense of the word, and the immanent goodness of a policy *always* depends on many more factors besides honesty. Be it even true that, in Nothnagel's famous words, *Nur ein guter Mensch kann ein guter Arzt sein*, a man can certainly be a first-rate doctor without being morally good *in every respect*, and of course many a morally fine man, even endowed with the necessary learning and technical skill, may never make a good doctor. And, whereas the manifoldness of the themes and configurations of practice is unbounded, in every particular dimension of moral emphasis a focal reference to the one privileged theme of the objective polarity of Good and Evil is still maintained. The 'moral signposts', though spread over the landscape of practice, do not actually map the geography of practice but indicate *one* supremely important network of orientations pervading that geography. Rather than supplying the traveller with information about the site of places he may wish to find, they warn him of areas of danger (this or that kind of danger) he should avoid, and press on his attention places of excellence (however significantly different among them) which he should visit in urgent preference to all else.

6

Existence and Ethics

1. THE IDOL OF AUTHENTICITY

If it is the case that whatever I do I do freely—more, that I choose freely even my inner evaluative acts, and my attitudes—how can freedom and unfreedom at the same time provide a criterion for the ethical judgement of my behaviour? In the framework of traditional Graeco-Scholastic rationalism, the answer would turn on the distinction between two meanings of 'freedom': (*a*) free-will, the natural 'faculty' ascribed to man *qua* man, and (*b*) the freedom of rational self-control and self-determination as opposed to brute impulsiveness or 'slavery to passion' or 'sensuality'; a distinctive quality of freedom proper only to the 'virtuous' man. Whatever the inherent defects and the possible relative merits of such a conception, the existentialists deviate from it in that they insist on the groundlessness of free choice and reject its interpretation in terms of rationality and prudence, let alone of conformance to specific codes representing a general guarantee or basis of a minimum of rational and prudent conduct. (Nor do they recognize the presupposition of such types of ethics: namely, 'happiness' as the universal and invariable 'final end' of man, not itself dependent on his free choice.) Yet, in a wider sense, something remains or returns, under the existentialist dispensation, of the distinction between the ever-present and ineluctable fact of free-will and the differential quality of freedom as a (highly exigent, perhaps unattainable) standard of conduct. It might indeed be suggested, though not without reserve, that existentialism *inverts* the rationalist-utilitarian schema of valuations. In its view, man's true freedom resides, not in his emancipation through reason from the dominance of his primal spontaneity but on the contrary, in the sustained manifestation of that primal freedom of pure indeterminacy as against its doctoring and stifling, its suppression and falsification, by the misguided demand of normative rationality. But, to state the necessary reservations, on the one hand rational conduct is not so much bad in itself as pointless because it is necessarily ungenuine, the alleged rational grounds being no more than an artificial sham which the agent thinks up so as to dodge the inexorable hardship of freedom; on

the other hand, original freedom is not the mere natural spontaneity of sensuous urges or biological wants but the vertiginous
abyss of conscious existence as such, the claim upon man of
Naught—which constitutes his core and essence—to create himself
out of Naught.

Let us stick to the assumption that this dismal mythology of concepts and moods, this nightmare of an anguish fleeing from itself
and veiling itself yet also haunted by the self-issued call to reveal
itself, *must* make sense in *some* fashion. How account for the
duality; and for the ethical preferability of one of its terms, damna-
bility of the other? If I am free, my craving to evade freedom and
sell myself into the bondage of 'thingness', to forge myself a mysti-
fying network of objective goods, values, rules, standards and
determinants of all kinds, also springs from my freedom. And if,
apparently, freedom does not take kindly to itself, why not allow
it the freedom to undergo limitations and indulge its thirst for
solidification and reification? In what way, indeed, could I 'create
myself' if not by submitting to a world of things, shapes, weights
and laws, adding something of my own to its contents and its
working-out? Further, what is wrong with shams, dodges, un-
genuineness and artificiality? Why not choose these freely, rather
than seek with desperate monotony to display my untainted freedom by an endless string of 'gratuitous' choices, i.e. by trying
always to obey one vacuous principle instead of actually choosing x
for being a greater good than y, and then z because it is an obligation or *non-q* because q is evil? And if insincerity *is* wrong, is it
wrong because my freedom has so decreed? Hardly. But why then
assent just to this one moral intuition or Divine commandment or
deduction from the utility principle or socially established standard,
and not to others as well? Should it be simply because Sartre has
so chosen *pour les autres*, including me? But are not all general and
immutable principles a fake, and might he not (perhaps, ought he
not to) choose anew and differently at any moment? Again, take the
famous young man who cannot serve two masters—the welfare of
his family, and the resistance movement—at once. No paragraph
of a universally valid moral code can direct his choice; he must
choose for himself, 'authentically'. Well and good. Sir David Ross
would presumably admit that this was a case of deciding between
two countervailing *prima facie* obligations or moral claims; and
Prichard's summary footnote solution—the greater obligation
should be chosen, regardless of which course is likely to produce
more good—though perhaps correct so far as it goes, fails to tell us
which in this case *is* the greater obligation. But why is the young
man's range of choice so narrowly limited? He might also consider

joining the fascist militia rather than the resistance movement, or sitting the war out somewhere in hiding, twiddling his thumbs, instead of intervening on either side *or* bothering about his family. Perhaps he has discarded these possibilities by a previous free choice; but perhaps he has already learnt from Sartre (*a*) that free choice must issue in commitment (are, then, duties to country and duties to family valid universal norms?), and (*b*), that anti-semitism, and therefore any cause tinged with it, cannot be an object of authentic choice. On the second point, Heidegger might object on behalf of a more generous conception of freedom; *das entschlossene Mitsein*, while in no wise implying anti-semitism, for some time at any rate seemed quite willing to take body in Nazi Germany.

But contents are not what matters in the first place; the divergences between the predilections (or 'choices') of different leading existentialists, Sartre and Merleau-Ponty the not quite orthodox communists, Heidegger the incomplete and disillusioned Nazi, Marcel the religious conservative, Jaspers the quasi-liberal humanist, by no means disprove the presence in all of them of a common emphasis. That emphasis is libertarian in a certain sense only; most expressly so in Sartre, but even Sartre gives me the impression of turning with more authentic vehemence against the acceptance of a blend of freedom and necessity, the commonsensical concept of a limited freedom and non-total determination, than against the idea of necessity itself: as if he were not entirely hostile to the sublime vision of absolute freedom coinciding with absolute necessity. Thus, freedom itself can neither be renounced nor really be made valid as against its fatal self-alienation; what seems to come nearest to authentic existence is our keen awareness of its impossibility, our tragic consciousness of the infernal circle in which we are irremediably immured. According to Sartre, we are responsible even for our wishes, and responsible for the world we live in, for we 'choose' ourselves and our world: if so, are we properly responsible for *anything* at all? For what precisely, before whom and under what code, in terms of what categories are we responsible? Nor can I see what choice means at all if choice is its own end; when really choosing we try to choose the greater good and lesser evil or the right course of action, we don't choose choice itself. (Similarly as the Kantian supreme duty of doing our duty is as such vacuous: we can only, with whatever 'purity of motive', do *that* which *is* our duty, and which cannot itself be the doing of our duty for its own sake. Sartre's pure choice and Kant's pure deontic will are similar in their self-stultifying formalism; so as to yield any hint for the guidance of conduct, they both necessitate a surreptitious recourse to independent, traditional standards—and given these, *they* are no longer needed.)

The 'fallenness' of man as Heidegger puts it, i.e. his 'being thrown into' a world of things and trivial interests, is akin to the Sartrian flight of freedom from itself and concealed but ineliminable responsibility; and Heidegger's 'conscience' the 'silent call of *Dasein* to itself, concerned about its existence', is very like the anxiety and nausea which in Sartre's landscape signalize the ever threatening suffocation of authentic choice. Heidegger's brilliant picture of *das Man* and Sartre's acute analysis of the modes of false consciousness or 'bad faith' as he calls it are obvious, if not identical, twins. Again, the Heideggerian 'conscience' implies an extension of the sense of responsibility which cannot but suggest, dialectically, its extinction. If my conscience is troubled about the fact of my being enmeshed in the paltry satisfactions, fears and cares, recreations and noncommittal beliefs, etc., of daily life, in a word, about my guilt in being human not divine, it is unlikely to worry a great deal about such trifles as my concrete specific transgressions against, say, the laws of honesty and the demands of neighbour-love. Putting it in theological language, if my personal feeling of guilt is centred on my 'contamination' by 'original sin', little of it may be spared for the secondary and consecutive things of which I am properly and distinctively guilty, i.e. my 'actual sins'. It has been said that socialism takes over from capitalism all that is bad in it, discarding all that is good; it might plainly be said that atheistic existentialism takes up and cultivates the chief source of a possible moral perversion in Christian theology while rejecting its positive substance. But such a displacement of emphasis is noticeable—not to speak of earlier traces of antinomianism in St Paul, St Augustine, or Luther—in Christian existentialists as well. That Kierkegaard's religious fervour is heavily infected with romantic vitalism and a hazy naturalism, that his overcoming of aestheticism by the Either/Or gesture of the 'moral man' is an ambiguous and problematical affair, may be seen from this passage (my italics):

In making a choice it is *not so much a question of choosing the right* as of the *energy*, the earnestness, the pathos with which one chooses. Thereby *the personality announces its inner infinity*, and thereby, in turn, the personality is consolidated. Therefore, even if a man were to choose the wrong, he will nevertheless discover, *precisely by reason of the energy* with which he chose, that he had chosen the wrong. For the choice *being made with the whole inwardness* of his personality *his nature is purified* and he himself *brought into immediate relation* to the eternal *Power* whose omnipresence *interpenetrates the whole of existence*. (In *Either/Or*, vol. ii, p. 141, quoted from Ronald Grimsley, *Existentialist Thought*, Cardiff 1960, p. 25.)[a]

If twentieth-century existentialist thought is also greatly indebted to Nietzsche—his neo-paganism, irrationalist vitalism, glorification of spontaneity, concept of 'will-to-power', etc.—the meeting of this line of filiation with the influence of Kierkegaard and his theological and mystical ancestry cannot be looked upon as wholly incidental; the fusion is far from inorganic.

Christian, Nietzschean, and furthermore Freudian, inspirations seem to converge in the existentialist version of truthfulness: the reaffirmation, in especial by Sartre, of the Socratic demand 'Know thyself'. In a different way again, Husserl's phenomenology exercised a kindred and very marked effect on Heidegger, Sartre and Merleau-Ponty alike. Though Husserl was himself a typical 'philosopher's philosopher' much like Meinong or Moore, the paragon of a respectable bourgeois and indeed of a correct *geheimer Hofrat* into the bargain, and in no sense the prophet of a new style of life or a secular salvationist, within the hidden chambers of professional Epistemology the attitude and claim of Husserl had something of the prophet's fine frenzy about them. His furious, titanic endeavour to pierce the pleasantly plausible concept-constructions of scientistic rationalism, or empiricism and psychologism, of Neo-Kantianism, with the view of penetrating and lighting up the inmost recesses of primal, precategorial and as it were world-constitutive mental experience—announced by the watchword *Zu den Sachen selbst*—belongs to the prehistory of existentialism. It has its place in the context of that spiritual revolution which ushered in, perhaps contributed to, and certainly accompanied, the collapse of the ornamental, compromise-loving and somewhat insincere high civilization of the world between, roughly, 1860 and 1914 with its peculiar decencies, illusions of security, tinselled superficialities and ponderous platitudes. The schooling and disciplining effect of phenomenological 'concept-intuition', itself partly a late derivative of scholasticism, is clearly perceptible in the modern existentialists: in the inflated but abstract and highly technical jargon they use, and the unmistakable concern about logical neatness they display in spite of their irrationalist bent and emotive preoccupation. And in their infatuation with sincerity and authenticity, there is undoubtedly something sincere and authentic, something deeply experienced and laboriously thought-out, although heavily overlain by reckless iconoclasm, a cheap antiphilistine obsession and often a frivolous delight in paradox—the havoc they play with language expressing *one* basic form of intellectual irresponsibility.

Whereas the emphasis on 'existence' and 'history', linked to a negation of 'human nature', is partly a reaction to the earlier

Husserl's essentialism, i.e. enquiry into 'pure' *Sosein* and 'bracketing' of *Dasein*, on the other hand it is in tune with Husserl's later interest in the 'perspective' character of the original cognitive acts and the 'horizon' in which the objects of all mental experience are incorporated. The contextual nature of all fundamental acts of apprehension, with the emotive and conative aspects attaching to them as already hinted at by Husserl, implies *Dasein* as somehow 'represented' in *Sosein* itself; and that insight underlies the concepts, prominent in existentialism, of situation, project, and temporality. This is obviously relevant to the ethics of freedom and authenticity. No significant action, it may be argued, is *merely* an 'instance' of a 'kind of action'; it cannot be fully understood and appraised except as a term in the unfolding of a project and in the context of a 'unique' situation. The mere mechanical 'application' of a static 'principle' to a 'case' means a frustration of freedom and an ungenuine choice. Nor can the motivation of conduct, and its *immanent* justification in terms of what the agent 'really wants', be validly deduced either from a fixed 'scientific' schema of the requirements of human nature or from an excogitated once-for-all system of ideal values: the personal texture of concerns emerges from history interwoven with acts of choice, from situations and projects, from the interplay of 'self' and 'circumstances' (Ortega), and is subject to spontaneous change and conscious redirection (as Stevenson would put it). It is, I believe, on these lines that the existentialist doctrine of freedom and authenticity has had, and can further exert, a valuable stimulating effect on moral philosophy proper, and perhaps more so on the theory of practice.

Deplorably enough, this positive contribution is outweighed by an overwhelming mass of unilateral and excessive formulations, provocative attitudinizing and strident accents. Sartre's exposure of the modes of 'bad faith' and Heidegger's analogous critique of *das Man*, i.e. of men's ordinary consciousness thriving in the medium of civil society, while rich in pertinent insights and beyond psychology relevant also to ethics, breathe the sterile spirit of nihilism in that they ultimately attack, not so much an erroneous doctrine or a specified kind of morally inferior conduct as human existence itself—which in its main body is first and foremost, inalterably, everyday existence—and aim at invalidating the moral demands which arise *in the context* of that existence. By showing up the inherent weaknesses and imperfections of man, and man as professing a set of standards of decency, the existential moralists mistakenly believe to have proved the inadequacy and inefficacy of those standards; they distort the necessary linkage of men's moral claims and civilized habits of mind with various non-moral and trivial self-regarding interests into an all-round identity, as if the frequent presence and general possibility of hypocrisy and self-deception meant that the whole treasure of decencies and loyalties was no better than a homogeneous fabric of sham. But the extraordinary, 'marginal', heroic and 'gratuitous' feats of authenticity, apart from being in strictness impossible—for man is doomed to be empty unsubstantial 'freedom', he can neither attain to divinity nor be sanctified by a non-existent God—themselves depend, for such meaning as they may be credited with, on traditionally approved principles and concerns like sincerity, benevolence, courage and the welfare of mankind or the self-assertion of a community. Seen from a philosophical point of view, then, the existentialist protest against human pettiness as such is caught in the dilemma of revealing itself either as an arbitrary conceptual jugglery, importuning an 'absurd' reality with a nugatory fancy of grandeur out of its reach, or as inconsistent, relying on a reference to homely values not 'chosen' by the sovereign creative genius of 'freedom' but objective and intuitively 'given', and renouncing the exorbitant pretension to one single, supreme and isolated mode of value which it originally meant to assert. Seen from a moral point of view, the existentialist position is plainly fraught with the danger of immoralism, as suggested by the polemics against priggish 'serious-mindedness' (or the 'righteousness' of *l'important* who 'sticks to principles') and 'respectability' (held in esteem by *das Man*). A graver danger than that of straight immoralism, however, seems to be implicit in the existentialist postulate of 'commitment' or 'resolution' coupled with the rejection of ordinary deontic morality. For it is not the sheer immorality of the pleasure-loving and self-seeking cynic or time-server but the *eroico furore* of the quasi-moral 'idealist' or 'activist' unfettered by traditional restraints that threatens to breed the greatest of evils, tyranny.

Applied, however, as a secondary and corrective principle, or injected into everyday conscience as an enlivening zest, the existentialist concept of Authenticity may certainly be turned to good use. The primordial standards of Right and Wrong, even though eked out with an elaborate semi-legal casuistry, are not the whole of morality; good sense, prudential maxims and assent to the received values of a settled civilization do not exhaustively determine the stature or express the level of the human personality. It does happen that conduct open to moral criticism drapes itself with a spurious semblance of correctness in virtue of *some* established moral precept to which it manifestly conforms and which obviously yet not in fact centrally and decisively applies to the situation and its dominant theme; that a schematically justifiable way of acting nevertheless

falls far short of the good the agent was, as it were, meaningfully
'called upon' to do by the inherent spirit of the situation; that an
uninspired life bogs down in the quagmire of over-rated externals,
sedative sonorities and a merely repetitive traditionalism; that,
stifled under the deadweight of conventional claims or particular
fetishes of his own, a person deludes himself into indifference to
what he deeply wants, or purblindly abandons what are, or might
appropriately be and in that sense 'ought' to be, his true aspirations.

In various phraseologies, long before existentialism was invented
and ever since, men would criticize the disvalues of self-deception,
false assurance, cramped regularianism, self-complacent super-
ficiality, hidebound repose in definitive classification, etc., which
may be comprehended under the common label of inauthenticity;
and whenever they praised a 'true Christian', a 'true gentleman'
and so forth, or again, 'true freedom', freedom and originality of
mind, genuine art, solid virtue or sterling qualities, perhaps also a
creative life fully lived, they had in mind a connotation of authenticity. Even the existentialist aberration, or shall we say paradoxy, of
substituting the value of authenticity for the primary, intrinsic
meanings of good instead of joining it thereto as a second-order
modality of value is much older than existentialism. It is embodied
in slogans like 'Become what thou art', '*What* you will is not so
important as that you should will it *wholly*', or *Peccare fortiter*, and
ambiguously suggested also by Kant's formalism with its primary
emphasis on 'consistent willing', by the Greek naturalistic identification of right willing with willing what the agent 'truly' wills,
and by the Christian rebukes against the 'lukewarm' and the self-
righteous as contrasted with a milder judgement of 'sinners'. None
the less, systematic moral nihilism fused with a sustained quasi-
religious claim—exhibiting a tint of austere moralism—is indeed
peculiar to the existentialist attitude, though, in this respect, it will
still remind us of some gnostic and millenarian heresies.

Again, the frigid schematic monotony of the existentialist outlook, with its strict indifference to concerns of welfare and to the
material world, itself presents a paradigmatic specimen of uncontrolled abstraction and deadening inauthenticity. It does not
follow that the quest of authenticity is necessarily self-defeating
and that the incisive manner in which the existentialists have pursued it deserves no positive response whatsoever. But the subtle
problems of authenticity and inauthenticity, their distinctive tests
and tangible signs, their moral and practical contexts, etc., require
to be explored in a more temperate and less partisan spirit; with a
theoretical interest subsistent in its own right rather than keyed to

one dominant emotive tune, and animated by the emotive attitudes of sympathy, patience and generous receptivity to values rather than by a scornful contempt for mundane existence and an obsession with 'crisis' and 'anguish' (all the more desperate, destructive and out of perspective for being atheistic). From a battle-cry endlessly reiterated in the gloomy consciousness of fatal defeat, authenticity should become a real problem of philosophical research; and from its imaginary rank as a key concept of ethics it should accordingly be demoted to its true status as a revealing note of moral rightness and of practical wisdom, and an auxiliary criterion for our assessment of conduct, character and performance. For why are we anxious to know whether some wine is authentic burgundy, or whether some canvas offered for sale is an authentic Cézanne? Not so much because we are interested in authenticity as because we are interested in burgundy and in Cézanne's painting.

To be sure, moral evil or inferior quality are made *worse* by hypocrisy or false pretensions; but the evils of dissimulation are parasitic on good and bad features which are not *themselves*, respectively, genuineness and dissimulation. If a man who does all kinds of immoral things yet at the same time poses as a champion of virtue, a pillar of society or a benefactor of mankind we feel an extra resentment at the pose—without which, he would be less of a scoundrel. However, what view shall we take of a man who usually or nearly always acts honestly, soberly, benevolently, etc., yet in a somehow cramped or crabbed or stunted fashion, with too much effort or too little daring, with an incongruous distribution of emphasis, lacking the limpid radiance of high virtue and the vivifying plenitude and lustre of goodness? We shall deplore his deficiencies, qualify our recognition of his merits, wish that his morality were of a purer quality or won through to a higher level; we should hardly prefer him to leave moral scruples well alone and turn resolutely to evil ways, transforming himself into an unmitigated, 'authentic' and 'harmonious' rogue. True, in regards other than moral we might take a different attitude. Of some dabblers in art, some 'idealists' tinkering at noble pursuits for which they were not made, we may indeed wish they gave up these inauthentic interests and confined their attention to, say, jazz or racing, or some worthier but humdrum avocations. Yet even such judgements should not be formed without great caution; cases of this kind may be sorted into vastly different classes. Thus, even a conspicuous and indubitable lack of genius does not preclude a measure of authenticity in a person's intellectual, artistic or reformatory interests, nor a possibility of objective value in his work.

In existentialist ethics, an echo of the romantic imperative 'Be a genius' is clearly audible. But the cult of genius in the sense of contingent personality and polychromous playful eccentricity is out of place in the age of 'masses' and machines, of human omnipotence through organization and the spectre of drab despair attendant upon it. The aestheticist idolatry of genius has been transposed into a key of philosophical abstraction and formal religiosity. Exceptional 'gifts' are rare and are ultimately irrelevant, but exceptional situations and modes of awareness—eccentric or marginal, that is, from the standpoint of the man entangled in the web of everyday mundane concerns, including intrinsic values and morality—are what actually constitutes existence: groundless and unguided freedom, naught, death, crisis, anguish and unspecified guilt are thrust on man as such, though perhaps only a few and only at rare moments will face them and make them consciously 'their own', thus ascending the steep path to the austere and elusive tableland of authentic existence which in a way corresponds to the 'genius' of old. Yet this may not be the *whole* 'message' of existentialism. Its primary, inward and quasi-religious ideal is likely to yield, as the demand of 'commitment' and other analogous phrases show, more widely applicable derivatives with an urgent, though in itself indefinite, bearing on practice. To what kind of pursuits will that *a priori*, and so far vacuous, 'commitment' tend to commit the disciple? No content can be, or is meant to be, deduced from its concept with anything like logical rigour; but that does not mean that it may 'receive' any kind of contents indifferently and that it cannot be essentially consonant with some types of contents rather than with others.

2. AUTHENTICITY AND ALIENATION

Much like 'the early Marx'—himself influenced by Hegel, Feuerbach and romantic ideals—although in a different setting of concepts and accents, Heidegger and Sartre regard the existence of empirical (fallen, falsified or self-adulterated) man as warped, veiled, debased and lost by reification and alienation. In other words, his being is seen imprisoned in a world of 'things' on which he confers an autonomous weight and of categories, forces, interests, claims, 'validities', etc., which make him, as it were, a helpless playball of *alterity* and deprive him of sovereign selfhood—yet at the same time, worst of all, throw him the sop of a deceptive semblance of selfhood and freedom, fuddling his consciousness of that deprivation. For, precisely, man is not just confronted, he does not just see himself face to face, with an overwhelming structure of otherness which constricts and coerces him and threatens to absorb him; he is actually engulfed and permeated by the glue of alterity (to borrow one of Sartre's expressive phrases), himself a party to the weird system of impersonality and a co-author of his own alienation. Hence, such corollaries of 'authenticity' as Sartre's *engagement* and Heidegger's 'heroic' mode of *Dasein* refer not so much to acts of resistance, rebellion or emancipation, or again of a contemplative withdrawal of interest from the alien ambit of the self, as to an 'authentic' style of intervention in the affairs of the ineliminable outer world which should issue from a 'restored' integral selfhood keenly conscious of alterity but, instead of playing its game, confronting it in an attitude determined by self alone, not by it. Nietzsche put it more picturesquely: 'They say a good cause justifies a war; but I tell you that a good war justifies a cause.' *Engagement*, then, has an aspect not only of self-assertion as against 'the other' or 'others' or 'things outside' but also of self-purification, as it were of 'conversion' or 'salvation'. It seems to me essential, *pace* the Christian existentialists, that this should not be presided over by a God outside self, but perhaps more essential still, more specifically underlying the existentialist scheme, that so far as we do imagine some phantom of a godhead behind it that must not be a God who speaks in terms of *commandments* or promulgates *standards*—which would mean reification—but a kind of deity who proceeds by *ad hoc* commands or decrees alone, or preferably by inaudible suasion, invisible predetermination or ineffable emanation; by intimate fusion with the agent's self. The authentic or heroic human will does not adjust itself or conform to God's will—that would be alienation—but itself is or comes to be, or represents or absorbs, the divine will.

Incidentally, it may be worth mentioning that 'commitment' with its all too moral resonance, evocative of promise and obligation, renders *engagement* somewhat inadequately: the French word has a stronger connotation of 'intervention', and perhaps it is only their fear of 'betrothal' or 'battle' that has kept English writers from translating it simply by 'engagement'. More important, Heidegger's pretty mythico-colloquial term *Zeug* is slightly misleadingly translated by 'tool'; 'instrument' would be even worse, while 'utensil' is rather better. *Zeug* is not a synonym of *Werkzeug* (tool, instrument); it means 'tool' more in the sense of 'equipment' (or part of an equipment) but connotes 'stuff', with the mildly depreciative flavour of that word. Again, *Zeug* is prevalently a collective noun, a concealed plural: *ein Zeug* is hardly possible German; my watch is not *ein Zeug* but *ein Instrument* (or *ein Werkzeug*), although, falling far short of chronometer standards, I fear it is rather *wertloses Zeug* (inferior stuff). There are five fitting synonyms, with slightly different connotations, for *Zeug* in Spanish, four of them plurals. In present-day philosophical English, 'furniture' is sometimes used in a fairly similar sense. The point is that *Zeug* emphasizes, along with the idea of 'utensility' (and more than that of 'instrumentality'), the idea of *functionality*. Certainly it subserves utility and is at the disposal of man; but this being 'to hand' (*zuhanden*) means not only being available as a means to preconceived human ends but also being part of a welter of tentative and competitive self-subsistent purposes in which man is entangled and at the same time too much at home, as if stuck in sugared mud, narcotized, corrupted and alienated: the *Zeug* is not just an available tool but an insidiously captivating little brute in a menagerie of man-eating teleologies. In a word, 'traps' are apt to entrap us.

Now, we are all familiar with phenomena of alienation and depersonalization that obviously constitute a form of grave disvalue. Thus, the behaviour of the kind of person who slavishly follows the directives of established authority or mechanically apes the latest fashion; the typical governess addicted to edifying clichés and in dread of the 'split infinitive', and the man who can only express himself in current journalese; the sectarian crank and the snob or gossip-monger diluted in the ivy-like shallow sociability of *das Man*; no doubt also the kind of person who *identifies* money or measurable utility with reality or practice as such, or again respectability or even mere reputation with morality as such. Pharisaical legalism, the cult of efficiency, uncritical veneration and romantic infatuation for specified persons may likewise be named. But these diseased or at any rate narrowing, impoverishing and perverting forms of reification and alienation should not be confused with reification and alienation as inherent in the human, and more particularly the civilized, mode of being. The reference to objective categories is the very core and nerve of the life of reason, and submission to alterity is not only what makes man moral and acceptable to other men but what makes man capable of comparison and discernment, of imaginative freedom and conscious self-direction. Resistance to outside pressure, compulsion and fascination itself requires the possession of knowledge learnt, beliefs received and habits inculcated; in other words, guidance by authorities and yardsticks borrowed from others. Dissimilation from outside influences is impossible without the assimilation of stuff conveyed from outside, and assertion of self inseparable from regard for alterity. In his critique of *casticismo* (i.e. the worship of ethnic, tribal or regional selfhood and distinctive originality), Unamuno, himself a thinker of partly existentialist leanings, has written the wise words:

There is no idea more satanic than that of self-redemption; peoples, like individuals, redeem one another. Civilizations are products of two-sexed generation, not of solitary burgeoning.

To vary Unamuno's phrasing—there is no conception of man more *inauthentic* than his conception as an ineffable, intangible and incomparable 'self' or 'person' dropped into a corruptive kettle of alien forces tending to absorb him, from which it were his business to emerge in unsullied glory, having recovered his pristine purity. As for the historic lineage of this barren myth, I may briefly point to the gnostic speculation about Light having fallen captive to Darkness and the manichaean theory of the Spirit being imprisoned in Matter. As for the historical explanation of its surge in the industrial epoch, we should of course have to consider the machine as a monstrous overlord of man, itself invented, installed, managed and fructified by 'others' (men but not 'oneself'), and the rise of social collectives and systems of administration which have come to control the individual, more and more frighteningly and bewilderingly, as so many huge, opaque, incomprehensible and impersonal 'alien' powers. Again Nietzsche is in point here: 'The State, coldest of all cold monsters!' Significantly, a Spanish fascist writer sympathetic to existentialism, V. Marrero, published some ten years ago a book entitled *El poder entrañable* ('State-power intimate', or 'rooted in the entrails', 'visceral' as it were) in which he expounds his loving vision of a 'hot' kind of State in utter contrast to the liberal *Rechtsstaat* and socialist bureaucracy but with some appreciation for Bolshevism; among various fascist ideologies, he is most attracted by that of Zelea Codreanu, the leader of the Iron Guard in Roumania (murdered at King Charles's behest) who dreamed of a peculiarly warm-blooded type of political community, founded on 'love'. A close connection in Germany between existentialism and the Youth Movement (grown from the *Wandervogel* league, founded in 1908 in a stylish Berlin suburb, chiefly vitalist and naturist in spirit, anti-bourgeois but not proletarian) should also be mentioned.[b]

What constitutes personal freedom is not, then, the absence of limitations imposed from outside and of dependence on others—which, on the contrary, underlie it, just as my possession of the truth is owed to the compulsive evidence of the object, to which my mind is 'subjected'—but the person's ability to balance, to revise and to modulate his limitations, ties and obligations. (In Professor Popper's language: not the erasure of traditions, the 'clean slate', but the additional acquisition of the *critical tradition*.) The existentialist contrast between a man 'all himself' and a man reduced to the worthless status of a mere vehicle of impersonal mechanisms or of a mere plaything of obscene devilkins (bred by himself and his like) reposes on an arbitrary, fictitious alternative and must be dismissed as the kind of myth usually concocted by extremist prophets and pragmatic aestheticists who, however familiar with the techniques of abstraction, are above all anxious to impress and to shock. It is not in a rapturous gloating over his own alleged 'uniqueness' but in his understanding, his intelligent handling and his appreciative conspectus of objects, objective categories, particular purposes and established value demands that a man reveals, and shapes, his personality; it is not in denying, ignoring or trying to cast off his limitations, but in making a prudent use of their diversities and flexibilities, that he asserts his freedom; it is not through the mirage of an escape from alienation but through the manifoldness and equilibrium of his alienations, and not through a self-insulating dread of otherness but through a sympathetic regard for it and a dialogic intercourse with it that he achieves and unfolds his selfhood. In their critique of *das Man* or of our wish for justifying our choices in objective terms, the existentialists have pointed to real inferiorities and dangers, but concentrating as they do on the deviant forms, the diseased fringes, the blind-alleys and clinkers of civilized life rather than on its paradigmatic modes of procedure, they largely offer jejune caricatures of it instead of a discerning, careful and helpful critical analysis; on the positive side, they have nothing to offer but doom-consciousness spiced with a high-sounding idealistic demand—or worse: a new version of the aesthete's surrender to active barbarism, an espousal of totalitarian tyranny as the next-best substitute for the impossible pursuit of total freedom.

Heidegger's picture of *das Man* is an amusing satire on a certain modality of bourgeois, or rather everyday and average-human, ways of thinking and evaluating: the world of ready-made and reach-me-down, conventional and fashionable, deodorizing and falsely comforting, titillating and titivated, ideas and idols; of rumours, parleys and opinions; of the *on dit*, of what 'is done' or not done, of the 'keeping up with the Joneses'; of 'living and letting live' and cheap sentimentalism; of edifying maxims, pooh-poohing gestures and prurient whisperings; of death as an accident which happens to others (morticians also must live and funeral parlours be kept going; though whether *The Loved One* is of directly Heideggerian inspiration I don't know) and sterilized into 'casualty', an aseptic material for the serene realm of statistics. Now in fact this ugly and ludicrous world of *das Man*, as dissected by Heidegger, represents one layer of social consciousness, discernible in every society and in almost every social medium but particularly conspicuous in liberal society with a strong note of commercialism and of low-grade literacy; it is nowhere by any means a true likeness of current or dominant social consciousness itself. The 'bourgeois', e.g., knows perfectly well, and not only theoretically but efficaciously, that *he* as an individual is going to die some day, like everybody else: that is why he makes testaments and takes out life-assurance policies. I can see no peculiar frivolity in death being sometimes decorously, but not incorrectly, referred to in such terms as 'If something happens to me': most people in fact do not die either as suicides or as centenarians submitting, having spent every particle of their vitality, to the law of nature, but death 'happens' to them with an aspect of contingence about it, and sometimes pretty unexpectedly. Even the boorish Hungarian squires of old who in their noisy carousals used to shout 'Yo-ho! We'll never die!' were not necessarily, for that reason, self-deluded fools or inauthentic cripples. Some of the moods and mental techniques characteristic of *das Man* are not illegitimate at all: they contribute to making life bearable and thus to making serious thought and action possible; they are inseparable from the tentative play of conceits and opinions without which no reflected judgements, mature convictions or firmly lodged personal appreciations could ever come into being. (In every field, the human mind proceeds by trial and error, involving a vast amount of loose and haphazard social co-operation, imitation, repulsion, etc.; it has rightly been said that but for a great deal of bad writing no good writing would exist either.)

But only to a hoodwinked—even though in some way sharp-sighted—eye can the archness, pomposity, humbug, irrelevance and petty hedonism inherent in the *das Man* type of attitude and relationships appear to constitute the focal spirit of civic society and the ordinary man's rule of life. Howsoever guiltily prone to inveigle themselves and one another into all kinds of shams, incongruities and unworthy satisfactions, men do in general distinguish solid and weighty concerns, lasting values and decisive moral principles and practical points of view from the dance of quasi-beliefs, nerve-twitchings, fakes and fopperies; they have a good deal of traffic (some more, some less) with what they at heart despise, and few of them would seriously place the confabs of fussy neighbours, the mouthings of agitators and advertisers or the fashions prevailing in the smart set of the day on the same level with ingrained ultimates and intrinsic evidences—seriously believe, for example, that the idea of Right and Wrong is a superstition fostered in their own interest by self-seeking conspiratorial groups, or that Not Using Amplex is the paradigm of the unforgivable sin.

But Heidegger's attack has a more serious meaning than a mere
moralistic exposure and scarification of the unsavoury nature of *das
Man*. Through the distorting medium of *das Man*, it is meant to
hit the target of objective morality and its proper *locus*, civic
society—a concept extending far beyond the limits of liberal-
democracy—as such.

Heidegger's starting-point is seemingly 'individualistic'. The
'fallen', 'inauthentic', 'alienated' puppet of *das Man* looks upon
himself with the eyes of the others, takes his cues (in thinking and
appraising) from 'them', interprets and judges himself as a self
among other analogous selves instead of being truly *himself*. But in
fact this is the fundamental law, not of the world of ephemeral
trumperies and slippery opportunism but of the world of *moral
reciprocity* as promulgated in the Golden Rule of the Gospel
(though, of course, expressing a moral intuition older than Christian and even than Mosaic revelation) and expounded, most specifically perhaps, by Adam Smith and by Kant. It is lodged in society
as a repository of moral consensus and an open medium of mutual
respect and evaluation; it informs Conscience—ordinary moral
conscience, to be sure, not Heidegger's objectless 'self-calling' conscience—as the 'inner spectator', the 'Man within the Breast'. It is
embodied, partly, in the institutional framework of impersonal
legality and the *Rechtsstaat*. A reflection of it is certainly discernible
in the *das Man* mode of consciousness, inasmuch as the latter is
parasitic on the relational pattern of the open society, of which it
represents both a pragmatic application and a falsifying misuse;
Heidegger fastens on that reflection alone, ignoring the moral conception of society which it presupposes, much like a critic of democracy who would describe the operation of the axiom that citizens'
choices shall exert a regular influence on their government as
directly mirrored in the practices of electoral fraud. Again, the
'reciprocity' and 'spectator' conception of inter-personal relations
is in fact individualistic in the sense of postulating the self-
purposeful, self-directing and self-controlling individual who
recognizes the different and alien individuality of others on an equal
footing with his own. Even *das Man* in its worst excrescences
reveals, by virtue of its competitive emphasis, a conception of mankind as a tissue of *relations*, as a kingdom immutably *divided* into
autonomous individuals. Consensual, conscientious and discursive
morality, with the model of the Constitutional Society or the Rule
of Law as its concrete counterpart, means an *individualist conception of human community*. That is what Heidegger's individualism
does *not* mean. What he has in mind (as a point of departure) is
sovereign and unlimited selfhood: the 'incomparable' individual

set apart as if he were the *only* individual in the world, a solitary godhead of the universe. Yet Heidegger is no Stirnerian anarchist; what he denies and denounces is not Community but only an individualistic community. Seen in a social perspective, his polemic against *das Man*, on behalf of an intact purity of selfhood, is in reality *anti*-individualistic. Its point lies in his positive conception of the 'resolute union' (*das entschlossene Mitsein*), that is to say, community as a closely-knit unique absolute, with which the individual *identifies himself* by a total decision, down to the innermost fibres of his being, without reservations and without any *other* overture to suasions from outside or regard for alterity. The 'self' is thus invited to become the co-bearer of the moral and metaphysical sovereignty, the unbridled power and sole validity, of the Totalitarian State. What is outside that is merely something that 'is there'; it is seen as deprived of authentic existence and is accorded no recognition or statute of reciprocity. The individual is restored to 'authentic selfhood' by his incorporation into one monolithic, integrally disciplined and self-contained collective with no moral curb or criterion imposed on it, no authority above it, and no being invested with any claim beyond it. The manifold and variable patchwork of the individual's alienations is replaced by one total, comprehensive and definitive act of self-alienation. The emphasis on Death (not quite to Sartre's taste), devoid of any reference to the fate of the soul in after life, chimes in with the ultimateness of heroic surrender to the community and the motif of tight-lipped militancy. *Sein und Zeit* is one of the more distinguished expressions of the creed of a refurbished, interiorized and consistently anti-civilian militarism which from 1919 on was establishing more and more completely its ascendancy in the public mind of Germany, particularly as concerns the mentally active elements of the younger adult generation whose earlier youth-movement ideology of authenticity, unconventional vitalism and naturalism, ethnic interest and the 'league' (*Bund*) as a mode of life had been hardened into a new cult of defiant and exclusive comradeship in arms through the experience of the war, the inconclusive defeat, the activities of the volunteer corps and a scornful revolt at the latitudinarian and hedonistic traits in the climate of the westernizing 'Weimar' Republic. Heidegger and his like were not the inventors of Nazism, nor did they ever adhere to it wholeheartedly and for good, but they decisively contributed to its sinister greatness by the armature of intellectual depth and spiritual substance, consonant to its own basic attitudes, which they put at its disposal.

The logical model of total self-alienation arising from the postulate of the individual's total self-sovereignty, however, had been constructed a great deal earlier and presented with greater clarity by Rousseau. Under the *contrat social*, the 'citizen' alienates himself wholly and without reserve to the community, *as a guarantee* that, the same being also true of every *other* citizen, in obeying social authority he shall never obey any *alien* will but always *his own*. In Jacobin 'democracy' as well as in Marxism-Leninism and in Fascist totalitarianism the model has been applied—in very different ways to be sure, and in the context of even more vastly different ideal contents and group interests specific to each. It may be worth while to add that Rousseau, particularly in his later life, took a sceptical view as to the practicability of pure and consistent democracy, and at least on one occasion declared his preference for frank and unchecked 'despotism' as against a limited set of liberties, which he not unreasonably associated with the concept of 'privilege'. Perhaps the existentialist dream of total alienation as a remedy for alienation is more specifically opposed to Burke's traditionalist constitutionalism or Burckhardt's concern about 'culture' and the balance of social powers than to the standard conception of liberal-democracy.

Sartre's unmasking of ostensibly justified choice is closely comparable to Heidegger's theory of *das Man*. Just as *das Man*, the concerted game and jelly-like shadows' dance of 'the world', is a product of inauthentic *Dasein* fleeing from heroic self-realization into dependence on otherness, the person in the state of inauthenticity invents rational, objective and communicable 'grounds' for his choice, in order to crowd out of his consciousness the ineluctability of freedom, and lull himself into the reassuring illusion of acting by a kind of objective necessity exactly as others would have to act in his place. He may follow some fixed intrinsic principles as required by respectability, or again choose spontaneously, on the stealth as it were, and *ex post* array the 'arguments' that have decided him to choose thus and not otherwise. Again, this is not sheer imagination on Sartre's part. As something like *das Man* exists, so also do habits of unintelligent conformity (with the illusion of self-evident validity) and plausible epiphenomenal justifications of what one does because one anyhow wants to do it actually occur. And again, Sartre mistakes the parasitical and degenerative fringes of orderly, moral and rational conduct for its central essence. For what *is* a figment of imagination is 'pure' freedom of choice. Our behaviour is primarily inclined, i.e. provisionally and incompletely determined, by our desires (many of them mutually conflicting, and many of them conditioned by reference to others and suasion by others), and it is within this field of forces alone that our free choice can operate. Were it not for grounds, arguments and objective validities, necessarily relative to *given* desires (including appreciative beliefs, the attraction of 'dignities' and the desire to comply with obligations), no deliberation and therefore no free choice could take place at all. It is true that new tonalities of desire and a discovery of new autonomous purposes can emerge in the very process of deliberation, that a tentative preliminary decision will gather momentum and force the issue on its own. Free choice does not *mean* 'rational' choice; it is not 'dictated' by reason and is not the result of a computation. Nonetheless, 'new motives' presuppose an antecedent personal field of valuation already furnished with contents, are invested with a meaning in that context of desires, axioms, codes, etc., and are subjected to the test of *given* (though not in all parts rigidly immutable) concerns and standards. What *else* should or could personal free choice mean? Indeed, in the very concept of choice the aspect of freedom is undetachably tied to the aspect of limitation. Choice is offered primarily between *given* alternatives, and the chooser's normal and meaningful aim is not to assert or exhibit his freedom but to end it—to consume it—by exercising it, and certainly not to 'choose' *it* but to choose, to the best of his ability, what is *best* and can *arguably* be presented as such. Far from being incompatible with, free choice is inseparable from reification and alienation; it is either limited, i.e. 'impure', or nothing.

It is, admittedly, conceivable to let one's choices be governed by the overall principle of maximizing one's freedom of choice in regard to future situations, coupled perhaps with a similar endeavour concerning the range of freedom enjoyed by others. This looks rather like a universal moral rule and ominously near to the liberal maxim of 'respect for the equal freedom of others'; freedom would thus appear to have undergone a measure of reification, and it is hard to see how a man could act on such a principle without consciously submitting to alienation. Pursuits would thus seem to become a matter of compromise, discursive morality readmitted, and 'uniqueness' jeopardized. More vulnerable perhaps than Heidegger to mental temptations of such a kind, Sartre's existentialism nevertheless points in another main direction, analogous to Heidegger's though not identical with it.

Solidarity with the freedom of others may be interpreted, rather than in terms of respect, compromise and normative arrangement, in terms of indivision, fusion and spontaneous harmony. And the promise of this is precisely laid down in Marx's vision of the communist society of the future, the utopian tail-piece of the Bolshevist ideology and system of life. Instead of recognizing the 'conventional' morality of justice, benevolence and equity in daily transactions and of supporting a scheme of government in keeping therewith, *engagement* at its highest will take the form of a free act of adhesion to the Communist cause, i.e. the social revolution destined to bring about a condition of the world in which everybody's similarly free, 'authentic' and wholly personal acts shall *a priori* fit in with everybody else's—without any sense of division and barriers, without any necessity for objective counters and abstract rules, for taboos and sanctions or for obligations, claims and reciprocal concessions. Here too, the war waged against alienations tilts over dialectically into total alienation; the vacuous sense of unlimited freedom finds its fulfilment in the act of surrender to an organized conspiracy, united by the bonds of a dogmatic creed and of iron discipline, for unlimited power. Lack of space prevents me from attempting a comparative analysis and appraisal of Heidegger's option for nationalist fascism and Sartre's for Marxist-Leninist communism. Nor can I expatiate on the fairly obvious fact that, while existentialists may 'choose' this or that brand of totalitarianism, or perhaps fall in love with several of them, the authentic representatives of any totalitarian creed will distrust, though perhaps exploit for their purposes, the allegiance of existentialists. This may apply more strictly to the Communist than, say, to the Fascist attitude, seeing that Communism implies a primary affirmation of ordinary human wants and 'welfare' points of view, whereas Fascism, though in fact much less intolerant and less destructive of freedom, is more markedly infatuated with the aesthetics of totality as a formal principle. Curiously enough, though not perhaps quite accidentally, it is Sartre the playwright-psychologist, placing a keener emphasis than Heidegger the professor of metaphysics on freedom, contingency and absurdity, who has 'chosen' as a cynosure of his 'commitment' the political system that is not only more flawlessly and oppressively totalitarian than any of its possible rivals but also distinctively necessitarian and wedded to sham-scientific dogmatism, certitudes and concepts of historical predetermination.

In view of its being on principle uninterested in the contents of life, in utility, 'human nature' or evolution, as also in God or any other *a priori* hall-marked moral authority, existentialist ethics is often counted as one of the 'non-naturalistic' types of moral philosophy. Yet it is significantly 'naturalistic' in that it fundamentally rejects the concept of diversified intrinsic qualities of good and evil, right and wrong, obligatory and forbidden as apprehended in moral experience, and reduces the moral problem of man entirely to the theme of his being genuinely 'existent': thus reducing Ought, not to what 'is good', but to *Is*. In Moore's phrase, I would label it as a form of 'metaphysical naturalism'. As in the case of many earlier variants of naturalism, the value-experience underlying it is unmistakably aesthetical rather than moral. Again, though 'authenticity' cannot be equated to *élan vital* or the display of energy, existentialism—as shown by its concept of *engagement* or 'resolution', and its totalitarian propensities—tends to value *intensity* at the cost of *direction*, and the presence of man's 'full personality' in his action rather than the goodness of its describable objective features. This is what I take to be the real point of the axiom 'Existence is prior to essence'; and it means extreme naturalism of one kind. It also means an undertaking to remove the set of alienations on which the properly moral being of man—his testability and his capacity to judge—is based, and to open the way to his supreme self-alienation into the hands of uncontrolled arbitrary power.

7

Moral Consensus

1. THE CONSENSUAL BACKGROUND OF MORAL INSIGHT AND OBLIGATION

It is my purpose here to argue for the reference to Moral Consensus as an integral aspect of moral experience and to attempt to throw some light on the meaning of Moral Consensus. Indirectly, this of course implies, at the same time, a defence of the 'Intuitional' view of Morality—in the broad sense of the not very felicitous word 'intuitional', for which I might substitute others such as 'intrinsicalist', 'non-naturalist', and above all 'non-reductionist'—in contraposition to the wide variety of reductionist and constructivist types of Ethics ranging, say, from utilitarianism to prescriptivism or from metaphysical perfectionism to situationism. For any such reductionist and constructivist theory, once granted its arbitrary (while perhaps plausible and by no means simply nonsensical) premiss, may within its own limits build on safe ground without needing any recourse to or support by consensual data, whereas 'intuitive' moral insights and valuations, or call them 'evident moral ultimates', necessarily depend for their validity on consensual confirmation available at least in some virtual, yet palpable, fashion. Such is, though, our commonsensical faith in 'people's opinions' that in practice most ethical thinkers of the constructivist type have shown themselves desirous to arrive at some linkage or correspondence with them at any rate in an occasional and haphazard manner—the prominent example being Aristotle who again and again points to 'people's opinions' in confirmation of his own, instead of relying with proud exclusiveness on his teleological (perfectional and utilitarian) construction. But my point is here that any intuitional and evidential or experiential theory of morals *needs* a consensual complement on pain of irrelevance.

Moral evidence is neither logical or mathematical nor 'plainly' factual or empirical. It is ineluctably valuational; and all kinds of valuational evidences, moral and other, suffer from an additional element of 'subjectivity' or, in respect of the mode in which the object presents itself, of 'opacity'. I may feel as sure that this French bread I am munching is good French bread as that it is French bread, and as sure that this Romanesque church I am looking at is beautiful as that it is a Romanesque church; but there is a difference. No doubt, in my plain sense-perceptions as such I am myself concomitantly 'given' as a perceiver; but this aspect, however inseparable from my object-experience, is peripheral and wholly unemphatic; my awareness of the object is what luminously predominates. On the contrary, in my reporting an evaluative experience my own pleasure, delight, satisfaction or admiration, etc.—or inversely, in the case of an unfavourable judgement my own dislike, unpleasure, horror, etc.—inevitably comes into play and fills an important place. I don't hesitate to say (on many occasions) with complete firmness, 'This is good', 'This is lovely', 'This is beautiful', etc.; but such judgements include a factual reporting of my own emotive response: 'I am enjoying the taste of this', 'The sight of this attracts me greatly', and so forth. And these factual reportings are invested with a status of objectivity quite on a par with my factual reporting of *what* I am tasting, looking at, conjuring up in my mind, etc.; whereas the corresponding value-judgements proper, *about* objects (that is, specified values and disvalues) not about my emotive responses, are precisely for that reason less objective. Essentially less objective, I mean: as if an additional layer of subjectivity, opaque to some extent, i.e. imperfectly transparent, intervened between my sense of evidence and the object it refers to. If I say 'I feel enraptured by this Cézanne or this Munch', or 'I shudder at the sight of this Toulouse-Lautrec or this Dali', you can only either question my sincerity or simply accept my statement, so far as it goes, as incorrigible (a more technical word for infallible). But if I maintain that the first two paintings are marvellous while the last two are hideous, many of you, including art connoisseurs, may well disagree without having to doubt my sincerity. Apart perhaps from some very complex exceptional cases, my awareness of my aesthetic tastes is infallible; but my tastes themselves, and my judgements depending on them, certainly are not. Tastes are not in general simply 'blind' nor simply at variance with the tastes of *others*; or else no aesthetical argument or indeed discourse would be possible. In some ways at least, we tend to expect others to share our tastes and like these to be hall-marked by the judgements of others, especially experts; and therein lies an element of recourse to Consensus. If a person sees no incisive difference of value between authentic Romanesque or Gothic and their inept caricatures in nineteenth-century historicistic architecture, we won't so readily say that 'our tastes differ' but rather that he 'lacks taste' or is afflicted with 'value-blindness' or at least one huge 'blind spot' in his vision. Yet anyhow we quite naturally 'tolerate' a great variety of divergent tastes or judgements in aesthetic matters and in some other, more practical, matters as well. Thus, within a constitutional framework at least and to some extent even outside such a framework, we regard the existence of more or less basically opposed political orientations ('parties') as normal and perhaps wholesome for the nation, although if we take any part in political life we cannot but take sides, e.g. vote for this as against that party, at least on given occasions. We may, however, extend no such toleration to advocates of high treason or workers for a movement sworn to the establishment of extremist tyranny.

In the ethical context and more particularly the context of strict deontic morality, the comparative opaqueness of valuational evidence is apt to evoke a keener sense of puzzlement, to inflict upon us as it were a more smarting sting of dissatisfaction. Accordingly, we feel driven here more urgently to look for support to Consensus. Although moral emphasis is by no means confined to the sphere of social co-operation and the problems and techniques of social co-operation are by no means confined within the area of moral themes, there is an essential conjunction between the two realms; a disintegration of the moral universe of discourse would gravely affect the business of life, and the breakdown of society as a far-expanding medium of communication would tend to render our moral experience and judgements singularly weightless and pointless if not vacuous. It can be brought to crystal-clear compulsive evidence that, say, Jones has made a grossly mendacious statement; but although it may seem equally evident to me that he deserves severe condemnation on that count since lying is wrong and blameworthy, on closer inspection the second evidence will prove to be inherently weaker than the first. Moral 'wrongness' cannot be 'seen' in quite the same sense as the wrongness of an inference or the falseness of a belief or the inadequacy to some definite purpose of a physical object. If many people have not so far detected Jones's lie or hesitate to recognize that his lie has been a deliberate and purposeful one I can still convince them by presenting them with a set of compulsive evidences which they finally cannot help accepting as conclusive; certainly their initial dissent will have no intrinsic bearing on my own well-founded conviction. My moral evidence, however, while definitely claiming a cognitive status (it is totally different from a feeling like 'I can't say why, Jones may be an irreproachable character for all I know, but somehow I don't take to him'), lacks the straightforward cognitiveness of sense-perception, logical inference or fact-finding. I confidently and in a way self-evidently expect 'others', in fact generally 'men', to share my conviction that lying is wrong; and indeed to feel so about as keenly as I do and hold the same belief with the same degree of evidence; but what if, e.g. on occasion of my reproving Jones's lie, I found myself confronted with an overwhelming body of opinion about the intrinsic wrongness of lying contrary to mine? I would not meekly surrender; but I would feel shocked in a unique fashion, and feel smitten with a sort of helpless wonderment as if the ground were being knocked out from under my feet. I should certainly not feel able to tell people with the same serenity as in the case of factual disagreement: 'But look at this, consider that, see for yourself.' Nor should I feel in a mood of dismissing the matter with a shrug as I do when meeting with basic and shocking disagreement in matters of art. Moreover, my sense of bafflement, bewilderment and giddiness as also of helpless resentment—for moral misjudgement is characteristically itself an object for moral indignation—derives partly from my awareness that I have, after all, been taught by 'others', by 'men', not to say by 'mankind', to despise and condemn lying and deceit and to attach a high value to truthfulness and probity. I do so now and have done so for long with a note of strong and self-contained intuitive certitude; perhaps I may have acquired that certitude very early and almost unaided by my educators' directions and admonitions; on the other hand, I also have acquired a great deal of my indirect fact-knowledge and perhaps even the 'rules of correct inference' through being instructed and trained—and yet there is a difference. Evidences in general are completely detachable from their origins in the person's 'apprenticeship' and the authority of their transmitters; but in regard to valuational evidences this separability may be much less complete, and particularly so as regards moral evidences—in virtue of the very close though not quite simple or uniform connection between moral experience as such and the experience of reciprocity, mutual responsibility, and 'demands' both binding *upon* the moral agent and represented *by* him in relation with others. Society as a medium of morality means an indefinitely open field of virtual accountability, of reciprocal inspectorship as it were, between men and their fellow-men, a tribunal extending beyond all particular group limits, with the correlate of *self*-judgement expected from everyone's part. A consensual attunement between claims and the recognition of claims constitutes, I do not say a definition but a focal characteristic of moral emphasis and meanings. A reference to actual Consensus, not so explicitly stated as, e.g. by Hume (let alone Descartes's ethical conventionalism), is nevertheless implied in the Golden Rule, in Pittakos's Law ('Do not do yourself what you condemn in others'), in the *Bystander*, *Spectator* or 'Man in the Breast' theories of the classic

British Moralists, in Kant's 'Universal Legislation' theory of a morally acceptable 'maxim of action', and in Hare's 'Universalizability' criterion of moral rules. None of these would invoke Consensus so bluntly and directly as does Prichard, or (more cautiously, though without adequate elaboration) Sir David Ross, or as I would do here (with still more reserve but also with more thematic attention). However, among more recent writers issuing from the dominant school of the last decades, Mayo at any rate goes so far as to set up Consensus as 'The Third Plane of Universalizability' (the first two being, of course, the identical moral status of the agent's descriptively similar or identically subsumable actions done on different occasions, and the same identity of valuation extending to different agents' actions subsumable under the same significant category).

If Consensus means something other than a haphazard empirical coincidence of individual insights, neither is it a sort of massive 'collective consciousness' which as it were lends me my own moral insights or whose pressure places me automatically under a set of moral obligations. My insight that lying is morally 'wrong' is not, say, like a patriot's reverence for the accidental colour-scheme of his respective national flag. Rather, it emerges in a somehow rational, not historical or conventional, context. It reflects, notably, the non-moral yet sharply characterized 'wrongness' of Error, i.e. of false belief: which, a non-moral 'blemish' or 'fault', in its turn presupposes that knowledge (and even true belief as such) is 'a good' —a non-moral good, a good *for* its possessor, of course—and ignorance, if not *per se* an evil (for the person who lacks the knowledge in question), at any rate an imperfection. Ignorance is not *per se* 'wrong' in however non-moral a sense, but error is non-morally wrong, and delusion, faulty or vitiated thinking, etc., are even more markedly so (in some cases, they are underlain by a moral lack of integrity). Yet these relations are complex and non-rigorous. Moral 'unfittingness' is not, as Clarke and Wollaston believed, a translation into conduct of an intellectual error, an incongruity of action with the true nature or order of things. A man's cruel treatment of his horse does *not* express his erroneous belief that the horse is not a sentient being; if he did quite genuinely believe that, his act might still be morally undesirable as are many acts based on a false belief and many involuntary character features, but could not be properly called a moral transgression at all. Surely if I cruelly ill-treat somebody, from vindictiveness for example, the more vividly I am aware of the suffering I inflict upon him the greater my cruelty. And if Jones voices *bona fide* an erroneous belief of his he is not lying at all, whereas if he states something that happens to be true but that he believes to be false he *is* lying. Again, in what ways are the duties of beneficence and the stricter duties of non-maleficence grounded in the goodness and badness of certain things for people; in what conditions and in what form do they apparently 'follow' therefrom? Our moral certitudes would thus, not simply vanish to be sure but grow extremely tenuous if we relinquished the enlightenment and support derived from Consensus as crystallized in moral codes and traditions and expressed in consultations, admonitions and other forms of moral discourse.

2. THE OBJECTIONS OF CIRCULARITY, NATURALISM, AND AUTHORITARIANISM

Let me state the fairly obvious reproach of circularity. On the one hand, I submit that the individual agent's moral insight and 'conscience' (including its wider meaning of 'sense of obligation') are not self-subsistent primary data but subject to a wide-ranging social consensus and indeed representative of it. On the other hand, I maintain that all collective states of mind, moods and pressures do not by any means deserve the name of moral consensus; that, on the contrary, moral consensus needs to be sifted out and ascertained by the critical tool of an independent and non-consensual once-for-all *distinction* between *moral and non-moral* principles, concepts or types of experience. But then what is the point of bringing in the reference to Consensus at all? If consensus is supposed to tell me what is right or wrong but not unless *I* am able to tell beforehand when it is bearing on right and wrong and when it isn't, we are faced with a sort of chicken-or-egg problem. Each of the two complementary partners seems to be asking of the other what they either both have got or are both unable to furnish: in the first case, the duality is redundant, in the second, unavailing; in either case, it is useless.

My answer to this objection is that apparent circularities are often highly useful clarifications of two inseparable aspects of one complex phenomenon. That chickens are hatched from eggs but in their turn lay eggs doesn't enlighten us about which of the two is prior to the other, but in fact we cannot draw chickens except from eggs and if we have no chickens we must do without eggs. If men grew up in complete isolation from their birth onward or even in quite narrow family groups completely insulated from one another, in other words if they were not *also* products of society with its co-operative requirements, it is utterly doubtful if they would ever develop any moral idea at all—and I mean this in respect of the 'self-regarding' just as well as of the 'other-regarding' virtues. But perhaps this observation, however sound, might interest anthropologists, sociologists and so on, rather than logicians, i.e. philosophers. More intrinsic to the question is my second counter-argument. It is true that (as against what a pure formalist might imagine) the agent could not possess the abstract concept of Moral Right and Wrong as distinct from other goods and ills without also possessing at least *some* inchoate and rudimentary idea about what kinds of things (of action or conduct) *are* right and obligatory or morally praiseworthy and what kinds wrong and morally forbidden. However, it may well be the case that his moral cognition and con-science would remain utterly poor, crude, hazy and uncertain, in-adequate to the purposes of moral orientation and the acquisition of virtue, but for the concourse and the impact of consensual moral codes and the life-blood of moral discourse which presupposes society, with its particular institutions, even with its lop-sided and ephemeral moral accents and its partly vice-riddled practices, as a medium of moral consensus. Moral *language*, evidently not the individual's private invention, is largely ambiguous (most of its terms, if not all, have also primary or derivative non-moral mean-ings), liable to arbitrary and one-sided emphasis and very often misused either impulsively or with a systematic intent of deception (e.g. a speaker would often call his political adversaries 'brigands', 'thieves', etc., or call simply a man who thwarts some wish or ambition of his 'that scoundrel', etc.). Yet, primarily, moral langu-age is informative and an expression of *moral* consensus rather than merely of the will or interests of some people around the agent or of some collective body. Even if some naive person may candidly be-lieve that Argentina is always right as against Brazil and that Brazil's designs on its neighbours are always sinister, or the reverse, he will very soon and easily come to distinguish the meaning of right and wrong from its application or misapplication to any con-flict between prejudged collective entities. For example, by having to turn his mind to the rights and wrongs possibly involved in a dispute between Colombia and Venezuela which does not affect his own loyalties and biases. In brief, the relation between indivi-dual moral sense or intuition and moral consensus is not circular but dialogic.

(*b*) Much less do I feel worried by an objection to the effect that a consensual conception of morals must be 'naturalistic' in that it places the criterion of moral truth or validity in the more massive reality of a large body of opinion as against the material tenuity of individual conscience. The objection falls to the ground if we only have clearly grasped that moral consensus has nothing to do with collective (and thus, superior) power as such, physical or psychological. The moral opinions that make up moral consensus, however vastly extended and perhaps potentially powerful and coercive, do not belong to any more 'natural' an order of reality than does any individual's highly personal, 'unique' and allegedly 'incommunicable' conscience, just as a million noses are neither more nor less 'natural' or 'factual' than one man's nose. The point is that they are *moral* opinions, that *all* moral opinions are facts, and that these facts are the only data on which any analysis and interpretation of morality, and not of something else arbitrarily substituted for morality, can be based. Consensual moral valuations are closely and manifoldly interrelated with *other*, i.e. non-moral kinds of practically relevant ideas and experiences (concerning our vision of human nature and of the circumstances in which men's lives are set: fears, purposes, preferences, etc.); but so is all individual moral experience as such. There is no question of any reduction 'without remainder', to use Broad's expression, of moral to non-moral valuations, strivings or interests; hence, the charge of naturalism is baseless. My moral conviction and conscience will not readily swing into harmony with any mob pressure or persuasion, or Gallup-poll majority, or institutional decree relating to some moral matter, for precisely I question their claim to represent moral consensus. On the other hand, if we insisted on describing a consensually orientated ethic as 'naturalistic', seeing that moral consensus is not independent of the biological and historical constitution of mankind and of societies, we should then equally be committed to call any ethic centred in the individual's moral intuitions and conscience 'naturalistic', for my moral experiences obviously cannot be independent of my non-moral personal data and history as well as of my own *de facto* moral character which obviously is not as such a principle of morality. Certainly my conscience can (and, normally, does in typical cases) set its face against such and such interests, desires and predilections of mine; but this basic (though not complete) definiens of morality equally, in some sense perhaps even more evidently, applies to the moral consensus of mankind as confronted with the interests, the dominant spirit and the maxims of policy of any particular collective, including of course a centralized One-World State should such a bliss or calamity ever fall to the lot of the universe of living and thinking creatures.

(*c*) The related but more specific objection that a consensus-orientated ethic must mean a form of 'authoritarianism' has largely been dealt with already in the foregoing discussion, but on this point I think I ought slightly to modify my counter-argument. Morality most certainly means a value *quality* of intrinsic right and wrong, of essentially good and bad wishing and willing, *not* conformance and disconformance to the 'imperatives' issued by any privileged and uniquely identified or designated 'authority'; at the same time, however, it doesn't mean either a so-called 'autonomous legislation' by the agent himself (hence the utter misleadingness of Hare's favourite phrase 'moral decision'). Rather, it inevitably connotes the idea of *some* kind of *submission* to 'authority', to something outside and above the agent of which some foreshortened aspect and reflection also comes to be incapsulated in the agent's own developing conscience but without ever coming to fully constitute it or to be completely embodied by it. When I started behaving agentially and thus passing under the jurisdiction of the Moral Law, the Moral Law was already there without waiting for my assistance in 'creating' it. It was transmitted to me and to a large extent divined by me and accorded my assent and endorsement. True, it has never been communicated to me in a total and absolutely definitive form, but from the outset has been claiming my ingenuity, skill and effort in applying it to the shaping of my life-practice, and has thereby even incited me to interpret it and re-formulate it at certain points—that is, to experience its directives not merely as the dictates of an extraneous authority or even a validity simply registered by my receptive insights but also as what is called 'the deliverances of my conscience'. But this irremovable aspect of 'autonomy' is secondary to that of 'heteronomy', seeing that it is based on the moral agent's *response* to traditional demands and consensual suasions prior to him, to his conscience as well as to his urges, inclinations and volitions. The right answer to the present objection is, then, in one sense that a consensus-orientated ethic is *not* authoritarian inasmuch as Consensus does not mean a specified alien will to which the individual is called to subordinate his own; but in another sense, that the consensual concept of morality *is* and 'ought to be' authoritarian inasmuch as the moral appeal does indeed invite the agent to conform to what he experiences to be the voice of moral consensus even if, *in the particular case*, he is unable to actualize a full intrinsic insight into the value which that voice calls to his attention and the obligation it is imposing on him.

3. THE OBJECTIONS OF RELATIVITY AND HISTORICITY

The most important objection to consensualist ethics is implied in the factual assertion of Relativity. If the moral views of men are multiform and contradictory, and are conditioned by and varying with different types of social organization and fast-changing social circumstances, then Moral Consensus cannot be the central principle of morality simply because it cannot be said to exist. Rational considerations of a general order and the here-and-now deliveries of conscience must then suffice by themselves, rather than receive their primary orientation from consensus and in their turn serve to bring consensus into the full light of consciousness and merely fill out its gaps and cast it in a more systematic or more directly applicable form. Pascal's contempt for earthly wisdom and moral insight would then hold—that what is truth this side the Pyrenees is error on yonder side, and *vice versa*. The more fantastic an exaggeration, indeed distortion, of facts as two contemporary and contiguous countries were meant here, almost identical in religion, scarcely less so as to form of government, and closely akin in language, race and culture. Yet, shorn of its bold paradox and forced brilliancy, the phrase expresses the relativist thesis fairly adequately. Pascal, of course, only meant it half seriously, but in striking consonance with Descartes's frivolous advice of moral opportunism: Conform to the customs and demands prevailing in the social medium to which you happen to belong. It is most unlikely that Pascal's own moral views and attitudes were in any conscious and systematic fashion 'French as opposed to' (or even 'as distinct from') 'Spanish'. But then, I would say in an authentically Moorian commonsensical vein, a philosopher who preaches to ordinary men a belief that he as a philosophizing man could not himself accept and follow is plainly teaching a false—a nihilistic and self-defeating—philosophy.

To be sure, relativism cannot be disposed of so cavalierly as Prichard (whatever my admiration and affection for this fine thinker) tries to do it in a curt footnote: objective moral obligations are intuitively evident to all people furnished with a developed moral consciousness, though not to others. There is no such thing as two kinds of peoples, societies or cultures, 'developed' and 'undeveloped'; nor does the late-Victorian or Edwardian Oxford intellectual gentleman necessarily embody the apex or the absolute and definitive standard of the 'developed' mind. And if I felt tempted to regard any living or extinct people as 'savages' it would certainly not be either the ancient Egypt of the three Dynasties or the ancient Iran of the Achaemenids, although it appears that in these two high civilizations incest (at least between brother and sister) was permitted or even respected. (It might even be doubted whether the incest taboo refers to a grave moral disvalue as unequivocally as men have usually assumed, though I believe that it does.) I would rather say that some high civilizations may at some limited points indulge in moral views somehow vitiated or out of focus, and discrepant from the all but universal consensus of mankind. One of the best, I mean the worst, examples is offered by our own extravagant, destructive and stupidly dogmatic belief in all-comprehensive Equality—self-contradictory too, for, in Tocqueville's splendid words, you can't have both equality of opportunity and equality of actual levels—though admittedly this aberrant ethos is not unconnected with certain valid moral postulates of justice and of charity.

It cannot be my task here to exhibit with encylopaedic completeness the perennial and universal stock of the Moral Consensus of Mankind; what I propose to do is to point out (following, partly, in Max Scheler's wake) the characteristic confusions on which the relativistic claim largely appears to rest. Before doing this, I would just put forward in the most condensed form, and in my own terminology as unoriginally chosen as I possibly can, the barest outlines of what I regard as the main contents of a Moral Consensus that may safely be called universal, and enduring in the past as well as surviving in our time. They range from formal, seemingly tautological and highly abstract principles or imperatives, such as *Bonum est faciendum, malum vitandum* (not *wholly* tautological in that it enounces the logical priority of evaluation over prescription) and *Pacta sunt servanda* (still in some sense tautological in that it is the *point* of a contract to be observed), across such rules, still apparently grounded in abstract 'reason', as the Golden Rule or the Rule of Pittakos ('Do not do yourself what you condemn in others'), to more concrete and substantive but still highly general dimensions of right-doing and wrong-doing, which I would quote here in the language of values rather than of obligations: that benevolence is good and malice, bad; that veracity is right and mendacity, wrong; and similarly with the contrast-pairs of courage and cowardice, self-control and intemperance, respect for others and arrogant self-assertion, yet on the other hand self-respect and servile self-surrender, adulation or pliancy, dignity and meretricious cynicism, magnanimity and cruelty, chastity and lust, self-control and intemperance, honesty and dishonesty, fidelity and treachery, loyalty and treason. With whatever modulations and differentiations and codified with whatever hidebound simplifications, and irksome omissions, and in spite of whatever philosophic mistakes of arbitrary and monistic reduction or again dogmatic empirical enumeration and neglect of interpretation in terms of some ultimate consonance may attach to these judgements, what we are facing here is a consensual perspective of feelings, insights, views and codifications. A great deal might be added thereto, including—to revert to more formal aspects—the belief that the

primary object of moral appraisal resides in the *intention* that underlies responsible choices, willings, actions and conduct, rather than
results and consequences on the one hand, the background of
interior 'motivations' and spontaneous 'stirrings' on the other. Yet,
seeing that man is not only a morally sensitive but also a non-moral
and thus inevitably also an immoral animal, Moral Consensus cannot but manifest itself psychologically in a somehow dimmed,
blurred, biased, lop-sided, adulterated or at any rate unevenly
weighted form; and this fact gives rise to the typical confusions
proper to relativistic speculation, which I will now attempt to
show up.

(i) Relativists are given to distinguishing different peoples, countries, nations, tribes, societies, cultures, civilizations, epochs,
generations and so forth, as if these were strictly distinct and
enumerable units, indeed collective and isolable units much like
distinct human or animal individuals, or beads of a string as it
were. In fact, this is not so. 'Abstract', universal mankind embodies
a largely intercommunicating, interpenetrating and continuous
manifold of consciousnesses; and the moral codes of Hammurabi,
the Ten Commandments, some Egyptian ethical texts or Cicero's
De Officiis convey to our minds today a far more meaningful, serious
and lastingly intelligible appeal than the thousands of immoralistic
or eccentric ideologies, aphorisms and 'systems' provided by misguided geniuses, clever charlatans and ephemeral journalistic
heralds of fashion.

Again, it is not true that 'concrete' personal relations based on
group affiliation (family, tribe, neighbourhood, nationhood, etc.)
and on particular friendship or enmity constitute a medium placed
somehow above or below or outside the plane of 'abstract' moral
principles. However close the bonds that tie persons together and
set them off from others, and whatever tensions and conflicts may
separate or oppose them mutually, they remain first and last incorporated in the person-to-person field subject to the claims and
category-pattern of moral standards. Men do not 'belong' to one
circle insulated from the 'outer' world, nor to one 'community' as
against 'the others', nor even to 'mankind in general' to the exclusion of 'the enemy'. While the dimensions of moral valuation are a
great deal more manifold than my own foregoing sketch would
show, there is no such thing as a 'pluralism' of possible morals:
there is only one morality. Its many different aspects are always
differently and imperfectly present to men's minds. Some of them
will be specially and felicitously underemphasized or only remote
and marginal in situations of close union and unanimity, e.g. within
the relational pattern of happy families or close friendships or

corporate styles of life and feeling; or again, deplorably under-emphasized or laid aside in possessive or servile types of familial or hierarchical relations; or again, suspended or in some sense extruded from consciousness in the spheres of wilful enmity and friction or indeed of inevitable conflict and hostility: but no limits are set to their *actualization* at any such points whenever it becomes necessary or when a strong experience of them, evoked by some salient feature or new turn of the situation, arises in the minds of some of those involved in it. The relativistic confusion I have here been discussing connotes a confusion between correlation, solidarity and continuity on the one hand and a fictitious concept of solid, identical 'oneness' on the other, and analogously therewith, between distinctness and variation on the one hand with the equally fictitious nightmare of discrete atomic units and blind alienness on the other.

(ii) At its crudest, relativism is prone to confuse the prevailing *practice* of men with their prevailing moral *appreciations*. It would only accept the fact of moral consensus if it saw the terrestrial world superseded by a uniform heaven of saints (or perhaps a uniform abode of the damned, under the sign of either *Lasciate ogni speranza* or *Evil, be thou my Good*). It tends to identify moral decay with a 'new morality' and *mores* with morals. Its favourite belief in homogeneous (and mutually alien) 'epochs', 'cultures' or 'societies' makes it overlook the potent presence of the Jeremiahs, Juvenals, Bossuets, Burckhardts and similar critics of their own societies, and its fascination by the moral indifference and moral-proof wickedness which often prevail in men's conduct will render it unaware of the primal *splitness* in collective as well as in individual minds that is precisely the root phenomenon of moral sense and conscience. At the back of relativism, we find a thinly veiled immoralism and an equally false but more shyly concealed moralism. Seeing that men's morals change and can sometimes appear monstrous to 'our' eyes, morality is obviously a mere function, reflection and plaything of interests, passions and power relations, and lacks any autonomous validity or weight; we may as well not mind it; what matters is that which 'is', not its pallid ghost and venal article of luxury: the idea of that which 'ought to be'. But this sham realism, this superior smile of matter-of-fact-mindedness, also betrays the idealist's bitter resentment at the fact that men are not all moral and certainly not nothing but moral (which last is indeed as it should be): that what 'Is' most certainly does not all along the line hasten to conform to what 'Ought' to be. If immoralism on the one hand is generated by an endeavour to lull awkward consciences to sleep, it springs at the same time from disappointed moralism reluctant to 'accept the universe'. And relativism may well be interpreted as absolutism turned inside out: since men are not uniformly nothing but moral but always something else as well and many different things else, moralities themselves must be different and at loggerheads with each other. This may appear to relativists all the more plausible as, in fact, tension and conflict between different moral *demands* often arises by reason of circumstances and is apt to create the illusion of multiple moralities. Moral laws, in spite of their intimate mutual nexus and consonance, are indeed *not* absolute in the sense of providing sure and handy directives for doing right in every practical situation; what *is* absolute is the validity and claim for earnest consideration of all moral points of view, always, everywhere, and in all circumstances.

(iii) By the same token, though the mistake is of a subtler kind here, relativism is guilty of confusing morality with '*ethos*', i.e. the variable and particular vividness of moral *emphasis* as displayed in locally and chronologically differentiated ideals, idols and ideologies, traditional code-phrasings and fashionable slogans, whose moral tenor is intimately amalgamated with the indefinite multeity of non-moral concerns, particular interests and aspirations, self-loves and selective sympathies, and the never wholly extra-moral but always mixed valuations attached to historically established institutions and emergent projects generally embodied in predominant or unfolding human 'types'. Without the operation of these more or less 'accidental' factors, morality would in truth lose its hold on the business of life and would be confined at best to a sterile protest against the reality of practice, or, more likely, would sink to the level of something theoretically conceivable but falling short of the status even of an inward experience of a few individual *rari nantes*: to the level of something thinkable but actually never even thought of. But for the animation drawn from and the animus provoked by particular 'ethos', no ethics would be so much as written for the benefit of quaint specialists or discussed in a vacuum. Relativists err in concluding therefrom that ethics cannot be anything but a differential description of kinds of ethos, with or without the addition of the thinker's own personal tastes and arbitrary one-sided preferences. They fail to perceive that, not in spite of but rather thanks to the existence of ethos, moral consensus and personal conscience transcending ethos and denouncing its immoral deviations or blatantly extra-moral accents also exist. It should be noted, moreover, that ethos, though itself only an imperfect manifestation of consensual morality, in its turn is only imperfectly expressed in the *institutions* thriving or emerging in its social area (just as a man's conscience, however erroneous or

deficient, does not invariably correspond with his will or habits);
the moral criticism of institutions often issues from the ethos of
the very medium in which they subsist.

Because there is no such thing as a smoothly effective, flawlessly
consistent and massively of-a-piece moral consciousness of men,
relativists assume that there are as many moralities as there are
men, or at any rate as many as there are 'societies', each with its
peculiar set of institutions and selectively cherished distinct
fetishes. They are gratified—not sensually, that is certainly not the
target of my attack, but intellectually—by the sight of tolerated or
even demonstratively displayed and quasi-institutionalized irregu-
larities and perversions, of Greek pederasty and Islamic polygamy,
of living by theft officially taught to Spartan boys as part of their
para-military training, of duelling and other un-Christian codes of
'honour' in the midst of Christendom, of a self-contradictory
'double standard' of sexual morality for men and for women in our
nineteenth-century world, of the peculiar jingoist and pacifist perversions of patriotic loyalty and of the negation of the collective
subjectivism into which that loyalty easily tends to be distorted, of
the ideological misuses of authority and the suicidal excesses of
freedom, and so on. But life is not, thank God, made of morality,
and therefore, deplorably, men's moral states of consciousness are
likewise not all made of morality. Yet, how much more striking is
the discordance between the factual beliefs of men, their religions,
their para- or non-religious outlooks, not to speak of their dominant individual and collective interests, than between their moral
beliefs all over the world and along its history! To become aware
of this contrast in its full proportions should suffice to establish the
fact of Moral Consensus. Why are 'western bourgeois' labelled
'imperialist brigands' and anti-communists of modest origins decried as 'class traitors'? Because brigands always are and have been
frowned upon morally and traitors have been morally despised
ever since and long before the times of Thersites. Why are so many
people apt to fling morally condemnatory epithets at whomever
would, ever so legitimately perhaps, thwart them in the pursuit of
their interests and ambitions? These very abuses of moral language
bear witness to the universal cognition and recognition of moral
categories.

A highly important example is afforded by Christianity, the outlook and ethos originating from the 'New Testament' which carries
a strong accent of innovation—a claim to constitute the record and
deposit of a new and 'definitive' special Divine Revelation—and in
fact certain antinomian overtones attaching to the central principle
of 'Love' in conscious antithesis both to Mosaic legalism and to

some 'Pagan', i.e. Graeco-Roman, scales of value. Yet Christianity did not abandon the Mosaic code of revealed imperatives, the 'Ten Commandments'; and it also drew upon the resources of the Stoic notion of an all-human *synderesis* as well as of Roman law-consciousness. Though the Christians believed that their special Faith alone was the road to salvation, St Paul (Romans 2: 14–15) warned his flock (with an eye to its members guilty of moral lapses) that the 'Pagans', who were 'without the Law' as explicitly revealed by God, nevertheless had the precepts of Morality 'inscribed in their hearts'. Again, traditional Christian apologetics ascribes the apparently miraculous spread of Christianity throughout the 'Pagan' Empire partly to the distinctive 'sanctity' of the lives of a very high proportion of Christians which invested them with a dignified moral authority in the eyes of the much more loose-living 'Pagan' majority of the population. Now this implies a presupposed *consensual* set of moral standards valid and at least dimly recognized by *mankind* as such, whatever its religious, metaphysical or other particular beliefs. If morally clean living were an 'entirely new' and exclusively Christian idea or ideal it would *only* have irritated the 'Pagans' (which it also did) but in no way impress or attract them. It is extremely unlikely that the sight of, say, Thugs living up perfectly to their Thuggish standards would morally bemuse us and convert us to Thuggism as a principle or attitude superior to our own Christian or humanitarian habits of mind.

(iv) It is still in the context of the objection of Relativity that I propose to deal briefly with the objection of Historicity. In order to actually review and exhibit the moral consensus of mankind as a whole, so the objection runs, the ethical thinker would have to garner an all-embracing knowledge and to build up a total conspectus of human history (opinions, philosophies, religions, *mores*) so as to extract from that monstrous assemblage of facts a time-proof objective code of Right and Wrong. Such a project would indeed be plainly impossible of achievement and self-defeating. The unhappy philosopher who were to embark upon it would, even on the supposition of unusual longevity, die before he had collected one-tenth of the required anthropological, cultural and historical information, and would certainly not have a minute left for philosophical, i.e. genuinely ethical, thinking. But such an interpretation of the consensualist thesis constitutes a crude misconception and a cheap caricature of it. In the first place, as has been argued above, it is not even possible to *approach* the phenomenon of Moral Consensus without an equipment of moral sentiments, intuitions and concepts partly derived from a *foreshortened* perspective of consensus and partly from the thinking person's own dispositions and reflections as well as from ethical discussions he is familiar with in his own primary social and intellectual environment. Secondly, the point about Moral Consensus is the mutual consonance and striking perdurability of basic moral valuations throughout the 'diversity of creatures', throughout the manifoldness of spatio-temporal particularizations of characters, situations and even types of ethos; not anything like a proof of their invariable identity with one another, to be held securely in the grasp of a comprehensive vision. An intellectual intimacy with several—and in some ways, divergent—moral codes, forms of ethos and other characteristics of historical plurality would in fact be of immense help to the moral philosopher in his quest for the sorting out of moral from extra-moral valuations and for the critical testing of his personal and environment-conditioned moral views and the apriorical constructions in Ethics that may impress and convince him. A poly-dimensional horizon of moral experience will aptly mitigate the austere jejuneness of linear and formalistic 'rigorous' argument. Without consulting one's own moral insights and sentiments, and confronting them with some standard modalities of the moral experience of mankind other than that of one's own traditional home medium of consciousness, one had, I daresay, better leave Ethics alone. But this has nothing to do with inviting the moral philosopher to transform himself into an anthropologist or historian of ideas aspiring to a totality of perspicuous knowledge, a new Hegel raised to the second power as it were. What matters, in general, for the philosopher is to be *world-conscious* in the sense of Husserl in his closing phase, not to pursue the inane dream of holding the world as a transparent crystal ball on the palm of his hand and gazing at it from all sides with equal facility and percipiency. Thinking in awareness of a mundane background, under a conceptual horizon methodically widened and capable of further widening whenever some special quest may call for it, rather than merely manipulating a machinery of selected and isolated—and thus dead and vacuous—concepts, is a possible and worth-while activity by no means identical with the utopia of historical omniscience or with the irresponsible wizardry of cosmos-pervading speculations.

But, having thus (I hope) succeeded in blunting the edge of the objection of historicity, I would admit to the necessity of a concession. My thesis asserts that Moral Consensus is a constant—absolute and immutable—as measured by the variety and the richness in change of human types, endeavours, objects of pursuit, practices and customs as a whole: not that it is rigidly permanent and, so to say, absolutely absolute in a timeless or eternal sense, taken out of all limitations of our perspective and grasped in a vision that were no longer perspectival. I cannot see the world except from the set of my own viewpoints (however multiple and elaborate) in the focus of my vision, and in a manner still embedded, despite all peeping-holes of transcendence, in the categories and specific emphases, of my own environmental world. Any desperate pretension to an absolutely detached objectivity can only usher in the delusions of some particular kind of uncontrolled and irrational subjectivism. Moral Consensus somehow reaches over oceans and aeons, but it cannot be independent of the realities of the human condition. While moral values and norms do not, as the naturalists imagine, mirror human nature and cannot be deduced from the fantasy concept of its 'perfection' as such or derived from its non-moral needs, on the other hand they have no meaning except in the frame of reference imposed by its reality. Basic structural changes in the human condition would also materially affect some elements in Moral Consensus; and if there is (or were) a universe of personal beings other than human—embodied or not—their moral codes are (or would be) quite unfamiliar to us on some or many points. Thus, should the place of mankind as we know and have always known it be taken in a distant future by more computer-like beings, still purposive and agential but self-perpetuating entirely without sexual reproduction and alien to venereal relations and pleasures, any form of what we know as sexual ethics would lose its applicability and perhaps even cease to be understandable at all. Or again, what cuts a great deal deeper: if our minds, without undergoing actual conflation, were to become mutually translucent, deception would no longer be possible and hence truthfulness no longer an obligation or virtue. Whether a world of persons is conceivable in which sins or moral defects would no longer occur and therefore no moral experience would exist is a matter for speculation—and pretty idle speculation at that. What I have been saying about Moral Consensus with its quasi absoluteness, unity and permanency is not a matter of cosmic inherence or ontological necessity but a phenomenological datum still confined within the horizon, however widened and rationally explored, of our empirical awareness of a world of persons that has existed and is enduring and reaching out into futurity.

4. CONSENSUS AND CONSCIENCE

I will finally try to rebut an objection to the consensualist view which is as obvious as it is plainly mistaken.

The agent's conformance to the moral positions prevailing in his social environment, so the objector will argue, is not necessarily equivalent to his goodness, virtue or moral perfection; moral dissent, i.e. a 'dissident conscience', is not always wrong, but may be the lonely voice of an authentic prophet—*vox clamantis in deserto*—and the herald of moral progress. A man (or a 'tiny minority') may hold a moral principle that far excels consensual standards, and is more exacting or more refined than the ordinary code of obligations; he (or they) may 'discover' moral experiences which balance or indeed outweigh the traditional conscience thus challenged. If that is so, if *conformisme* does not mark the apex of true righteousness, if moral innovation may prove to be valid and mean actual moral improvement, then surely a consensualist ethic breaks down.

Does it, really? Not a bit of it, I answer. The premisses are ambiguous, and the conclusion is not only false but self-refuting. The objector fails to distinguish between Moral Consensus and an historically given particular ethos; he fails to distinguish between ethos itself and the non-moral (and perhaps largely immoral) traditions, fashions, moods and ideologies which happen to attach to it; accordingly, he fails to distinguish between pliant conformance to environmental pressure and contagion on the one hand, and reflective and responsible submission to moral consensus on the other; he confuses the non-conformity of an incorruptible conscience with the non-conformity of the anarchical self-assertive impulses of individuals and minority groups; he mistakes for a negation of moral consensus what really aims at recalling, reconstituting, representing and promulgating that consensus. Putting it more briefly and with some simplification, 'moral rebellion' with its glamour of 'originality' and 'creativeness' may mean two diametrically opposite things: to wit, rebellion *against* morality (and such social powers as may stand for it), and rebellion *on behalf* of morality (as against such powers as tend to embody and enforce Moral Wrong of some kind). The former sort of 'dissentient conscience' does of course defy Consensus; usually, it is not wholly selfish (as is the ordinary immoral person, who often employs the tactics of moral hypocrisy) but is bent on emphasizing some genuine or specious non-moral values, some 'ideology', and loves to toy with the concept of a 'new' or 'higher' morality and to glory in the 'transvaluation of all values'. Rather than 'all-too-human', its favourite tactics will be diabolical. On the contrary, the 'dissentient conscience' that in fact *is* moral conscience, far from challenging or deriding moral consensus, strives to lift it from the abyss of oblivion and indifference, to reawaken it in men's minds and to place it once more in the focus of their attention. It endeavours, not to abolish the Law but to restore it. It *appeals* to moral consensus as against the layer of amoral interests which hides it from sight and the sway of immoral idols which overshadow it. Dissentient conscience of this type is of an eminently consensual character; it marks a resurgence of consensual as against degenerate or impoverished forms of morals, and so far as it claims moral 'reforms' it is actually meant to *re-formulate* moral consensus.

Now, as I have admitted in advance, the contrast as here sketched between an anti-consensual dissentient conscience which is sham conscience and a true dissentient conscience which is only ostensibly opposed to consensus is over-simplified; I had to resort to this black-and-white picture to bring out my point. In reality, most cases of dissentient conscience are situated somewhere between the two poles. Whoever is out of sympathy with a received code of morals or a type of ethos prevailing in the social medium around him will, however immoral he may be and however amoral his motives, very likely point to some actual defects in the code or ethos he is revolting against, in particular to such aspects about that ethos as appear to subserve certain non-moral interests or stand for a remnant of certain (perhaps magical and arbitrary) habits of mind rather than for any surviving genuine moral insight. And on the other hand, whoever, motivated by a moral experience no matter how deeply genuine and justifiable in consensual terms, attacks a recognized and overemphasized moral point of view or a dominant ethos is likely to lapse into some countervailing one-sided emphasis so as to override or sweep out of sight even what is unassailably valid in the beliefs and attitudes he is criticizing. This is only another way of saying that, while man is an incurably or, say, indestructibly moral animal, still this moral virtue is irremediably defective and his moral consciousness itself is far from being all-comprehensive and infallible, and therefore also liable to some degree of perversion. In matters of some importance, his practical deliberation will rarely, if ever, fail to involve a feature of moral *conflict*. At times, he may rightly feel in duty bound to rise in opposition against the dominant ethos of his social ambit—and, of course, more often to disobey some instruction of a concrete authority to which he is subject—; but even so he cannot rely with certainty on his voice being simply that of Moral Consensus or even the premonitory voice of the future authority of a more purified and refined, or again a more plainly manifest, a more universally conscious and recognized form of Moral Consensus. In some important sense, St Augustine's amazing dictum *Securus judicat orbis terrarum* holds indubitably; but if the status of that solidified universal judgement cannot be pre-empted by any collective ethos (and much less, by any decree of magistrature), *a fortiori* no

individual conscience, whatever its inspiredness and the force
of the arguments it commands, can arrogate that status to itself.

Moral dissent is nearly always an irritant and is very often
impressive. On many occasions, it may in its turn come to generate
new fashions, changes in ethos, and future 'conventions'. It has,
generally speaking, a claim to open-minded consideration but
never a claim to unconditional *a priori* respect. Its claim to respect
is evidently the stronger in proportion as it stresses and reinforces
a hitherto underemphasized moral demand, and the weaker as it
urges or implies the abandonment of *other*, so far established,
moral demands. For, inasmuch as the former aspect prevails, dissent has a greater chance to vindicate Moral Consensus, and to make
it more explicit, perhaps actually to contribute to its treasury;
whereas in so far as it runs in the latter direction, that of permissive-
ness and relaxation, it incurs a greater risk of its attack upon ethos
being levelled at Moral Consensus itself.[a]

8

The Concept of Hierarchy

I. PRELIMINARY APOLOGY

The concept of Hierarchy, as well as various problems, aspects and doctrines attaching to it, was preposterously overrated in Greek philosophy, especially Platonic and Neo-platonic; probably even more so in medieval Scholastic philosophy which attempted to rationalize its supernaturalistic obsession with arguments taken from Greek, chiefly Aristotelian and thus semi-Platonic perfectionalism as a putative 'natural' basis for it. Some great exponents of the modern German philosophy of Value, Scheler and Nicolai Hartmann, represent the same tradition in a doubtless more critical and more properly philosophic, less naively metaphysical, but still in a pretty dogmatically intuitional fashion. The counterpart to this we find to be rampant in modern English-speaking philosophy dominated by the thought-style of Logical Positivism, though many of its more recent representatives would disown that label. Mouth-pieces of an egalitarian, machine-ridden and (at least apparently) utilitarian and functional society intolerant of the idea of kings, aristocrats, slaves, serfs, even rich and poor, nay literate and illiterate, these thinkers idolize human 'wanting' as such, whatever its contents and characteristics, would reduce all value to 'needs' or 'desires' and their different 'intensities' and in their turn, I venture to say, seek preposterously to evade the very concept of Hierarchy, not only on the plane of social philosophy but also in the context of Axiology. They postulate a flattened world from which the experience of Verticality is all but wholly excluded.

Both parties, if I may simplifyingly call them so, take advantage of the peculiarly obscure and complex nature of the world of values. Dogmatists enamoured of 'Degree'—to use Ulysses' word in Shakespeare's *Troilus and Cressida*—take verticality for granted as a linear dimension (although Christian religious doctrine, with its limited but strong egalitarian aspects, might be apt to puzzle them a great deal). They do not think it necessary to take any pains to embark on an accurate analysis of the matter—a reproach that would certainly have to be qualified in regard to N. Hartmann in spite of the grandiose vision he expounds in his early work *Ethics*;

and even more to Meinong, whose cast of mind, if certainly not positivistic, is predominantly analytical. Again, the positivists (in a broad sense of the word) proclaim their profound lack of interest in whatever is not accessible either to straightforward empirical verification or logical 'rigour'. Yet, *pace* the famous phrase of Hume, philosophy *is* precisely about what is *not* accessible to scientific calculation and rigorous logical clarification, but at the same time is *not* simply a matter of empirical contingency. As Findlay brilliantly wrote in defence of Meinong's theory of values, '*Why should it be necessarily wrong to discuss the nebulous in a businesslike manner?*' And this is exactly what I should like to do here, confining myself of course to one or two salient and phenomenologically tangible points. Phenomena, especially such as play a great and manifold part in man's mental and practical life, after all *do exist* and cannot be explained away as '*mere* appearances' or *reduced* to more massive and more universally indubitable data of experience, however difficult they may be to analyse and however meagre the results we may directly obtain in analysing them. If, as I firmly believe *with* the positivists, arbitrary high-flown speculation is the *worst* pitfall in philosophy, the *next* worst is, and here I am turning *against* the positivists, the idol of the rigorously ascertainable. No one can have more respect than I have for the positivist appeal to honesty, modesty, intellectual integrity, self-criticism and self-control. But there is a fallacy implied here against which we must be most strenuously on our guard. There is nothing disingenuous or irrelevant about non-rigorous evidence or reasoning so long as it does not *pretend* to be rigorous. If I say 'The value of π is (exactly) 3.14', I do indeed utter a falsehood which may be practically, and *is* theoretically, perniciously misleading. But if I say 'The value of π is *approximately* 3.14, and for *some* practical purposes this is a safely applicable approximation' I am uttering a plain truth, indeed in some sense a 'rigorous', an arguable and demonstrable truth. Similarly, if I say 'Moral rules are above the level of pleasure and pain' I am speaking apodictically, insufficiently aware of possible objections, exceptions and qualifications, and taking for granted an evidence not obviously present to everybody's mind; you might accuse me of *frivolous* dogmatizing. But if I say 'To my mind, and to that of many other and diverse types of men in many places and epochs, it appears evident that moral rules possess an inherent dignity superior to men's sensuous concerns', I am stating a fact which is universally known and at the very least arguable; whereas if I am *a priori* resolved to ignore it, to minimize it, to reduce it forcibly, to level it down and to explain it away, I shall be speaking untruthfully and anti-philosophically, i.e. in a way apt artificially to circumscribe and diminish our world-knowledge. Similarly again, 'Mankind divides into noblemen and common men' is sheer nonsense; but the negation of degrees of nobility and commonness in men likewise flies in the face of facts widely known and frequently referred to by quite ordinary as well as by more sophisticated persons. And with this I conclude the apology proffered by a phenomenological temper (as mine is) averse to speculative dogmatism but in revolt against the tyranny of the positivistic, monistic and naturalistic outlook. The proof of the pudding is in the eating: shall I be able to produce a few, two or three, sober, defensible and problem-raising remarks in support of the phenomenon of 'higher' and 'lower' levels, of aspects of verticality and hierarchy?

2. A RUDIMENTARY SURVEY OF THE METAPHORICAL USE OF 'HIGHER' AND 'LOWER'

With very slight shades of difference, all (European) languages make use of expressions like 'Higher or Lower', 'High', 'High-level', etc., in an identical sense. It is not a question of English idiom or some foreign-language idiom. A reference to verticality is firmly, stably and ineliminably built into our very thought. These 'hierarchical' usages differ significantly from one another, not however according to particular languages but according to the main, I would say paradigmatic, meanings or objective points of application of the expressions in question. I will not try to list here all such typical references to 'height' but select the most common and important ones. It appears to me that these are *six* in number, though of course there is some overlap between them and some of them present a closer kinship between them than with others. Let us take them in order—a kind of order, at any rate.

(1) The simplest and least distinctive sense of 'high', yet one that requires mention, is just *quantitative*; it coincides with 'large', 'great', 'much', 'very', etc. We speak of a high amount, a high power (in mathematics), a high temperature, a low degree of something, a highly doubtful assumption. (Only this last, adverbial, usage is a bit, not entirely, specifically English.) Why exactly do we on many occasions use these metaphors, which are nearly always expendable? Why do we thus import verticality in what appears to be just number or intensity? Must it be a purely contingent freak of language? For such too occur. But it somehow doesn't look like that. I cannot offer any explanation except one, admittedly hypothetical. The operations of counting, of measuring major extensions and of assessing greater intensities involve a

7

surplus of effort. I can more easily count six objects than sixty or the number of primes up to 40 than up to 400, or pull a weight of ten ounces than one of ten pounds. This, in itself, still does not seem to bring in the idea of verticality. If you stick into the earth a pole three yards long and one three feet long, the former will certainly appear taller; but here verticality has expressly been posited. Three yards laid along the earth are not taller than an inch laid along the earth. Nevertheless, when we count from 1 upward to, say, 1000, we do often call this 'ascending' in the series of natural numbers; and it is customary to call fever a 'high' or a 'raised' temperature. Why? First, because verticality exists in nature: thus, waves mount *high*, a *high* hill or mountain threatens to bar our way, and we may be struck *down* by an aggressor. Second, because lifting, raising or rising, climbing and ascending movements naturally symbolize the experience of *effort*, of 'going out of our way', of 'overcoming our inertia'. Mounting four flights of some five yards each may put a more onerous claim on our resilience and energy than walking half a mile on a smooth level path. The effort required by counting from 1 to 1000 really subserves an act of progress rather than of rising or ascending, but it somehow reminds us of the tiring act of ascending a thousand steps. In every resolute 'onward', an aspect of 'upward' seems to be implicit. So far for the merely quantitative connotation of height.

(2) In close connection with the preceding point, we are in the habit of associating the notion of the *elementary* with that of the *lower*, the notion of the *advanced* with that of the *higher*. In English, it was or at least has long been customary to speak of elementary algebra, higher algebra and (higher still) advanced algebra. In American, a 'high school' means an institute of secondary as contrasted with elementary or primary instruction; in German, a *Hochschule* means a university or some special training-school of more or less university rank. An English boy who has achieved success in the *n*-th form of his school is *promoted* to the next *higher* form. Progress, once more, is seen as ascent; here, however, we are no longer moving in the medium of pure quantity but are approaching the concept of a 'qualitatively' higher *mental level*. To this I would not for the moment add any further interpretation, but I would as early as at this point add a warning remark. Lower and higher levels may be seen in a contrasting and even an antagonistic light, as when we are contrasting a low and a high type of mind, a shallow or *terre-à-terre* and a 'soaring' or 'elevated' mentality, distinction and vulgarity, and so forth. But even more naturally and essentially we may see a *complementary* relation between the lower and the higher, or perhaps rather the lower as

the indispensable precondition of the higher. Whatever higher and lower mean, they do not generally and essentially mean *value* and *disvalue*. This only happens when we have good warrant to expect something 'high' and find in its place something 'low', e.g. a university professor owing his place to brutal patronage only, whose knowledge and intellectual power we find inferior to that of an average undergraduate in his field. Still less do 'lower' and 'higher' essentially correspond to immorality and morality. When we speak of 'basic' we do not mean 'base', and when we speak of 'fundamental' we are not alluding toa certain less dignified part of the human body; indeed, when in English we speak of 'finding our feet' in a tangled situation we are not hinting at a low and relatively crude part of our anatomy as such. And this is an important consideration as against certain idealistic misrepresentations of the concept of hierarchy.

(3) A classic locus of hierarchy, which indeed some would without hesitation regard as the primary source of the concept, concerns social *super-* and *subordination*: the correlation between command, leadership, government, law and degree on the one hand, obedience and service on the other.[1] This is, howsoever significant its varieties and variations, an aboriginal phenomenon of every ordered society, human and to a large extent animal, civilized as well as tribal, constitutional and absolutistic, liberal as well as totalitarian (communist or fascist). But again the question obtrudes itself upon our minds: why do we so self-evidently, mostly unaware of using a metaphor at all, designate command positions as 'high' or 'superior', obedience or instrumental (servantship) positions as 'low' or 'inferior'? To be sure, the king or chairman sits on his elevated dais, we subjects or members sit or kneel low down at his feet. But this fact itself is of human institution, not a datum of cosmic nature, and presupposes the dignity we associate with lofty height and the respect for alien dignity we associate with a lowly and

---

[1] Standard types of subordination differ between them significantly in particular as regards their teleological pattern. Personal 'servants' (in the widest sense) are most unequivocally 'subordinates' of their 'masters' in that they are instrumental to their masters' ends. The lower members of a military or civil hierarchy, however strict the discipline they are subject to, are only 'subordinate' to their 'superiors' in the limits of their being all ordained *to a common end*. Members of a society (even, normally, of the same estate or profession) who hold an 'inferior' position or rank are not properly 'subordinate' to 'superior' ones at all. Thus, the First Sea Lord is not *the* or *a* superior of a colour-sergeant of infantry. In the subordination involved by expertship (cf. 'Doctor's orders'), and again by education, the teleological relationship is *reversed*: the physician's authority exists 'for the sake' of the patient's health; parents and teachers are 'superiors' of their children or pupils, but the latter (predominantly) embody the 'superordinate' ends.

crouching position. Besides, an inverse position may also play a symbolic part here: my superior may fill comfortably his ample arm-chair, while I stand before him erect on my feet, awaiting his orders in trepidation. In the former case, the elevated level embodies distinction, the status of being lifted from out the common multitude; in the latter case, the sitting superior displays an attitude of stable repose, while the vertically placed subordinate expresses the attitude of effort and of a disposition to instant physical execution of instructions and directives. (It also happens that the typist or other subordinate is rigidly sitting on a low stool while the dictating superior, towering above her or his head, rambles freely about the room.) In any event, the social hierarchy of command and obedience or more informal leadership and followership appears linked to the contrast between mental (volitional) direction and instrumental (absolutely or relatively physical) execution: it conjures up the age-old analogy of the relation between the *head* and the *limbs*. Now, to the extent at least as man— and, less markedly, most other animals—are concerned, the head is in plain, *non*-metaphorical parlance the topmost, the highest part of the body. Whereas, if I may refer to a specifically English term, being a *footman* constitutes the lowest, again I am far from saying the 'basest', occupation.

A certain very important ambiguity arises at this point, peculiarly relevant to divergent conceptions of ascent or progress, at which I must briefly hint. 'Height', like other dimensions, is susceptible of a twofold interpretation. It may be conceived of as an indefinite continuum (like the series of the natural numbers or the prime numbers): e.g. Brown is taller than Jones, Robinson is even taller than Brown, Smith again is taller than Robinson and some fourth man will be even taller than Smith, etc. On the other hand, a 'perfectional maximum', a 'highest point' may be imagined, and all objects of the same order inferior to it may be measured by that absolute standard. In an emphatically monarchical order, the social position of everybody will, ideally at least, be determined by his proximity to and distance from the 'Crown', the 'Throne', in a word the Royal person. In an emphatically aristocratic order, at which, say, the Roman senatorial republic seems to have aspired, no such absolute and unique headship is accorded any place and the criteria of assessment will be of a more direct, contentual and intrinsically qualitative or quantitative rather than of a strictly positional nature. Any man may surpass another man in regard to such points of view as lineage, virtue, public-mindedness, talent or wealth. The typically monarchical mode of valuation is more akin to a *theistic*, the aristocratic mode to a properly *axiological* and a more *open* view of the universe. Similarly, our thought of progress may be either of a more Utopian or Marxian type, postulating a 'final' state of perfection, with every stage in social evolution being evaluated by the criterion of its dialectical function in hastening the march of mankind towards the ultimate heaven on earth; or it may be more properly evolutionistic (and probably more Engelsian than Marxian): one stage in social progress being thought superior to the preceding one, the next stage again intrinsically higher than the former, and so on indefinitely.

(4) In conformity with the above distinction, an inegalitarian but less properly hierarchic conception of Society exists or has existed in men's social thought, a conception that puts emphasis not on military or bureaucratic subordination but on social authority and prestige, quasi 'natural' leadership and followership, intrinsic quality and 'ordinary' men's appreciative submission to it. One extreme aspect of this conception is expressed in Plato's perfectionist ideal of the 'rule of the wise'; another, in the phrase 'I know a gentleman when I sees 'im'; another again, in the problematic and partly imaginary traditions of racial aristocracy. The *opposite* aspect, that of discipline and subordination independent of, as it were mystical, superiorities was expressed by a Lacedaemonian who, in answer to the flattering remark of a foreigner extolling, in view of the impressive achievement of Sparta, the fine capacities of its rulers, drily countered: 'Nay, our successes are not due to the extraordinary virtues of our kings and ephori, but to us Spartans in that we readily and punctually obey their injunctions.' Qualitative and distinctive 'degrees' of men and particular social groups are extremely unpopular in the sharply egalitarian atmosphere of our present world, which is much less reluctant to face the inequality even of tyrannical rulership than the recognition of 'higher' and 'lower' types, breeds and strata of men which appears to hurt our sense of justice (too univocally tied up with a sense of the absolutely equal importance of all men's destinies); our tendency to supinely obey institutional rulership and command seems to be inspired by Rousseau's and the Jacobins' dialectical masterstroke destined to persuade us that by deferring to unlimited power we really obey a 'General Will' equally omnipotent over all of us and thus embodying 'the will of each of ourselves'. Yet the idea of qualitative hierarchy, as ineradicable as are all basic categories of human thought and valuation, survives in our various and largely incoherent beliefs in family traditions and in special forms of education, in careful Communist party training and selection, and in the bent for nationalistic exclusiveness which characterizes many older and all the recently created independent States as well

as many fragmented nationalities cleaving to their distinctive 'identities' and aspiring after independent statehood.

(5) From the particularly entangled problem-world of social philosophy, I now return to the more familiar and more unequivocally accepted 'height'-category of *natural evolution*, which displays a peculiar analogy to our concept of intellectual or mental level which we are wont to call a 'higher' or 'more advanced' one in contrast with the crude, primitive or elementary. We quite automatically tend to distinguish 'higher' forms of life as opposed to the 'lower'—especially, the unicellular—ones, to regard animals as higher beings than plants, to speak of 'higher' and 'lower' animals and especially mammals, and to place monkeys 'above' other mammals, the primates 'above' other apes, and man 'above' the primates and all other animals in general. The criterion we use here is that of a more differentiated, complex and functionally richer form of life. Perhaps, however, with this complexity and wealth of life we also associate a notion of concentration and focal unity. We can mutilate or dissect lower types of living individuals more easily than higher ones without necessarily killing them; and we (rightly or wrongly) credit man with an individual selfhood, an indissoluble and in some sense 'simpler' centre of consciousness rather than we do the 'lower animals'.

Two remarks must be made in this context. First, we are siding here with the 'maximum'-emphasizing and 'perfectional' variant of the conception of height: perhaps somewhat naively and uncritically, we establish man as the ultimate standard of 'height' and the degree of similarity to man as the unequivocal criterion of relative 'height' in the lower forms of life; this is not altered by more or less vapid speculations about the 'superman' or anyhow 'more perfect type of man' we sometimes expect to evolve or to 'create itself' in the future, nor by religious or mystical speculations about the possible existence of 'higher' beings than man, either purely 'spiritual' and 'disembodied', or equipped with a 'finer', an invisible and perhaps immaterial body. Second, it is obvious in the perspective of natural evolution (though in fact also in that of social hierarchy) that 'height' is *not* experienced as a strictly univocal and linear dimension. The highest *plants*, say trees as familiar to us today, do not merge into the lowest form of *animal* life; on the contrary, an elm-tree is a far more evolved being than an amoeba or other protozoon. Again, we do not like to think of highly evolved state-building insects, e.g. the ants and bees, as 'higher' beings than mammals, such as bears and some monkeys, leading a comparatively solitary and anarchical life. The line that leads 'up' to man appears to us to represent the classic and central line of evolution;

but all its 'degrees' by no means appear to us to be 'higher' than *all* 'degrees' or levels emerging in *other* lines of evolution. Nor do we necessarily see in an average philosophy undergraduate or a middling artist or writer a 'higher' type of man than, say, in a chancellor of the exchequer. Perhaps we regard *anything* living as something 'higher' than *anything* inert; yet we do speak also of 'precious' metals and 'exquisite' stones or magnificent mountains and rivers. It is not my wish to destroy my own case utterly by pointing out the anthropomorphic, inconsistent and circumstantial use of hierarchical terms; but neither must I attempt to veil the difficulty of the subject and foist upon you a dogmatic picture by forced, simplifying and disingenuous interpretations.

(6) Finally, I beg to be allowed to point to the etymology of the word *hierarchy*, which suggests a reference to something 'sacred' or 'sacral', the inherent and ever-recurrent yearning of man to something outside him and above him, be it the Deity as conceived of in the great historical diversity of religions, or some less unitary and apical zone of possible supra-human entities, or perhaps not even any such entities but a mere region of qualities and values not 'natural' to man, even to man *qua* rational being, but in some sense 'supernatural' to him and compelling his attention and deference. In other words, a need of 'self-transcendence': a need felt by man of ordering his life with an eye on something over and above him. In our own utilitarian and technological civilization this yearning or need appears to be most effectively repressed, but there are many signs of a deep-reaching dissatisfaction of man with such a purely humanitarian and positivistic order, a sense of discomfort, malaise and mutilation. Again, we must be very careful here. The phenomenon of the 'supernatural need' of man cannot be taken for a metaphysical proof of the existence of God or of any supernatural entities or even of an impersonal supernatural order. History has shown that men can *somehow* live without anointed monarchs who represent them in their relation to the Deity and the Deity in face of them. (Indeed, Christ's own strict disjunction between 'God' and 'Caesar' bears in it a certain germ of republicanism and of the de-sacralization, the secularization of secular life as such.)

Another point should likewise be emphasized, which N. Hartmann in his *Metaphysik des Geistes* has worked out very tersely, perhaps a trifle too much so. There is no *proportionate* correspondence between man's deferent attention to 'higher beings' or 'higher things' (real or imaginary) and the mental levels he has *himself* risen to. On the contrary, it would seem that his theological and metaphysical preoccupations have been somehow premature and short-circuited; and that his own intellectual height has reached its earliest and most impressive peaks in his dealing with the *lower* rather than with the *higher* domains of objects: in mathematics and in mechanics rather than in physics proper and in chemistry, in these rather than in the biological sciences and particularly in psychology—whose subject-matter is more elevated than that of biology—while metaphysics and theology cannot have so far attained to a 'scientific' level at all. In other words, that the simplest, most tangible and most *value-free* matters have furnished the human mind with its most fertile occasions for deployment, elaboration and brilliancy. It is in its confrontation with the 'humblest' objects that it has risen to its most soaring 'heights'. But, while this observation, in some form anticipated by Comte, is certainly worthy of our closest attention, it betrays a one-sidedly 'scientistic' and positivistic outlook. Moreover, it does not account for the strange fact, which is unlikely to express a *mere* historical contingency, that in spite of the magnificent achievements of the ancient Greeks in the field of mathematics and to some extent in that of empirical observation, the great and distinctive modern venture of the human spirit, to wit the *experimental science of nature*, has been specific to the area of *Christian* religious predominance, though undoubtedly it has developed *pari passu* with the weakening of the religious hold on men's minds since the Renaissance and the Enlightenment. But the more important point, I would suggest, is that our spiritual level does not unequivocally depend on our attainment of scientific rigour and the wealth and progress of our scientific research either. To be sure, religious beliefs and metaphysical fancies may be crude, intellectually irresponsible, and abundant in contradictions (papered over by dint of verbal constructions and sophistical sham arguments), and the religious art of, say, the eighteenth and nineteenth centuries is very inferior, even *qua* art, to the grandeur of, say, late nineteenth-century French impressionism or early twentieth-century German expressionism. But this is not the whole story. In mediaeval Romanesque and Gothic architecture, Byzantine icons, mediaeval craft, mediaeval and early modern music, in some manifestations of mediaeval and later religious poetry, in some modern initiatives in Christian arts, and even in some aspects of mediaeval philosophy we encounter monuments to the heights to which the human spirit has risen which we rather take for granted or simply disregard or have forgotten than have any reason to disdain; and I would add, not just as an expression of my personal preference but as a fact of the history of civilization, that modern philosophers of the greatness of Brentano, Meinong, Moore, Ross, etc., have derived at least as much inspiration from Aristotelian and Scholastic as from modern rationalistic and empiricistic sources—not to mention the astounding crop and utterly impressive level of the British eighteenth-century moralists, who were for the most part Christian (if anti-Papist) believers.

No doubt, we can approach 'low' objects in a 'high' spirit and inversely; this is what the Eleatics and Platonists—who saw the symbol of perfection in certain regular geometrical figures—naively overlooked.[2] But on the other hand it is also true that in our 'upward look', our genuine appreciation of divine or royal majesty and our concentration on dignified rather than trivial objects we *eo ipso* tend to nurture and as it were to prove our own dignity. Certainly in our positional superiority to what is 'below' us we assert a kind of 'height' on our own side; but, without arguing the point, I would make the suggestion that our humble bow to what we feel to be above us (in Aristotle's idiom, 'things better than ourselves') lifts us higher even more decisively. It may easily happen that you write a wretched novel about a great hero and a skilful, perhaps a sublime, novel about grocers and insurance agents. But if you succeed in writing both a first-rate novel about heroes and an equally first-rate novel about everyday people the odds are that the former will significantly surpass the latter.

3. THE PARADIGM OF THE RAISED POSITION

A cynical Italian proverb runs *Loda il monte e tienti al piano*: 'Praise the mountain and keep on the flat.' If we disregard that counsel of cheap admiration and creature comfort and climb the peak of a fair-sized hill, we shall note certain changes in our direct world-vision, in the optics of our ken as it were. Beyond a mere awareness of height, which of course we may possess also sitting or lying on the level ground, we have gained a more existential experience of physical height: we can still look up to things well above us, but at the same time we can now look down at things well below us; we have entered ourselves a scalar position of height. The perspective proper to the flat earth is no longer ours. We can, moreover, estimate more exactly the vertical order of many objects below us and of some above us. Our horizon has *widened*; our perspective has become *enriched* and more *articulated*. The enhanced verticality of our position implies a more adequate, a more graded and more *comprehensive* vision of things and their connection in space. This is not gratuitous speculation but a piece of quite matter-of-fact, I would willingly admit of a rather trivial, psychophysical descrip-

[2] The Eleatic-Platonic attitude survives in Aristotle's 'Physics' in the shape of the 'spheres', the stars and the 'regularity' of their movements.

tion. And herein lies the tangible hard core of the more or less metaphysical patterns of hierarchical relations to which I devoted the foregoing section. The paradigm of the raised position of the perceiving subject underlines our variously ramified experiences of 'mental height'.

There are two more points that demand to be stressed here.

(1) The raised position lends our perspective not only a stronger aspect of extension and comprehensiveness but also a more *focal* character. No doubt, wherever I am placed space and things somehow surround me and are round about me, and I am in their 'centre' whether I choose to be or not. But this centrality is of a uniformly contingent nature: aside from the possible intrinsic significance of the things in whose midst I may be placed I possess, on a horizontal level, nothing like a *privileged* or distinguished focus of perspective. Once, however, I contemplate things from a *vantage-point* this situation has in some sense changed. I have now gained a focus of vision into which the lines of vision that constitute my perceptual world synoptically converge. Thus, I see a moderately large and high hill or house much as I would also see it from the flat ground but now I see at the same time its top far more exactly, and what matters more, I see what is *behind* it: my position provides me with the *positional value* of objects in a rather new sense. I am able to make comparisons, estimate distances, and penetrate spatial structures as I could not otherwise do. I no longer merely represent an *automatic* focus of vision but embody a privileged and nameable focus of visual perception and thus, in a sense, an enhanced *centrality of consciousness*. In some respect and some measure, I have also gained a certain *distance* from the earth and a relative *independence* from it. It would be illusory to imagine that I have therefore become a 'master of my fate' and a 'captain of my soul'—on the contrary, I might well feel beastly tired after the climbing—but it would be near the truth to suggest that my raised position *has* freed me from certain shackles and conferred upon me the germ of something like a position of *dominance*. Instead of crouching at the bottom of a modest house-gate, I may now find myself on a level with a tall Gothic spire. I may see distant and high objects without the use of a telescope, and *with* a telescope I may achieve a power of vision and conspectus I would not have dreamt of while confined to the flat earth. As a general, I may conduct a battle of which the soldiers fighting down in the valley are no more than modest executants and whom the concatenation of its details escapes altogether.

(2) This capacity of man to set himself at a distance from the earth, this dimension of verticality virtually inherent in the natural

fact of the upright gait—the top location of the brain and the far-gazing and percept-garnering mobility of the eyes—compels our admiration for our own species, which in biblical language is 'only a little lower than the angels'. We only know it in an embodied, material and matter-dependent condition; but at the same time we feel it to be a 'spiritual' kind of animal, by no means only in virtue of its being endowed with object-grasping 'intelligence', ratiocinative 'reason' and sustained purpose-consciousness and will-power, but also in view of the relative looseness of its ties (however intimate) with materiality and its capacity to cancel and neutralize its bodily urges and material 'interests' for the sake of knowledge, objective judgement, self-judging conscience and all that dedication of self to nonmaterial concerns that we are wont to call 'spirituality'.

Yet all this, including the perspective of the 'raised position', has also its reverse side. That man is a moral and conscientious being is inseparable from the fact that he is also an *im*moral and unconscionable being, sensual, selfish and self-worshipping, a tyrant and a truant, in religious parlance a 'sinner'. My point here, however, is not so much that he is capable of indifference and effort-shunning aversion to 'heights' accessible to him—*tienti al piano*—as that the perspective of the 'raised position' *itself* involves loss and virtual 'fall' as well as gain and ascent. On the moral side, a height position *achieved* naturally tempts me to assume a pridefully downward-looking attitude as opposed to an upward direction; a false and premature consciousness of 'perfection'. On the perceptual and intellectual side, the loss is perhaps even more obvious. My expanded and enriched conspectus is inevitably balanced by a weakened grasp of details, a hazier appearance of single objects, a less intense contact with reality. While the sense of sight is the noblest—this has often been emphasized; let me forbear from its analysis now—and most informative, it is not the only vehicle of our world-consciousness. The sense of *touch*, our awareness of the resisting and yielding, compressing and malleable, character of things that directly surround, impale, support and serve us, is more properly our 'existential' sense on which our experiences of limitation but also of security and expansibility directly depend. And accordingly, if none but foolish slaves of the egalitarian obsession would deny, largely with their tongues in their cheeks, the types of distinctive wisdom proper to rulers, international aristocrats and financiers, diplomatists, military leaders, and the so-called aristocracy of the intellect and of high art, there is also on the other hand a *distinctive* wisdom of craftsmen and manual workers, of peasants and labourers, nay of the 'common people' and even of the so-called illiterates as such.[3] (Widespread literacy, for example, seems to be incompatible with the creation of new languages.) When, therefore, we speak of 'height' or 'high levels' we should do so with respect, indeed with reverence, but not with unbalanced admiration and perfectionist ecstasy; and when we speak of 'hierarchy' we should have in mind, not so much the contrary opposition between value and disvalue as the extremely complex and but very obscurely penetrable *complementary* manifoldness of 'higher' and 'lower' levels of value.

4. 'HEIGHT' AND 'DEPTH'

Whereas in some physical contexts we refer to depth as a negative dimension of height, a diametrically opposite direction (cf. a deep-level and a high-level crossing), in the intellectual context we sometimes use the adjective 'deep' as almost a correlate, not to say a synonym, of 'high'. We mean here, of course, their common contrast to 'superficial' or 'shallow', their common cognitive and experiential transcendence of '*mere* appearances'. But even here—I can only just touch upon this matter in passing—we do not use the two words in an exactly synonymous way. I don't know if there is much difference between high thinking and deep thinking, but we do prefer to speak, e.g., of high-mindedness or a high-souled man on the one hand, of a deep insight or a deep-reaching train of argument on the other. 'Height' emphasizes the aspect of a wide and rich perspective of comprehension; 'depth', the aspect of penetration and subtle discernment of the object. At the same time, depth and in particular the German cult of depth may be linked to imprecision, nebulosity and vacuous mystagogic moods just as well as may height, if not more so. Perhaps, unless I misunderstand Husserl's teaching about the *Außenhorizont* and the *Innenhorizont* of things, a 'high' view is more interested in exploring their 'external horizon' and a 'deep' view, in searching out their 'internal horizon'.

Bernard Shaw somewhere offers to young men embarking on the career of their lives a most interesting advice: 'See to it that you get what you like, or you'll end up by liking what you get.' On the surface, and not a merely illusory surface, this seems to be a counsel of

---

[3] There exist not only certain specific aspects of dignity in some peasantries and some types of small craftsmen but also certain specific aspects of vulgarity in the middle and upper classes. This applies to many 'upstarts' but also to the disproportion, necessarily present in *some* upper-class people, between their awareness of their social position, of their genetic past, etc., and the actual contents and levels of their mental lives.

'height'. Shaw had a strong sense of pride and independence; he understood the upright manliness of fighting for one's loves and indeed one's tastes, and rightly despised their supine adjustment to mere availability—a danger besetting the feeble, the unsuccessful, the meek and the mediocre.[4] But to a deeper insight his phrase reveals the basic baseness of his soul: the soul of a man who in 1914 failed to understand the nobility of the Allies' cause and whose pseudo-virile power-worship, or perhaps life-worship, later inveigled him into admiring such energetic monsters as Lenin, Stalin and Hitler, and even a histrionic worm as contemptible as Mussolini. He took it for granted that unless we pretty soon 'get what we like' we are *doomed* to come to like what we get. He did not understand that, although the danger of degenerative adaptation and inward atrophy is indeed common enough, the greatest glory of man lies precisely in defying and resisting that danger rather than in fleeing it and discarding it *a limine*: that our *ungratified* and even hopeless loves (and even many such tastes) are among our most precious possessions.

But the distinction between height and depth, in spite of their common antithesis to the shallow, the smooth surface and the level average, serves on us another warning against the manufacturers of schematic hierarchical systems from Parmenides and Plato to Scheler and Hartmann, even though it would be very unjust to deny the greater awareness which such 'hierarchistic' thinkers as Aristotle, Aquinas or again N. Hartmann possessed of the complexity and manifoldness of these matters.

5. TWO REMARKS ON THE 'HIERARCHY OF VALUES'

According to the traditional picture, the 'Hierarchy of Values'—at some points, but by no means exactly and all along the line, corresponding to the metaphysical hierarchy of 'levels'—may be approximatively ordered in about this way. From inert and unconscious being (including perhaps some lower forms of the organic) we ascend to life proper and, a 'leap' emphasized by Hartmann, further to consciousness; and from the matter-bound level of the merely hedonic values, the agreeable and disagreeable, pleasure and pain (or rather the pleasant and unpleasant) we rise to the level of

---

[4] The Latins of the East, the robust and remarkable Roumanian people, have long been the victims of alien oppressors: Turks and Tatars, Phanariotes (a thin aristocratic class of Constantinopolitan Greek origin), Hungarians, Russians, and even for some time a Serb ecclesiastical hierarchy. Among Roumanian peasants, a saying used to be current which picturesquely expresses the attitude fustigated by Shaw: 'Dăcămusăi, bucuros' (Since you must, better do it willingly).

'vital' values, by which Scheler means both the values of 'welfare' and the values of 'nobility'; again from here to the level of 'spiritual', i.e. intellectual, moral and aesthetic values; and finally, to the values of 'holiness', i.e. the level of 'religious values' whose experience refers directly or indirectly, but expressly, to the supreme or Divine being. Professor von Hildebrand, mainly a disciple of Husserl and Scheler, but perhaps influenced in this respect by Meinong, denies the hedonic the status of 'value' altogether and contrasts the pleasant and unpleasant with value and disvalue as such; he accords only an ambiguous status to what he calls 'the category of the objectively good *for* me' and ascribes the full character of 'value' to spiritual and religious values alone. Hartmann, whose outlook was atheist (whereas Scheler continued believing in a Divine Person even after his break with the Church in the early 'twenties), not unnaturally questioned the category of specifically religious, over and above the spiritual, values. But it was on two more tangible and concrete points that Hartmann came forward with original and emphatic theses of his own. He, utterly rightly I think, attacked Scheler's inclusion of the values of 'nobility' in the category of 'vital' values; and, certainly in keeping with his atheism but not, I think, in any necessary nexus with it, nor *wholly* rightly I believe, he established an *inverse proportion* between the *strength* and the *height* of values. On these two important points alone I shall have a few more words to say. As regards the value status of pleasure and pain, I shall merely state without arguing the matter that I am inclined to accord a definite value status to the hedonic (though sheer pain seems to me to constitute a disvalue more unequivocally than sheer pleasure a value); and as regards the specific value category of 'holiness', I again feel inclined to admit it (i.e. I feel reluctant to *reduce* religious to a mere high degree of moral values, though I am convinced that without a close reference to moral values they would collapse in an utter vacuity of meaning).

(1) That 'nobleness', whatever it may be, has its particular locus in the 'vital' sphere is a phantasmagoria Scheler has uncritically borrowed from Nietzsche. Like most fashionable errors, it possesses some partial basis in reality which then comes to be inflated and misinterpreted. We mostly connect with the concept of nobleness a notion of spontaneous, effortless, as it were self-evident grace of body, gestures and behaviour we often meet with in the social nobility of old lineage; we attribute it to a certain amount of inbreeding ('noble blood') and to 'good breeding' in the sense of early, organically formative good education mainly through example. It has precious little to do with properly 'vital' values such as health, energy, robustness, well-being and welfare, though something

like 'harmonious development of body and mind' may present an actual connecting-link. In fact, nobleness exhibits a certain contrast with the specifically Kantian moral ideas of duty-consciousness and the merit due to moral *effort*. (Kant himself, while more or less crippled in body, was a thoroughly noble person: naturally kind-hearted, highly civilized and cultured, a friend of good food and a man of very agreeable and witty conversation—he was an eighteenth-century man of partly Scottish blood.) Scheler fell a victim to his not wholly unjustified but morbidly excessive aversion to Kantian deontic ethics; he was infected with the Nietzschean and Bergsonian error that if not moral virtue as such —this he would have denied—a peculiar modality of human goodness came from an overflow of 'life', a superabundance of 'vital force'. Hartmann, while scrupulously avoiding the pitfall of identifying the goodness of 'nobility' with moral goodness as such, keenly saw through Scheler's mistake and trenchantly rejected the thesis that, e.g. noble-mindedness had anything to do with 'vital values' such as welfare, etc. (Kant, who had something of an authentic 'saint' about him, and Hartmann, who had nothing of that but was a Baltic nobleman by origin, were both incomparably nobler men than Scheler.) In my own surmise, nobleness is not so much a special value modality besides vital, moral and aesthetic value as the mark of a specially intimate *compenetration* between a concrete being (notably, a person) and some salient modality of vital, aesthetical, intellectual or moral values. We would call a man 'noble' whom we could not as it were *imagine* to act or behave in any situation otherwise than with intensity, grace, genius, originality, grandeur, justice, generosity or high-mindedness. Scheler may be right in so far as the typically conscientious and scrupulous and the typically 'noble' sort of man will rarely be one and the same person, though perhaps Kant could be suggested as a counter-example.

(2) Hartmann takes the 'optimistic' view that men always act for the sake of *some value*; never in pursuit of a *disvalue* as such. To do so is a privilege of *satanic* beings ('Evil be thou my Good'), if there are any; it is inaccessible to mere *human* beings. Nor is, as Hartmann rightly says, the pursuit of a *lower* value in itself 'evil' at all. What *is* evil is to *prefer a lower to a higher value* when the situation requires a choice between them: thus Scheler and Hartmann alike, while another phenomenologist, Reiner (who I think is still alive) calls such a preference merely wrong or incorrect (*unrichtig*), reserving the qualification 'evil' for cases in which the preference for the lower value entails a violation of another person's rights or harm done to his significant interests.

My own views differ from these too much to leave me any scope for their exposition here. The point is merely that Hartmann, like Aristotle, sees concrete right action in the *synthetic* realization of moral value aspects which by their nature stand in a certain tension to each other; only, while Aristotle interprets virtuous conduct as a 'golden mean' between two unvirtuous 'extremes', Hartmann interprets it as a harmonious combination of two antithetic aspects of good. Aristotle says that 'true' courage is a golden mean between cowardice and imprudent temerity; Hartmann would say that we ought to act with well-weighed, rational courage rather than either with courage alone (which is *per se* good but not a sovereign, absolute norm of action) or with prudence or with an eye on 'safety first' alone (to which the same valuation applies). Now Hartmann introduces the specific antithesis between the *strength* and the *height* of values, a point of view in which I seem to have little difficulty in recognizing an echo of the Aristotelian principle *Primum vivere deinde philosophari*. Hartmann attributes to values a mode of being of their own, one kind of merely 'ideal' being which nevertheless is endowed with *strength*, for it inevitably exercises an *impact* on men's *real* conduct. Thus we *tend* to shun evil and do good not only because of the probable harmful consequences of at least many transgressions and the probable good consequences of at least some good actions but because of the shame and guilt attaching to evil and the satisfaction which accompanies good conduct; more fundamentally, the essential repulsiveness of evil and attractiveness of good. But lower values, though in no evolutionary sense do they 'engender' higher values, are a *precondition* to them, while the converse does not hold. Thus, the imparting of goods to others is incomparably higher than their selfish enjoyment, and this new, higher goodness cannot be deduced from, or 'explained in terms of', the primary lower goodness of self-enjoyment; but this lower goodness exists massively in its own right, whereas the imparting of goods to others would lose all conceivable meaning if the goods themselves were not goods fit for straightforward self-enjoyment: if I offer you the gift of a box of chocolates that is incomparably more virtuous of me than if I eat them myself, but if we all knew that chocolates are mere gravel unfit for human consumption or any other significant use the virtue of my offering them to you would reduce to absolutely nil. Hartmann expands this truth into a theory stating that the lower a value the 'stronger' it is, and the higher the 'weaker'. We can eat without feeding one another, however deplorable and blameworthy such a state would be; but unless we eat there is simply no *point* in feeding one another. Similarly, common honesty is a strict duty whose omission rightly entails (in some cases at least and in various forms) retaliation, but whose fulfilment is not particularly meritorious; whereas generosity, charity or exemplary virtue embody very high values and are greatly meritorious but they do not constitute strict duties and their omission (in any given case) will not arouse disgustful indignation nor entail grim retaliation. In other words, with some simplification it can be said that the higher a value is the weaker the natural or imperatival *pressure* it exercises upon us.

There is a great deal of evident truth in 'Hartmann's Law', both in the sense that natural wants assert themselves more imperiously than higher-level desires and yearnings and in the sense that within the *moral* sphere the exclusion of crude and elemental disvalues translates into strict universal *duties* while subtle and positive goodness tends to be admirable rather than obligatory and to appear an *optional* matter entrusted to men's individual conscience—or, better, sensitivity—and assigned to single occasions with their selective thematic contents. Yet on closer inspection I would not hesitate to accuse Hartmann's view, in a non-Moorian sense of the term, of a kind of 'naturalistic fallacy'. Psychologically speaking, the impact of higher values is *sometimes* definitely *stronger* than that of lower values; men's awareness of higher demands *may* take on the form of an *imperative* that overrides the *imperiousness* of more primary urges or universal postulates. It sometimes occurs that a man voluntarily sacrifices his very life or at any rate his basic comforts for the good of his family, his country or a close or admired friend. Ethically or axiologically speaking, we might even erect the primacy of the service of higher values over the *cult* or *elaboration* of lower values into a universal principle. To live *honestly* is a duty, to live '*well*' is *not*; to live on a high spiritual level is not a duty but constitutes as it were an incommensurably more *valid* value than to live in comfort and security, let alone to live in luxury. Wordsworth in 1802 complained:

> The wealthiest man among us is the best:
> No grandeur now in nature or in book
> Delights us. Rapine, avarice, expense,
> This is idolatry; and this we adore:
> Plain living and high thinking are no more.

(I wonder what he would say if the mishap befell him of being re-awakened to life today.) To be sure, without a 'minimum' of food, shelter, clothing and other basic comforts there could be no such thing as 'high thought', nor—Hobbes is right here—any generous and unselfish modes of life without a fair measure of legal order with a massive power to sanction and enforce it. But the Wordsworthian ideal of 'plain living and high thinking' plainly *is* practicable. There is no reason why I *could* not have several thousand books and only three or four suits, nor why I *could* not go to museums and picture galleries nearly every day and to the moving pictures only once or twice a year or not at all. Furthermore, among the classic 'spiritual' values the moral values are undoubtedly the 'strongest', but it cannot be said that either the intellectual or the aesthetical values are the 'highest'; the only thing I would venture to suggest is that, both intellectual and—in a different way—aesthetical values extending over a very much broader spectrum than the moral values, *some* of them are in all likelihood lower than the lowest and *some* of them very probably higher than the highest moral values. Disappointingly as it may sound, while higher and lower values and categories of value undoubtedly exist and can to some extent be explored, no linear schema of a 'hierarchy of values' can stand up to closer scrutiny; in a somewhat lesser measure perhaps, this applies also to a linear gradation of the 'strengths' of values—apart from the ambiguity in the very concept of 'strength': for Hartmann fails to distinguish between the empirical 'strength' of vital wants and the ideal 'strength', no doubt expressed also in terms of *real* pressures and urgencies, in duty-forming as contrasted with supererogatory or otherwise optional values. None the less, maintaining all these provisoes I think that by pointing to a generally and vaguely inverse proportion between 'height' and 'strength' Hartmann has made an important and fruitful contribution to the theory of values.

6. NOBILITY IN SOCIETY AND THE NOBLENESS OF A SOCIETY

Abstaining from any critical discussion of this most complex theme but mindful of the social origin of the very concept of Hierarchy, I would conclude this survey with an *aperçu* which has both a conservative and 'élitist' and a democratic or egalitarian edge.

The scheme of any point-by-point correspondence or mutual translatability between the 'Hierarchy of Values' and the 'Social Hierarchy' (including political, administrative, economic and even cultural) is mistaken as an idea and pointless as an ideal; it is neither a possible nor a desirable reality. Neither are values *generally* representable by concrete beings, nor do established degrees of authority, power, charge, etc., *generally* breed anything like a scale of corresponding values. Naturally, just, competent and stable rulership depends *among other things* upon excellence of various kinds in the rulers, but administrative, functional and social leadership or precedence constitutes a hierarchy, or rather a system of hierarchies (of skills, capacities and prestige-embodiments) *of its own*; and similar considerations apply to the hierarchy of values in its more proper and abstract sense. The Platonic postulate of an identification of the two is an arbitrary fancy and an inane utopia. Wisdom and knowledge as well as moral qualities in the rulers are highly desirable, but *A* being wiser or more intelligent or juster or more merciful or more chaste than *B* is far from making *A* necessarily fitter for rulership than *B*. Inversely, while Lord Acton may have been wrong in saying that power corrupts—he was nearer the truth in going on to say that absolute power corrupts absolutely—power of any kind *can* make a man more conceited, more stupid, more lazy, more selfish and more self-indulgent than he would otherwise be. *Normally*, i.e. given a certain amount of division, equilibrium, control and manifoldness of social hierarchies, positions of authority, power, rank, prestige, wealth, etc., deserve being respected and honoured not because they warrant personal excellence but because they stand for a vital necessity of social order and are conducive to the recognition by and *in* society of the hierarchical distinction of values, along its equally various dimensions, in the proper sense of the term. So far, an 'aristocratic' society is both possible and desirable. In this interpretation of 'Conservatism' or 'Toryism', I more or less closely follow Christopher Hollis attributing, with approval, similar ideas to that great eighteenth-century genius in his excellent book on Samuel Johnson.

But a society is not a 'noble' society *in proportion* as it accords a prominent place to nobility *in its midst*. The nobleness *of* society depends, not merely on the nobleness (in the widest sense of the word) of its *leading* members but also on the nobleness of its members in general, as a whole, and the possibilities it affords for the unfolding of the nobleness virtually present in its average, I would venture to say in its *humblest* members. Moreover, beyond this principle of 'meritocracy' and selective élite-formation, it also depends on the degree of justice, beneficence and value-directed guidance it bestows on its individual members as such, even without regard to their actual and their virtual distinctive merits. In other words, it depends on the democratic *correctives* of diverse kinds it applies to its aristocratic features. In Hartmannian language,the height of values embodied in a society depends, not only on the high values *conspicuous in it*, but also on its readiness to do justice to the principle of the *urgency of values*. If the expression 'a good society' has any meaning at all, it can only be measured by the standard of vigour, wealth and temperateness in *all* directions.

If society exists for the sake of anything at all, it exists for the sake of itself and thus for the sake of its ruling, leading and tone-giving members, *and* for the sake of the distinctively valuable, eminent, virtuous, ingenious and creative members *emergent* in its midst, *and*, last but not least, for the good of its members *pure and simple*. Such a pattern may appear very vague and lacks any panacea-like applicability: an avowal from which I draw the supreme comfort that at all events it is anything but utopian.

9

Aesthetic and Moral Experience

1. ON THE KINSHIP BETWEEN 'THE BEAUTIFUL' AND 'THE GOOD'

Whereas there are many, perhaps I should say countless, forms of value experience *other* than either aesthetical or moral, many (but not all) of them displaying both an aesthetical and a moral aspect, in my view it may well be said that the aesthetical *and* the moral constitute the most paradigmatic types of our experience of Values as such. I cannot here undertake anything like a proof of this thesis, but I propose to adduce a few arguments in its support. First I will point out the tendency of ordinary language to conflate, I do not mean to say identify, the concept of the beautiful with that of the good. Second I will try to contrast the aesthetic and the moral with four other modalities, still standard but somehow less prototypic, of value experience.

'Good' is a blanket term for anything we find compelling, or deem worthy of, a *pro* attitude. Very often it has no moral connotation at all, but by a good action, good conduct, a good person we usually mean a *morally* good action, conduct or person. Again, when a work of art is called 'good'—usually by artists, experts or at any rate people familiar with the branch of art in question—what is meant is certainly that the work is well executed, as also conceived by a true artist, and thus *beautiful*. The term 'beautiful' itself in this century at any rate—and not only in the English-speaking world—is often avoided by people who 'understand about art', for to their ears it has come to acquire a somewhat derogatory sound: a suspicion of the obviously and conventionally beauty-emphasizing, the cheap and sugary—in a word, of *kitsch*. 'Kitsch-phobia' may attain a degree of morbidness preventing some snobs from appreciating the beauty of certain *natural* objects, say the full moon or the red glow of the sinking sun, which can after all only be called 'beautiful' or 'a marvellous sight' but not 'good'. But this is not all. As every grammar-school boy knows, ancient Greek *kalos* means 'beautiful' but may often usurp the place of *agathos* (the proper term for 'good') and can be applied to human conduct as such—by no means only to the grace of young athletes' bodily movements. And in modern German *schön* ('beautiful') may play a similar part. *Er hat schön gehandelt* (he has acted nobly, generously) and *Das war nicht schön von ihm* (that wasn't *nice* of him, it's slightly objectionable) are quite ordinary German phrases and express unequivocally judgements of *moral* value. In English an action, an object, a person and a state of affairs alike may be called *fine*; and the secondary idiomatic sense of *nice*, though not the same, is similarly multivalent. Unless I am mistaken, Russian *khoroshiy* is pretty analogous to Greek *kalos* (while for *agathos*, properly 'good', the adjective *dobryi* exists).

There is also an inverse extension of usage, at any rate in English and Spanish. English has for *beau, bello, schön*, Dutch *schoon*, etc., only the synthetic and relatively clumsy word *beautiful*. This is often, as the case may be, replaced with such non-moral words as 'pretty', 'handsome', 'comely' or 'personable'. But in older, perhaps antiquated, English we have *goodly*, and in present-day English the term *good-looking* is constantly used and is scarcely if at all sub-standard, certainly not slangy like 'quite a looker' or 'easy on the eye'. In Spanish *bello* and *hermoso* (Portuguese *formoso*) certainly ought to fill the bill, but alas! they don't. *Bello* sounds so formal and stilted that it can hardly be used outside very formal and oratorical language (and satires on it). *Hermoso* is nearer to the normal key but in standard speech the Spaniards are little given to using it; they call a handsome, well-built young man *guapo*, a girl *guapa*; and in quite normal, standard conversation they would nearly always call the cathedral of Burgos *muy bonita* or the no less marvellous Gothic district of Barcelona *muy bonito*—'very pretty' (or 'nice') as it were. *Bonito*, a perfectly standard word, corresponds of course to 'goodly', and indeed in older Castilian *bueno* ('good') could also sometimes mean 'fine' or 'beautiful': even in today's popular idiom *un buen mozo* means not a virtuous youth but a sturdy, good-looking young fellow. Not without blushing at the vulgarity, I would add that in English and in some other European language media erotically-minded men are apt to credit a woman possessing shapely limbs with 'good legs', though in standard speech this expression should indicate a high capacity for walking, racing or football-playing.

Ordinary language is not 'all right', as Wittgenstein said in one of his moods; it needs a great deal of critical tidying-up for the purposes of serious methodical thinking. But it certainly *is* the main source for such thinking and immeasurably nearer to being 'all right' than any 'perfect language' invented or dreamt of by Utopian prigs or the universal 'deep language structure' of Chomsky's phantasy could be; and any philosophy placing itself *outside the framework* of ordinary language is bound to lose touch with common sense and thus in my firm view—though I cannot argue the matter here—is doomed to be totally pointless and irrelevant to our reading of reality. Thus I conclude from the foregoing linguistic considerations to something like a close interpenetration between our experience of beauty and that of goodness; and while goodness need not at all mean or imply moral goodness, moral goodness certainly does mean goodness *per eminentiam*. It is hardly necessary to add the proviso that good, i.e. beautiful, representative art (e.g. literature or painting) need not therefore be 'edifying' and represent either morally good or morally qualifiable objects. But then it need as little represent beautiful objects: Rembrandt's portraits of ugly-looking persons are no less aesthetically first-rate than Shakespeare's or Dostoyevsky's portrayals of abject evildoers. Despise as I do the modern excesses of '*kitsch*-phobia', far be it from me to embark on a paradoxical 'neo-primitivist' or sham-naive defence of *kitsch*.

2. COMPARISON OF THE ETHICAL AND AESTHETICAL WITH FOUR OTHER MAIN TYPES OF VALUES

In support of my contention about the axiological primacy, in some sense, of the ethical and aesthetical, let us now compare ethical and aesthetical with four other main types of Values.

(i) Purely *instrumental* values, which may be of indeterminately diverse kinds as to the objects and the purposes they bear upon and which cannot meaningfully be divded into any sub-species of their own, are not properly *values* at all in that they are strictly *extrinsic*. Whatever is nothing but useful or has nothing but market value may be highly important but is only called 'value' in an improper sense; it is established use to call it value in an economic context, but it would be tidier to speak in such a context only of 'goods' and 'prices'. Such values are, for example, embodied by drugs. Quinine, mepacrine and their more modern successors are excellent things in a social medium in which malaria may occur; but outside such regions, or once malaria has been wiped off the earth, what can they be used for and in what manner could we *value* them? In so far perhaps as they still form part of the objects treated in the history of medicine; but hereby we have passed from the domain of instrumental into that of scientific or cognitional values, a wholly different matter on which I shall touch in subsection (iii). Again, while it would be the peak of silliness (or hypocrisy) to deny a paramount importance to money and its equivalents (cheques, etc.), the type of purely instrumental value, it would be even sillier, in fact bordering on logical impossibility, to value money 'for its own sake', that is otherwise than *exclusively* in view of the objects and services it can buy in virtue of state-imposed stipulation. The only exception relates to beautiful gold and silver coins—a thing of the past, save perhaps for Dutch silver currency; but here we have unequivocally stepped back into the realm of *aesthetical* (and also, perhaps, once more that of historical) interest.

Importance as such does not, philosophically speaking, constitute 'value' at all; for awareness of it lacks that tinge of 'upward-looking' *reverence* which is one aspect inherent in every experience of value. Far from hating or despising the rich, I warmly respect them, because mainly and generally wealth is closely tied either to tradition or to ability and industry, very often to both, and in these I indeed sense high values; but the connections I was just stressing are anything but proportionate and therefore the abstract 'worship of wealth', i.e. an uncritical reverence for the rich and greater reverence for those who are even richer, *is* indeed servile and contemptible. If my neighbour, hitherto perhaps as poor as I am myself, suddenly gets rich by winning the highest premium in the lottery, I shall heartily congratulate him with a gesture of good-natured envy but not find him immensely more worthy of respect than before: in other words sheer luck deserves at best joyous sympathy but not respect, nor of course, contempt or resentful envy. I will now deal with two conceivable objections.

(*a*) In a work of art, especially one bound up with 'craft' (in consonance with the ancient sense of *ars*), beauty and usefulness, that is instrumental value, often go together; this may even be sometimes true of objects of nature. A fine-looking fruit, especially within one species, is to some extent likely to be also a tasty and wholesome fruit. But above all it has been said, rightly I think, that a work of art or, say, of aesthetically ambitious craft that is ill suited to the purpose it is designed for cannot be beautiful either, no matter how costly the stuff it is made of and how lavishly it is (possibly even 'in good taste') decorated. If not absolutely true, this may on the whole be true; I would expect an uncomfortable arm-chair or an all too high table to be also an eyesore, an irritating sight. But the reverse is hardly true. A useful and functionally well-designed object may at the same time be ugly—for various reasons. More important, the *Neue Sachlichkeit* style of *Wohn-maschine* flats and houses and of *Seelen-Silo* churches as well as aeroplane-shaped 'racers' offer, to the eyes of many of us at any rate, an ugly and depressing sight, apt to arouse suicidal temptations. Indeed, while usefulness *per se* suggests an inchoate and rudimentary beauty rather than ugliness, all boisterous emphasis on utility and conspicuous puritanical evasion of the ornamental, the picturesque, the playful and superfluous as it were, is *eo ipso* ugly and repulsive. Naturally so. For on the one hand *ne peut pas qui veut*: there are *some* values that, as Scheler and Hartmann insisted, cannot be realized by the direct and deliberate pursuit of them at all, or only to a very limited degree; yet on the other hand deliberate *exclusion* of a value, for example of beauty, is always certain to succeed at least to a very large extent. Even with the utmost effort, had I such wanton desires, I could not contrive to evoke the impression of an elegant gentleman; but if I set my heart on displaying the credible appearance of a vulgar and indecent-looking ragamuffin, I trust I could easily achieve *that*. Whether the style of utility-emphasis always ensures the maximum of actual usefulness is of course a moot point. I, for one, nurse the suspicion that the cult of ugliness springs less from aesthetical indifference than from aesthetical perversion, and is mysteriously devoted to the service of Satan rather than soberly confined to the service of human wants.[1]

(*b*) An analogous objection on the ethical side might even more plausibly be proffered. According to the Utilitarians moral values *are* instrumental values; moral conduct is 'nothing but' useful conduct—useful to 'Society' and 'ultimately' to the agent himself. It cannot be my task here to refute the Utilitarian doctrine; suffice it to state that it is false, flying as it does in the face of moral experience and consisting in the fake-scientific *reduction* of a thing more subtle and difficult to grasp to *another* thing (to echo Bishop Butler's words which Moore chose as his motto) more crudely and reassuringly tangible. Yet I am ready to admit that round the abysmally false core of the Utilitarian doctrine there is a peripheral layer which contains an element of essential, not purely contingent, truth. Moral appraisal bears on the quality of action, intention, will, conduct and character; but these things—character as the fostering-soil of the others—are goal-directed and necessarily productive of effects, wherefore their quality *cannot* be simply and completely independent of 'foreseeable consequences'. And this fact lends colour to the objection: though no more than colour, not real strength. *Every* morally good intention, action, etc., tends, as Findlay justly wrote, to *benefit* people, *some* people at any rate and *somehow* the agent himself: thus if in a context in which I might pointfully feel tempted to lie or deceive or mislead or cheat I in

---

[1] I owe the phrase *the cult of ugliness*, and largely its interpretation, to a friend more aesthetically sensitive than I, who, however, being neither a professional philosopher nor a writer on art, prefers to remain anonymous.

fact speak and proceed with scrupulous honesty, my conduct is morally good *in itself* and not primarily in virtue of its (possible, probable or certain) good consequences; but it is true and *relevant* to its value that the practice of honesty as a rule is conducive to social co-operation and its desirable fruits, but also to the building of my own 'character' (i.e. that which above all else determines my 'worth') and furthermore to the *trust* people are likely to accord me in future (i.e. one of the most precious *extrinsic advantages* that may fall to my lot). From this valid consideration it is only a step to the Utilitarian assumption that it is these beneficial effects that *constitute* the moral goodness of my honesty. The step is utterly fallacious, for apart from extreme marginal cases I ought to be honest even if it doesn't seem likely to 'maximize good' but may well produce more harm than advantage; it is, further, partly circular, inasmuch as a great deal of the good effects moral conduct tends to bring about *presuppose* the fact that men on the whole approve of, view with satisfaction, and in some cases admire moral (honest, temperate, benevolent, just, magnanimous, etc.) conduct. Moral goodness is closely similar to *beauty* of any kind in the highly important respect that it is a good thing to *contemplate*:[2] this consideration alone has sufficient force to cut the nerve of all 'consequentialism'. It likewise goes to confirm my attribution to the ethical and the aesthetic of a prototypal pride of place in our experience of values.

(ii) I shall say very little about our value-experience of *ontological* or *metaphysical*—whether 'natural' or 'supernatural'—*perfection*. By no means do I wish to deny that such concepts may be meaningful or that if they are, they must also be of very high importance and most intimately linked with men's awareness of value. But in so far as perfection means no more than that a thing or entity is a perfect example of its kind, or means no more than power, strength, vitality, etc., I can only see very vaguely anything valuable about that, unless it be instrumental or technical value of some kind. Again in so far as perfection is meant in a sense connoting holiness, the value I can see in it is precisely a superelevated form of *ethical* value. If God exists, which I believe to be the case and could perhaps

---

[2] See Pepita Haezrahi's fundamental work on Aesthetics, *The Contemplative Activity* (1954), esp. Chs II and III. The condensed enumeration of the (four) 'features of the aesthetic object' (p. 40) marks, I think, the apex of the book. Haezrahi's description, while sharply illustrating the contrast with moral *preoccupation*, is yet to some extent applicable also to moral *appraisal*—at any rate on an Intrinsicalist view, as opposed to both Utilitarianism and Prescriptivism. The reader is reminded of the 'spectator' approach in eighteenth-century British ethics and of Herbart's 'aesthetical' theory of morality (the five basic 'pleasing' features of moral conduct and inter-personal relation patterns).

argue but certainly not prove, I see and revere in Him mainly
the Moral Legislator (or rather the supreme fountain-head of our
moral orientation) and above all the Supreme Judge (that is to say,
the Guarantor of the decisive weight of moral values in the order
of reality). Again, in so far as natural objects of 'perfect' build and
stature impress us with a sense of value, the modality of that value
is clearly *aesthetical*. Most certainly the aesthetically valuable, the
'beautiful'—especially, but not exclusively, as regards works of art
—may be of a more or less 'perfectional' type (e.g. whatever
instantiates the 'classic' style in the arts), which however is not to
be confused with the greater or lesser degree of value attributable
to it. As regards certain human or personal dimensions of value like
dignity, distinction, stance, bearing, impressiveness, etc., they
seem to me to be interpretable as blends (in varying proportions)
of the ethical and the aesthetical with each other, and in some cases
of either or both with the intellectual value modalities.

(iii) The reader may most understandably wonder why I should
assign to beauty and to moral virtue, not indeed a greater or higher
but so to speak a more typically *axiological* value than to the world
of *cognitive* correctness, wealth and depth: the domain of validities
and achievements that go by the names of reasons, truth, legitimate
inference, intellect, insight, knowledge, well-grounded belief, intuitive evidence, learning, and so forth. (Perhaps he may even suspect
me of being an irrationalist: a reproach that would afflict me as
grievously as that of being morally unprincipled, and cause me far
greater pain than being contemptuously dismissed as an aesthetically insensitive, a banausic—in high-flown German *amusisch*—
person.) Indeed Franz Brentano, with whom most later anti-
idealist and anti-positivist, i.e. neo-objectivist, phenomenological
and intuitionist thought originates, taught that there were only
two fundamental and irreducibly evident classes of values: (*a*)
pleasure; (*b*) cognition; or as he—more incisively and more felicitously, I would say—put it, *consciousness* as such.[3] And according

[3] My reference to Brentano's doctrine of values is somewhat oversimplified here
and needs a brief rectification. Instead of pleasure and unpleasure, Brentano
sometimes speaks of joy (or gladness) and sadness; but gladness and sadness
mean pleasure and unpleasure relative to states of affairs as distinguished from
objects. Again, it is his contention that all consciousness is germinally *directed* to
(true) judgement, i.e. cognition; but consciousness is precisely the more *fundamental* value-embodying phenomenon. Finally, I have not mentioned Brentano's
radically intuitionist definition of *moral* value. This resides in love and hatred
(in the sense of *dilexio* and *abominatio*, in English emphatic and effectual *like* and
dislike) characterized—given to the agent's or appraiser's consciousness—as
evidently right, correct, appropriate. This third category is not reducible to the
first two but plainly presupposes them and is thus not in the same sense fundamental. See J. N. Findlay, *Axiological Ethics* (1970), Ch. II.

to an age-old and ineradicable tradition which on the whole pre-vails throughout the history of philosophy, there can be nothing we should, and on the whole ultimately do, *value* higher or esteem more reverently than Truth and Reason.

My answer to the charge will, I fear, indeed sound meagre and apologetic; and I do plead guilty of being able to express what exactly I mean so imperfectly only as to involve a risk of being misunderstood. But it is precisely my respect for truth that compels me to speak my mind, however haltingly.

To repeat: my contention is *not* that aesthetical and ethical values *surpass* cognitional or intellectual values. (It is well to em-phasize at this point, incidentally, that what we designate and revere as intellectual *integrity* or *probity* is only partly an intellectual but pre-eminently a *moral* quality; and that an able, lucid and forceful *exposition* of scientific, juridical or philosophical thought connotes a good deal of *aesthetical* value: it is not for nothing that, although mathematics is the most purely rational thing on earth, it is customary to speak admiringly of the 'elegance' of a mathe-matical deduction.) My contention, then, is that the aesthetical and the ethical have their locus *in a more strictly valuational context* than have the truth of a proposition, the validity of an inference, the treasury of knowledge, the precious and basic good of conscious-ness, or again wisdom, wit and brilliancy of mind. All aesthetic and moral judgements are *ipso jure* evaluative; judgements as such, however true (e.g. 'The Netherlands are divided into eleven pro-vinces, Belgium into nine' or 'My father and I were dark-haired'), are not. Admittedly judgements about judgements (e.g. 'The above judgements are true' or 'Jones is right in holding that there are four primes between 100 and 110') are also evaluative. But I can-not get away from seeing a *difference* here. That all non-axiological judgements can in the way just indicated ('this view is right, that view is wrong') be turned into value-judgements is, of course, trivial. On the other hand intellectual value-judgements proper ('Jones is bright', 'Brown is shallow-minded', 'Robinson is a genius', 'This is a deep insight', 'That is a fallacious argument', 'Smith is a skilful and efficient actuary') are not value-judgements in a merely trivial sense, and they are hardly less intrinsic or more instrumental than, say, ethical judgements.(Even aesthetical judge-ments can, fairly trivially, be 'instrumentalized': 'This landscape is calculated to enchant us and gladden our hearts', 'That Surrealist painting with a fish gloating under a chair is apt to induce a sick feeling in the pit of my stomach'.) The point, however, seems to me to be that the full-blooded value-experience expressed in ethical and aesthetical appraisals contrasts with the radically 'neutral' or 'value-free' nature of knowledge as such, the knowledge of facts and logical relations which somehow reflects also in our appreciative knowledge of knowledge and our depreciatory knowledge of ignorance and, particularly, of fake knowledge. Whereas in our intellectual valuations we are always ultimately concerned with a dry factual or logical kernel of 'This is so' or 'That is because . . .', in our moral and aesthetical valuations our perspective likewise always includes some similar references: 'He kept—or broke —his promise', 'This portrait of X really resembles X', 'The statue on the Place Saint-Jean in Brussels is meant to represent the heroine Gabrielle Petit', etc., yet it is in a fashion *inseparable* from our emotive and evaluative attitudes. The keeping of promises is inherently right, their breaking inherently wrong; the artistic rendering and, so to say, eternalization of a personality cannot but be admirable, and in some way even the fact that a personality *can* be thus grasped and re-created is so; the bronze statue just mentioned appears to me a fine work of art and moreover I dearly cherish the memory of the brave and ingenious young woman who paid with her life for her active and righteous patriotism. As I have already admitted, great art may depict ugly or dreary objects even without a balancing background or a contrasting feature of beauty, and may depict moral evil, including evil triumphant; and moral awareness is in fact more engrossed in the experience of transgression than in that of virtue. But there are certain limits set to this. Art is meant to *create* beauty and thus it must connote at least some reference to beauty and make the experience of what is contrary to beauty subservient, in a discreet and subtle manner at any rate, to its contrast. Again, it is true that Hamlet does not simply kill Claudius and then live happily for ever with Ophelia; but if he kills Polonius, more or less drives Ophelia to suicide and is killed himself, he *does* kill Claudius, and with the succession of Fortinbras a liberating storm cleans the air. And awareness of moral evil is only meaningful against the background, less emphatically but more permanently experienced, of moral principles and rules, and the possibility—the manifold occurrence—of living up to moral standards. On the contrary intellectual quest is directed to the true and the false, to whether p or its contradictory is the case, *indifferently to which*, by any standard, *would be preferable*. As Frederick Price's *Text-Book of Medicine* states drily, cerebrospinal meningitis is (or used to be) more often mistaken for influenza than influenza for meningitis. The diagnostician should *equally* avoid both blunders; it is better for the patient to have influenza but not, independently thereof, better for the physician to *hold* that he has influenza. If, in fact, it is more *dangerous* for the therapist to mistake meningitis for influenza than the reverse, that of course is contingent exclusively on the *instrumental* aspect of cognition. I conclude, then, that while the cognitive or intellectual modality of value is an intrinsic and securely established one, the ethical and the aesthetical are more saliently paradigmatic types of value.

(iv) Finally we return to the question of Utilitarianism, but from another angle: instead of dwelling on instrumental, we raise the problem of hedonic values. Is not *pleasure*, rather than beauty or moral goodness, the fittest candidate for the position of the basic and prototypal value? One thing is certain: pleasure, as Aristotle saw it clearly, is not an instrumental but a fundamentally and evidently *intrinsic* 'good'. On the other hand, as Aristotle saw it almost as clearly in spite of the strong Utilitarian note of his ethics, it is not a *bonum honestum* (that adjective, in ancient and scholastic language, and still, sometimes, *honnête* in literary French, meaning not 'honest' but honourable, gentlemanly, respectable) but merely the *bonum delectabile*. For Aristotle and the scholastic guardians of his tradition this means that pleasure as such is not distinctively linked to the specific rational nature of man. We prefer to say that the differentia of our pleasurable experiences *qua* such, in contrast with our awareness of value, lies in the fact that they do not connote a feeling of *reverence* and that we experience the objects of pleasure, again *qua* such, as 'instrumental' (*scil.* to our pleasure), whereas the object of value-experience 'compels' esteem rather than subserves it. Thus, in a significant sense, value-experience is object-directed while pleasure is self-directed. The distinction stands out in clear outline and to try to blur it would amount to an artificial restriction of our world-knowledge; but to very many concrete cases it is but vaguely applicable and for a more detailed treatment of the matter it would need some modifications. Every value-experience, every *pro* attitude, is *somehow* 'pleasant' or 'pleasing' (cf. phrasings like 'It is our pleasure to confer ...' or '... during Her Majesty's pleasure') and thus bears *some* note of pleasure; conversely, every pleasure proper, however sensual, self-regarding and perhaps selfish, confers *some* value on its object (mainly aesthetic value, e.g. when on a sultry day we enjoy a 'pleasant breeze') and is certainly compatible with a most intense emotional penetration of the object. Hence it is not surprising that some philosophers should have strayed into the blind alley of identifying the valuable with the pleasurable or defining value in terms of pleasure and 'measuring' it in proportion with the intensity of pleasure; and that others should have yielded to the opposite temptation of banishing the hedonic from the axiological realm and denying all relevance to the 'merely psychological' relations between value and pleasure or valuation and enjoyment. I would steer clear of both these extremes and definitely accept the notion of hedonic value but as definitely stick to its distinction from *bonum honestum* and deny it the paramount axiological status of the ethical and the aesthetic. The structure of the relations between *dis*value and so-called 'pain' (or, rather, *Unlust*, displeasure, 'unpleasure' or suffering) presents no complete symmetry with that of the relations between value and pleasure: suffering has a much more obvious claim to the status of a disvalue than pleasure has to the status of a value, while yet asceticism may lay claim to a high value of its own.

3. CONTRASTING THE ETHICAL WITH THE AESTHETICAL

1. *The Universal Range of Aesthetic Valuation*

The most conspicuous extrinsic contrast resides in the universal object-domain of aesthetic as opposed to the narrowly confined area of moral valuation. It is true that very many things fail to strike us as either particularly beautiful or particularly ugly. But what kinds of things *can* be beautiful or ugly? It is hardly hyperbolical to answer: Every kind of thing. Material and immaterial, psychic or conceptual, human or personal and extra-human or impersonal, animal or vegetable, living or inert; plots and schemas, artifacts and wild-grown things as well as their compounds (e.g. urban and rural landscapes), manners of exposition and involuntary gestures. If perhaps moral right-doing of a hum-drum and conventional sort is neither beautiful nor ugly, noble and high-minded moral conduct is also eminently beautiful, while base, sordid and corrupt ways of behaviour are also disgustingly ugly. In contrast therewith what kinds of things can be the object of moral appraisal? Their range, though I feel it cannot be quite exactly delimited, is incommensurably narrower. It would be false and parochial—as Moore rightly insists—to define it as the range of *human* intention, will, conduct and character alone. First, I do not regard it as proved that 'transcendental', unembodied personal beings cannot exist and that, notably, there are no such things as holy and fallen angels. Second, to balance the Christian with an a-Christian emphasis, I am not absolutely sure of the 'irrational' character of all, including the 'higher', animals and thus of their being completely deprived of choice and will. (While I am only second to the ancient Egyptians as regards cat-worship, the tendency of cats cruelly to maltreat smaller and weaker animals arouses in me an emotion very like moral indignation.) Finally and principally, the Aristotelian statement 'Man is a rational animal' may be correct as a classification but is wholly unacceptable as a definition. We simply do not know whether there are not, be it on Mars or elsewhere, *embodied* beings as 'rational' and 'spiritual' as men (or more so), as much endowed with free-will and as capable of being consciously virtuous and deliberately wicked, yet definitely *not* part of the human species—e.g. seven-legged, acting chiefly with their trunks, and equipped with substantially different sense-organs—whose genetic history is totally unconnected with that of mankind. (The late C. S. Lewis, a deeply and emphatically religious Anglican, much appreciated also by a multitude of Roman Catholics, thought this hypothesis to be probable and based part of his splendid and inspiring fantasies on it.) In a practical and empirical sense, to be sure, all our moral appraisals and ethical speculations bear on things human—'human nature', men's actions, and so forth. But the point is that they only bear on actions, intentions, wishing and willing, and situations and institutions in some way resulting from these and representing them. Even these not in a comprehensive sense, for 'Philosophy of Mind' is not Ethics though indispensable for the study of Ethics, which considers them only from certain evaluative and prescriptive/prohibitive points of view, in the perspective of a 'system' or *corpus* of norms, codes and standards. In other words, the very core of the ethical object-world is Intention (in the volitional modern, not in the object-reference meaning of the word): that is to say, *the direction of willing*—I do not say 'the Will', for although being 'strong-willed' is *per se* not only practically but morally preferable to being 'weak-willed', an exceptionally strong will may at the same time be an utterly *evil* will, whereas a weak will may be an essentially, yet imperfectly, *good* will. (One of the grandiose Nazi *Parteitage* at Nürnberg, following Hitler's ascent to power, was officially entitled *Triumph des Willens*; yet most of us would demur to call that indubitably tough and effective will a morally good will.) Intention or Will in the sense thus clarified is, I say, the core of the ethical object-world; to be sure, its core is not the whole of it. The central point is surrounded by a vast aura of more peripheral layers: putting it briefly, habitual and even routine conduct; practical wisdom, rationality and efficiency; the direction of the agent's mere wishes this side of actual willing; and even the nature of his purely spontaneous desires—in the language of Moral Theology, *motus primoprimi*—which, as such, fall short of any trace of responsibility, imputability and guilt. The area of what is susceptible of moral *evaluation* far transcends the orbit of applicability of moral imperatives, condemnation, retaliation or even unqualified praise. What is not morally imputable is not therefore of necessity morally 'neutral'; failure to recognize this was one of the most flagrant errors of Kantian ethics, an error of which some faint traces still subsist in Sir David Ross's ethical writing. Granting that, the territory of the moral none the less appears tiny in comparison with that of the aesthetic. It would be erroneous to infer from this consideration, even combined with the one to follow presently, that the moral could be soundly interpreted as a sub-division of the aesthetic. Mind, as we know it empirically, is also but a tiny enclave in the material cosmos; but we can gain no understanding whatever of its peculiar nature by observing and analysing the data and regularities of the physical world and the events it displays.

2. The Primacy of the Evaluative and Contemplative as Against the Deontic and Practical Emphasis

Another consideration similarly appears to favour a subordination of the moral to the aesthetical. In some important sense our receptive and responsive way of being definitely precedes and underlies our properly elective and practical acts. *A* pleases us and *B* displeases us, or *A* pleases us more or displeases us less than *B*: 'therefore', or at any rate consecutively upon this, other things being equal, we choose *A* and reject *B*. To be sure, 'other things' are rarely 'equal'; and this provides space for our complex and subtle deliberations, our *liberum arbitrium indifferentiae*, our taking 'calculated risks' and sometimes our acting 'at random'. But in principle we 'first' sense, perceive, know, imagine and evaluate, and 'then' decide, bring ourself to act, and make or urge others to act. Goethe's Faustian *Im Anfang war die Tat* and Fichte's primal concept (much more consistently fitting in with his outlook on life than Goethe's phrase) of *Tathandlung* turn things upside down and put the cart before the horse. Perhaps this seems to me the more evident as, like the 'great' Fichte's better son Immanuel Hermann Fichte, I entertain a theistic view of the world and am thus inclined to conceive of men as creatures, children and guests of God, receptive in the first place and only secondarily active and 'creative'; but my thesis by no means logically depends on belief in the existence of the Deity. I do not know how far and in what manner Napoleon held such a belief, and in the passage I am going to quote he certainly did not refer to God or to 'Providence' (so frequently invoked by a more recent emulator of his ambitions); but I do know that he could hardly be accused of unduly passive, contemplative and sedentary proclivities. Yet in a letter sent from the boat that carried him to Egypt, which he intended to conquer, he wrote:

8

Brutus est un esprit médiocre, il croit à la force de la volonté. Un homme supérieur n'a pas cette illusion: il voit la nécessité qui le borne, il ne s'y brise pas. Être grand, c'est dépendre de tout. Pour ma part, je dépends des évènements, dont un rien décide.

(Instead of sending this great man into unfruitful exile, I would have tried to persuade him to accept a professorship of Philosophy in a Scottish university.)

Seen in a biological perspective, it is true, we are born with various urges and wants which undoubtedly *condition* our likes and dislikes. But on the mental level our likes and dislikes precede, stimulate and selectively engender not only our willing but even our wishing and desiring. To use scholastic jargon once more, *amor complacentiae* is prior to *amor concupiscentiae*, and all the more to *amor benevolentiae*. (And while for the Christian *odium inimicitiae*, i.e. hatred proper or ill-wishing, is declared to be sinful as such, *odium abominationis*, i.e. dislike however vehement, is *not*— it may be sinful in as much as it perversely responds to *good* qualities in others.) Where is the lover who does not love his beloved because he *finds her lovely*, but just registers that he has fallen in love with her and thereupon 'decides' that she must be lovely, as it were appoints her to be lovely; nay, 'means' by her loveliness the fact of his being in love with her? Such subjectivistic paradoxes may be popular among sham-educated amateur (or professional) psychologists; they play ducks and drakes with reality and presuppose a sovereign indifference to what is actually the case. Of course I do not deny that *secondarily*, once the unfortunate man *is* in love, he will very likely tend to detect more and more traits of loveliness in the woman who has bewitched him; it is natural for love—by no means only for sexual love—to *overestimate* its object. But that does not mean that the lover does not first of all *estimate* and *appreciate* it.

Very cautiously, well aware of indulging in tentative simplification, we might then suggest that aesthetic value experience, pervading the whole of experience more universally and embodying a more primal mode of experience, is prior to moral and a precondition to it; whereas moral experience definitely is *not* a precondition to aesthetical. For, as emphasized above, the *core* of moral experience is certainly deontic or 'obligational', 'normative' or 'prescriptive/prohibitive', less closely related to the contemplative attitude and more intimately enmeshed in the machinery and the problem-world of *practice*. On *this* side too the ethical theme is confined to a more limited section of the whole. Professor Nowell-Smith has luminously exposed that we could at least *conceive* of a life in which there were goals but no duties, yet hardly even conceive of a world in which duties subsisted without any telic framework. Somewhat analogously to this we could more easily imagine a sort of utopia in which no moral tensions, rules and categories existed than one from which greater and lesser degrees of beauty, and also disappointment aroused by lack of beauty, were absent while consciousness and perhaps conscience were to survive in it.

Herbart, a most acute and perceptive, and undeservedly forgotten, analytical and 'realistic' German thinker of the early Victorian age, propounded a schema for the interpretation of moral categories in terms of the aesthetically pleasing and unpleasing, which, if somewhat artificial and not altogether convincing, is far from appearing nonsensical. Hume, whose ethics compounds a utilitarian perspective with that of consensual intuitionism, also injects an aesthetical element into his ethical thought; indeed, he goes so far as to raise the odd-sounding question 'Why Utility is pleasing'. But even philosophers so obsessed with the experience of duty as Kant or Prichard were did not attempt to account for the aesthetic in terms of the moral. The highly gifted but crude and half-crazy thinker Otto Weininger, a Viennese Jew who wrote at the turn of the century, did assert, though, that woman, being essentially amoral, couldn't be even beautiful; his conclusion, albeit not his argument, derived from Schopenhauer, one of his masters. (The poor fellow, like Schopenhauer, suffered from a robust and irrepressible heterosexual instinct but, unlike Schopenhauer, from no overdose of practical common sense; about a year after taking his Ph.D. degree he shot himself. He saw in woman not so much *laqueus diaboli* or the incarnation of evil as 'the incarnation of the guilt of *man*'.) I am well aware that it is not for nothing that we speak of an 'artistic *ethos*', e.g. that we incline not only to contemn pretentious trash aesthetically but to condemn it morally. But who, within the boundaries of sanity, would identify the great artist with the particularly virtuous person or, worse, pretend to perceive in the colour and the scent of a rose or the sweet rush of a silvan brook the expression of a moral quality?

Nevertheless I would warn against oversimplifying matters, and insist on the 'autonomy' of the moral in relation with the aesthetical as well as with the practical. If evaluative and contemplative attitudes are more tightly bound up with aesthetical, and deontic and agential attitudes with moral experience—the former being somehow prior to the latter—the co-ordination is far from being unequivocal. We come to be *moral* beings not so much by deliberating (or being told) 'what we should do' as by appraising—commending and condemning—the conduct of others and the intentions that seem to have informed it, and, more definitely and penetratingly, *kinds* of conduct and intention whose appraisal we cannot but apply to our own past behaviour and tentative projects, i.e. by developing an accusing, warning and demanding *conscience*. (This happens, of course, to a large extent under guidance and pressure from outside.) But from the outset these reflective appraisals, prior to directly action-compelling 'obligations', are distinctively *moral*, even though a discreet note of the aesthetical may adhere to them. It was, I think, a mistake on the part of Prichard, repeated by Ross (less bluntly) particularly in his earlier book, to start from a primal experience of 'obligation', to identify 'obligation' with 'the right' and to separate 'the right' in a somewhat artificial and forced manner from 'the good'. Again, if man *qua* moral being is an appraiser even more fundamentally than an agent, man *qua* aesthetical being *may* be an appraiser only; but on the whole he is not only an appraiser but also an *artist*, a 'creative' (or 're-creative') *maker*, and that means a kind of *doer* beyond *mere* contemplation and evaluation. (We may count in of course the craftsman, the gardener, the breeder or 'fancier', the city-planner and the 'maecenas'.) The analysis must be broken off at this point; I hope to have established so far a balance, slightly to the advantage of the aesthetic as the more primal and basic sentiment.

3. *The Contrast Concerning Reality, Taste and Style*

In the preceding argument I omitted to mention that there is also such a thing as aesthetic 'criteria' and 'canons', as well as artistic 'rules'. An unbiased mind, however, neither obsessed with a set of particular aesthetic dogmas or predilections nor sunk in the morass of ethical relativism, will immediately descry a neat, indeed a shrieking contrast between aesthetic and moral 'criteria', 'principles' or 'rules'. Let us for a moment—we might do worse—accept the Ten Commandments as the paradigm of a moral code: no one will be able to point to an even remotely analogous 'code' in the field of aesthetic valuation or artistic creation. But we need not abide by the Decalogue: purge it of its religious and historical preamble (together with its veto on 'idolatrous' representative art) and its repetitive phrasings, expand its all too vague or narrow modes of expression ('Thou shalt not commit adultery', which is too narrow, probably meant in the original 'Thou shall not commit lust', which sounds too vague), add to it a more Christian or more humanistic and up-to-date set of injunctions directed towards charity, self-criticism and rationality or responsibility and fuse it with the Greek cardinal virtues or any more modern extensions of moral subtlety and sensitivity. A moral code thus revised and amplified will perhaps lack the monumental compactness and majesty of the Ten Commandments but would otherwise mark a great improvement of it and satisfy many or most of us more fully, although no two men would construct the new 'perfected' code in exactly the same manner. You may, on the other hand, also try to compress the Commandments into a more concise and more evidently coherent set of abstract principles. Neither attempt will conjure up the vision of an aesthetical counterpart any more than does the Decalogue itself. We shall continue distinguishing between the beautiful and the ugly, between great art or successful artistic achievement and trashy imitations, lame dilettantism or forced and unavailing simulacra of originality, intensity or overall 'perfection'; but all such distinctions will appeal directly to effect, impact and *aisthesis* as such rather than repose on established criteria, and if they evoke reasoned discussion, it will lean upon *ad hoc* arguments however ingenious, impressive and sometimes convincing. In spite of some marginal truths we may incontestably find in the teaching of ethical relativism, historicism, evolutionism, etc., and in spite of aesthetic argument being possible and by no means *a limine* pointless, ethical valuations somehow decisively surpass aesthetical as regards their tenor of objectivity and their claim to perennial durability. Correspondingly such aspects as style, distinctive taste, successive fashions, 'creative' or 'degenerate' innovations, profound variations of genuine experience, and extrinsic philosophemes such as '*Tout genre est permis, hors le genre ennuyeux*' have played and will always play an incomparably more important part in the aesthetical than in the ethical field. If a man tells me that 'classic' or Renaissance architecture is immensely superior to Romanesque and early Gothic, that Shaw's plays are greater than Ibsen's, or that Mengs was a painter towering high above Cézanne, Van Gogh, Nolde or Munch, I feel 'shocked'; if a man tells me that there is nothing wrong with deceit or promiscuity and nothing particularly good about self-control or altruism, or that the butcheries and the mental corruption perpetrated by the Totalitarian dictators are fully justified by their dedication to vast projects and comprehensive ideals, I likewise feel 'shocked'—but though the word is correctly used in both cases, the tint and substance of my feeling 'shocked' are highly different. A feeling of rank absurdity is equally present in both, though more intense in the face of the second type. But perhaps I may best put it briefly in these terms: in my first kind of reaction the sense of a gulf of alienness predominates, whereas in the second it is the sense of being challenged and outraged, and of having entered into a situation of implacable conflict—a sense of *ceci tuera cela*. In the first case I feel overwhelmed and disconcerted by the immeasurable and incomprehensible vastness and chaotic manifoldness of the world; in the second virtually speaking lethally threatened and as it were transpierced by its pin-point narrowness and unevadable stringency. No doubt the contrast *partly* springs from the fact that while social peace, co-existence and co-operation by no means *define* morality, they *depend* on moral incomparably more than on aesthetical consensus. For divergent and even mutually disharmonious contemplations can thrive side by side very much more easily than mutually clashing maxims of action and thus even contradictory evaluations of kinds of conduct.

What I have tried to establish here should not be distorted into some such simplified picture as that aesthetic valuations are 'subjective' and moral valuations 'objective'. If extra-moral goods and concerns, desires and interests, etc., did not exist, moral values would make no sense at all; again, our moral 'glimpses' of a situation or a character are *de facto* sometimes swiftly and directly intuitive, inspired by an unanalysed emotive attitude, not so far supported by any cogent argument—and yet substantially correct. On the other hand the expert or even the more reflective sort of man will habitually, and often very keenly, distinguish between what he holds to be 'beautiful' (or 'good' as a work of art) and what peculiarly enchants and prepossesses *him*, i.e. be on his guard against automatically erecting his *taste* into (his) *judgement*. I submit that even quite ordinary people do not fall into the error of confusing 'beautiful' and 'what pleases them' *invariably* and *consistently*: that is, they are inconsistently and fitfully, unreliably but yet essentially, aware of the distinction. The same ordinary man will on one occasion call a girl 'beautiful' or 'lovely' simply because her appearance and demeanour exactly answer his erotic predilections, but on another occasion quite naturally utter the phrase: 'She is a very beautiful girl but not "my type" at all.'

To round off this set of considerations I would refer here approvingly, but pushing it one step further, to Professor Hare's famous 'two apparently altogether similar paintings' argument against Moore's infelicitous (and later strongly modified if not abandoned) theory of 'good', in the sense of simply and absolutely valuable, as an independent and straightforwardly perceived primary quality comparable to 'yellow'. Hare rightly insists that a differential evaluation of two similar objects *must* be tied to *some* element of *descriptive* dissimilarity between their features. Suppose, overriding the Leibnizian axiom of *identitas indiscernibilium*, that two paintings, distinct in the sense of individuated—one perhaps a supremely cleverly executed copy of the other—are seen side by side: can the spectator find them to be of unequal value to the point perhaps of calling one of them 'good' and the other 'not good'? This is plainly impossible. (We must of course assume that the man is not cognisant of the irrelevant historical circumstances that the painting, say, to his left is, for example, an authentic Rembrandt or Gainsborough and the other its copy.) Either *no* inequality of value, much less a contrast between 'good' and 'not good', is perceived by the spectator, or there *is* some descriptive, 'featural' difference, perhaps barely perceptible yet perceptible to a keen vision, and *that* somehow underlies a different, perhaps decisively different, evaluative impression. 'Good' and 'not good' or even 'less good' cannot be the *only* difference; it must be 'consequent upon' a sizeable, tangible difference describable in non-evaluative terms. This is, I trust, a fair rendering in my own words of Hare's train of argument, which, I hold to be unanswerably cogent. But let us now compare this with an analogous problem in *moral* appraisal. In apparently identical circumstances two men, say Jones and Smith, have behaved in apparently identical ways; for example, both have kept a serious promise regardless of the definitely and similarly undesirable—and equally foreseeable—public consequences of their respective acts (coincident in time but completely independent of each other). Now can I, an 'impartial spectator' in no wise connected either with Jones or with Smith, in the same breath (i.e. the factor of changing convictions or alternating moods being likewise excluded) judge that Jones has acted rightly and Smith wrongly (or the inverse)? Plainly not. Either I am secretly, perhaps half-consciously, swayed by *some* preference for one or aversion to the other agent, in which case I am *not* a truly impartial spectator and my 'moral appraisal' is disingenuous, adulterated and illegitimate; or else I *am* aware of *some* difference in the circumstances (e.g. a more or less well-founded suspicion that one of the two men has kept his promise from a sort of automatic, hidebound legalism, while the other has painstakingly deliberated and pondered the matter until his conscience arrived at the conclusion that the evident duty of promise-keeping could not in this case be invalidated by the foreseeable harmful result, etc.), and this contradicts the initial supposition of the two acts and their respective circumstances being descriptively identical. That is to say that in the case of moral appraisal Hare's argument applies, in some sense, *more rigorously* than it does to his own aesthetical example. For it is extremely hard to imagine that the moral appraiser should, say, praise Jones for his action and at the same time blame Smith for his (relevantly) identical action, or even praise Jones heartily and Smith no more than half-heartedly, without being able to say *what* was right about Jones's action and wrong about Smith's or *why* he is inclined to accord a more unstinted praise to Jones than to Smith. He may express it clumsily or inaccurately but he will point to the essential difference he sees between the two apparently identical acts. If he just says 'I don't know' or in any other fashion shrugs away the *onus probandi*, he exposes himself—unless he is exceptionally stupid and inarticulate—to the well-founded suspicion of being partial and 'interested', i.e. of being pro-Jones or anti-Smith from some (very likely non-moral) motive irrelevant to the matter, and of his utterance being a fake-moral disguise for the expression, on this occasion, of his biased attitude. As for the evaluative comparison between two quasi-identical paintings, the situation is markedly different. Even the art expert may at first sight find only that 'although they seem to be exact likenesses of each other, *this* is much superior to *that*'. It may take him some time to detect the subtle descriptive nuance or nuances that make the two paintings really *not* identical, and he may have considerable difficulty in subsuming the descriptive differences under some general and arguable aesthetical principles or testing them by some known and more or less widely accepted aesthetical criteria. The non-expert, like the present writer, may rest content with saying '. . . and yet I much prefer *this* to *that*, heaven knows why' or 'There *must* be some difference in the pattern of shapes or the shade of colours, but I can't find it' or again, perhaps 'This slightly broader yellow stripe and slightly narrower blue patch is what evokes *in this case* a so much more vivid impression: but *why?*— you should ask an expert'. Perhaps we might indeed put it in the words that to be an expert on art and beauty is a specialized profession or that to be expert in this domain is a special quality which only a minority of people are fortunate enough to possess, whereas a fair degree of moral 'expertise' is *demanded* of every one of us. Anyhow, while aesthetic valuation is more universal than moral in that it extends to an incomparably vaster range of objects, it is most definitely, inalterably and on principle less dependent on universalizability.

4. *The Unequal Thematic Primacy of Values and Disvalues*

It is a fact consonant with our foregoing considerations of the contrast we are dealing with that men's attention is turned primarily to beauty rather than to ugliness but to moral evil rather than to moral goodness. Our primal aesthetical experience is, I suggest, a response of enchantment to 'beauty' (in a very wide sense of the term, of course); our primal moral experience is indignation at wrong—transferred and deepened to assent to the pressure of duty. Thus bluntly put the thesis may sound arbitrarily selective and overemphatic to many. The objector is likely to point to the frequent occurrence of positively ugly, dreary, repulsive and nauseating sights of objects with which we cannot always escape contact at will; on the other hand he will point to morally praise-worthy and even admirable conduct which is far above the merely irreproachable. I must admit the force of both objections; and, as I still think that I have in mind something real and valid, I must seek to qualify my phrasing. I shall say that we somehow experience beauty as a gratuitous and superabundant gift and ugliness as something we may at least often easily or with comparatively little effort remove from our ken; whereas we feel not only disturbed but defied by moral evil in others and oppressed by our own sense of guilt; again, that we tend to praise and even to admire constant and enduring duty-fulfilment while any single act of duty-fulfilment *as such* appears to be no more than 'irreproachable' (except in the face of what to most of us would constitute an exceptionally strong temptation). And whenever our heart goes out in enthusiasm to an act of gratuitous self-abnegation and generosity, the *absence* of which could in no way be censured as condemnable or even blameworthy, our moral admiration—without ceasing to be such—will take on a slightly *aesthetical* tinge: it is then that we speak of not merely 'good' but of peculiarly 'noble' and quite explicitly of 'beautiful' behaviour.

To note that the core of morality is 'deontic' or 'obligational' or 'imperative' is after all but to echo a securely established—and often overstated—truism; though people do not always realize that this means a *thematic* primacy of the *infringement* of duty, which is more conspicuous than the fulfilment of it, and, in general and on principle at least, raises the problem of 'retribution' or 'punishment'—which is not on a par with 'compensation'. Salaries, bonuses, prizes, distinctions, fame, etc., are accorded not in general as a recompense for duty-fulfilment as such but for services and accomplishments into which a moral component usually enters in different forms and measures but which are primarily required for their utility or appreciated and admired for their intellectual, aesthetical or 'practical'—'political'—rather than for their moral value. As F. T. Vischer, a German writer in the last century—significantly enough, chiefly devoted to aesthetics—put it with some simplifying exaggeration, *Das Moralische versteht sich immer von selbst*: 'Morality is a matter of self-evidence.'

It is characteristic for beauty in general and for artistic excellence in particular that it is *not* a matter of self-evidence. People did not say before, e.g. the rise of Shakespeare or of Beethoven: 'Now it is time for Shakespeare to emerge' or: 'Beethoven cannot tarry any longer—it would be outrageous if he did.' Those who do entertain beliefs, not indeed to that extent preposterous but conceived in a similar vein, such as that the rise of artistic geniuses largely depends on security and prosperity, the amounts spent on museums, art schools, faculties of letters, art scholarships and the like, think—to put it most flatteringly—in terms of culture or of history of civilization, not in aesthetical terms. I do not mean that artistic creation, like most human accomplishments, demands no effort, dedication, bitter self-sacrifice and even perhaps habits of self-discipline and regularity. But when Goethe said *Genie ist Fleisz*, he surely did not seriously mean that mountains of industry can produce so much as an atom of genius; he very likely meant what I think is perfectly true: that in contrast with mere *das Genialische*, velleities and moods of 'feeling a genius', authentic genius *compels* industry, and that the belief in great artistic creation being a mere effortless pleasure is a 'bohemian' myth.

5. The 'Non-existential' Character of the Aesthetic

The dimension of *urgency* inherent in deontic morality, somehow analogous with that of survival (as symbolized by the Christian concept of 'mortal sin'), strikingly contrasts with the valuational mode of aesthetic experience. The great Meinong in his fourfold division of the basic types of valuation, or types of 'goodness' as he called them, assigns the aesthetical to the category of *Vorstellungsinhaltsgefühle*, i.e. feelings that attach to *presentational contents*. (Pleasure-feelings for him are linked to 'presentational acts'; we might also say to the experience of agreeable objects with the emphasis placed on the pleasant condition of the experiencing subject; feelings of cognitive satisfaction are linked to 'acts of judgement', the quality of the object being *per se* indifferent; and what he calls 'values' proper, I think in the main moral and otherwise 'practical', e.g. welfare values, form the objects of 'contents of judgement'.) Professor Findlay, who—though this is far from exhausting his significance as a philosopher—is, I suppose, the greatest living Meinongian, has developed this interpretation of the aesthetic into a thesis affirming its 'non-existential' character. The phrase may be somewhat obscure and perhaps slightly misleading, but it seems to me to express a profound truth, and feeling at a loss to discover a pregnant and more neatly intelligible term, I will try to expose its point as I understand it. 'Content' should be taken here as contrasting not so much with 'object', in the sense of a subjectivistic emphasis on, say, 'emotion', as with 'state of affairs' or 'being-the-case' (*Sachverhalt*, in Meinong's language *Objektiv*).

Beauty or aesthetic excellence *is* of course predicated of objects, including works of art, but does not depend on something being or not being actually the case. Thus we may aesthetically enjoy the mellow grace and sweet tenderness of cats *regardless* of their being also nasty beasts of prey, a *fact* we *overlook* in our enchantment, and similar aesthetic attitudes are likewise possible though less sustainable in regard to human beings; that the moral *Either-Or* was alien to the aesthetic mode of experience was probably the most valid and fruitful of Kierkegaard's thoughts. Again, the picture of some personage in a novel may be of supreme excellence independently of whether any such person ever has really existed; indeed, a figure 'faithfully modelled' on a person who has actually existed is likely to be second-rate and less 'living' in the novel. Some arts are by their nature 'un-representative', and various distortions and poetic licences may enhance rather than diminish the expressiveness of a 'representative' work of art. 'That long-ago place', which is not grammatically possible English, is I think one of the most marvellous phrases in Hardy's poetry; to be sure, it could not very well have flown from the pen of a person with an inadequate command of English, just as the most impressive and expressive 'misdrawings' and 'disproportions' in early twentieth-century painting could not have been produced by persons who didn't know how to draw. Inverisimilitude as such is anything but a guarantee of high art. Moreover beautiful and enthralling sights —as well as sounds, odours, tastes and tactile surfaces—exist in wild nature and in nature wrought upon by artistic craftsmanship; nor would it do to say that the objects exist but their aesthetic qualities are merely superimposed by arbitrary subjective fantasy or 'empathy'. That is why there is *something* misleading about the term 'non-existential'. It is hardly necessary to remark that beauty and art, like anything else, only make sense in an 'existential', a 'mundane' *framework*. (Even entities 'ideal' in a far stricter sense, such as numbers, including fractions, irrational numbers, transcendental numbers and imaginary numbers, etc., would make no sense in a world in which denumerable and divisible individuals did not exist.) Yet for a moment I shall just grant the objection and go on to extend, in one sense, the concept of relative 'non-existentiality'.

At the time of the First World War I was an adolescent boy in Budapest. Although passionately and integrally pro-Ally—that is, at odds with my environment—I could not repress a smile when (in 1915) reading in a comparatively sensible local newspaper article, which mildly protested against the excesses of cultural chauvinism, the phrase: 'After all, we cannot dispense with the spiritual treasures of a Dostoyevsky or an Anatole France.' What we cannot dispense with, I thought, was the victory of the Allies; the spiritual treasures of a Dostoyevsky or an Anatole France (the pairing, accidental and time-conditioned, did not yet suffice at that epoch to throw me into fits of laughter) we could dispense with if need were. Today I would say that the anxiety and zeal of the culture-builder or the guardian and collector of works of art, though surely *per se* necessary rather than despicable, are fairly different and only obliquely related to aesthetic experience; and that their objects, major and minor alike (as coupled in the quoted example) lack the existential *weight* of the 'indispensable', the imperative and the decisive. No iconoclastic tendency whatever makes me think so, but simply the consideration that in a world from which a thousand canonical objects of aesthetic, including artistic, appreciations were absent a lavish abundance of such objects would still exist, and perhaps some that were superior to all those we know of. Whereas if children starve somewhere or epidemics flourish from lack of adequate means to cope with them, if tyranny rages unchecked, or if I tell a boastful lie or wantonly betray a trust, these are things which imperiously demand remedy, or such compensation as it may be possible to make for them. In some way, then, which I admit I can but very imperfectly express, aesthetical values are 'non-existential' in that they, by no means unrelated to or outside existence, 'hang loosely' on it or sit lightly to it. However embodied in singular concrete objects, they escape the existential 'responsibility', as it were, that attaches to values and problems of welfare and of morality: to Praxis in the wider sense of the word. This is not a matter of inferiority but of some kind of incommensurability. If certain churches or certain regions or street corners in certain cities I peculiarly admire and love did not exist, it 'wouldn't make much difference'. Yet it is in their contemplation and tangible nearness, undoubtedly an *aesthetic* experience, that I seem somehow to become aware of the ineffable goodness of existence more deeply and vividly than in any experience of benefit or thriving, and even of moral virtue.

Forgiveness

Forgiveness is pre-eminently an ethical subject, and a paper written about it cannot help being a paper in Ethics. It need not therefore be sermonizing, which I wish to avoid in the highest possible measure (either with a 'soft' or with a 'hard' emphasis); it may well be properly philosophical, conceptual and analytical, as I intend it to be. In fact, I intend it to be chiefly *logical* in nature: the *central* question I wish to discuss is not how far and in what sense forgiveness is commendable or perhaps objectionable, but whether, and if so in what manner, it is logically *possible* at all. In Section 2, then, the core of my paper, I shall expose what I call the Logical Paradoxy of Forgiveness; this I preface in Section 1 with a straightforward analysis and delimitation of the concept, and finally in Section 3 I shall try to show that the paradoxy can to some extent be solved by a more subtle version of the 'rigorous' logical analysis implied and that something at any rate of the idea of Forgiveness remains tenable. The question is of obvious ethical significance, for the value—and possible disvalue— attaching to Forgiveness has, in spite of the Christian tinge of the concept, engaged and is worthy of engaging the interest of moralists, Christian and non-Christian of various shades.

1. DELIMITATION OF THE CONCEPT

1. *The interpersonal context. Introduction of 'Fred' and 'Ralph'*

Forgiveness primordially refers to a context of 'interpersonal' relations, in the narrower sense of relations between two parties 'on a footing of equality', neither of them being the other's 'superior' or having 'authority' over him. It presupposes an affront, injury, transgression, trespassing or offence committed by one person against the other and consequently the other's readiness or refusal to 'forgive' him. It is not of course excluded that the two parties should in some respects be unequal or that either of them should in some sense stand for certain collective interests or points of view. But I would rather steer clear of such complications, and that is what I mean by restricting myself to an interpersonal context. For clarity's and brevity's sake, I will call the supposed offender, i.e. the party who inflicts a wrong, 'Ralph' (phonetically alliterating to 'Wrong'), and the one who is or feels 'wronged' and feels inclined or reluctant to forgive, 'Fred' (alliterating to 'Forgive'). 'I' or 'myself' are to mean in this paper, not the offender or person who forgives or refuses to do so, but only the writer as expressing an opinion or trying to apply an argument.

2. *Hurting, Wrongdoing and 'Wronging'*

In biblical language, we hear a great deal about its being commendable to forgive 'our enemies', 'those who trespass against us', and 'sinners', as if these things meant one and the same thing. Yet the three concepts have sharply different meanings, though of course in the given circumstances they may coincide. A person may behave towards another as an adversary, or in a way displeasing him or with foreseeable harmful consequences to him, yet his conduct may be wholly defensible or indeed justified, perhaps *the* right action in the given case. For example, he may point out the other's errors in a discussion, justly assign to a third party a post also coveted by the first, confer some other selective privilege on a third person instead of on the first, and the like. The person thus combated or 'left out' or 'harmed' may nurse feelings of revenge, but that is simply a moral defect on *his* part, and if he has no such feelings or laudably suppresses them that is not 'forgiveness' but only normal behaviour which conforms to his strict *duty*. (And further, if he in the sequel tries to refute what *he* believes to be faulty in his adversary's arguments, or tends to keep aloof from the person who apparently does not greatly appreciate him, that *again* is normal behaviour and not vindictiveness.) On the other hand, if Ralph commits moral transgressions which do not infringe Fred's rights and are not even indirectly calculated to hurt Fred, again Fred is not strictly speaking the victim of an offence and the question of his forgiving or not forgiving does not properly arise. Here I felt compelled, though, to use qualifications like 'strictly speaking' and 'properly'. For, although by supposition it is not part of Fred's office to punish Ralph's sins, he may well feel indignant about them and in some sense hurt by them and thus inclined to 'cut' Ralph henceforth; in cases relevant to the criminal law it might also be his duty to denounce Ralph to the proper authorities and testify against him in court. If Ralph commits his iniquities as it were 'in Fred's sight', or boasts about them to Fred, that may actually make him an offender *in relation to Fred*. However, the classic case of 'trespassing against' and thus raising the

problem of forgiveness consists in Ralph's hurting *Fred* illegitimately and behaving immorally *towards* Fred. The previous
example is only a less direct variant of this. The standard type,
then, is that of Ralph's *inflicting wrong upon* Fred: briefly, *wronging* him. Historically speaking, the biblical phraseology seems to
take for granted a social medium in which *vindictiveness* was rampant and people tended to identify it with *retribution*. Whereas in
fact vindictiveness is itself a damnable vice, the retributive attitude
as such is nothing but the correct primary response to immoral
conduct as such, and above all to 'wronging', i.e. immoral conduct
specifically hurtful or offensive to the person 'concerned', the
primary claimant to retribution.

The vindictive person as such cannot properly 'forgive'; he can
only, and ought to, overcome his own vindictiveness and, if he did
feel originally any indignation, not mere frustration or even anger,
come to understand that his indignation was baseless—itself a *false*
response to disappointing but in no way wrongful behaviour.
Punishment, on the other hand, is quite outside our context: it can
only be inflicted by the proper legal or administrative authority
(maiming or killing an aggressor in self-defence is not punishment,
however justified); and though it necessarily presupposes retribution it no less essentially includes other important goals such as
deterrence, the securing of social peace and order, and possibly
reform. 'Pardon' in the English sense (German *Begnadigung*) may
or may not connote acts of 'forgiveness' on the relevant authorities'
part.

3. *Forgiveness as distinct from Non-Imputation or Indifference, Exculpation, Remission, and Reconciliation or Atonement*

Non-imputation, indifference and exculpation or 'excusing'
mean forms of 'not taking offence' where offence might *prima facie*
be taken. They are somehow similar or akin to forgiveness but
differ from it in that they omit to actualize the primary indignation
and retributive attitude. They typically, though by no means
always, refer to matters of slight importance. While forgiveness
digs deep into its object before it sets aside indignation and
cancels the retributive attitude, the above-named acts *a limine*
'look away from', or 'shove aside', the wrong in question. Non-
imputation or indifference may be due to Fred's own amoralistic
world-view (coupled with his not being gravely harmed or
humiliated); exculpation and excusing also 'minimize' the guilt
incurred by the offender but with a stronger emphasis on (putative) 'explanation', linked to Fred's taking the position that Ralph's
wrongdoing or insult is not worth a quarrel with him. 'Excusing'

in the second Austinian sense of 'not finding guilty at all' is of course a much more above-board act and is absolutely unrelated to the problem of forgiveness.

French is poorer in this respect than English; its equivalent for 'forgive' is simply *pardonner*, whereas in English 'to pardon' is a legal or quasi-legal act of authority, though in colloquial English and in reference to superficial matters we also say 'Pardon me' or 'Excuse me', not 'Forgive me'. In German, 'forgive' means *verzeihen* (noun *Verzeihung*), which would literally mean 'dis-accuse', i.e. 'excuse'. On the contrary, the literal translation of German *vergeben* (noun *Vergebung*) would be 'forgive' and 'forgiveness', but in actual usage it means 'remission', which can only be granted by God and has its place exclusively in a religious context. 'Reconciliation' is likely to be largely based on forgiveness but it emphasizes the *result*, not the essence, of forgiveness; and is a *reciprocal* return of Fred and Ralph to friendly relations, not a one-sided change of Fred's attitude to Ralph. It can occur that forgiveness is not *accepted*, in which case no reconciliation ensues. The form of reconciliation, called in English 'atonement', is again a purely religious category: it means a restoration of (sinful) man's 'being at one' with God, and presupposes 'penitence' or 'penance' ('atoning for'), which belong to religious language alone.

4. *Forgiveness as distinct from 'Emotional Prescription' and from Revised Insight or Judgement*

'Emotional Prescription', the noun being patterned on its legal sense (German *Verjährung*, as it were 'superannuation') means something akin to non-imputation or indifference but is closer to forgiveness in that it postulates 'a long lapse of time' in the course of which the wound ceases to smart and the original indignation and retributive attitude come to be toned down and finally to vanish, fading away without any (even purely mental) explicit act of forgiveness. Not so, revised insight and revised judgement, whose similarity to forgiveness is purely external and which really mean something totally different. Revised insight means that Fred comes to discover or believe that Ralph's apparent offence has not in reality taken place at all: that he, Fred, had owing to intrigues or deceptive appearances credited a slanderous statement or insinuation or suspicion concerning Ralph's behaviour. Revised judgement means that Fred has in time changed some of *his* moral beliefs and no longer holds that the thing Ralph actually did do was *wrong*. In either case, Fred may perhaps *repent* and then, rather than forgiving Ralph, may ask Ralph to forgive *him*. Some such cases *may*

cast discredit on Fred's rash judgement or his gullibility, or indeed
his own increasing moral looseness or lack of moral principle.

2. THE LOGICAL PARADOXY OF FORGIVENESS

1. *Forgiveness as distinct from Condonation*

Condonation means that Fred is clearly aware of Ralph's
wrongdoing, insult, offence or viciousness and *per se* disapproves
of it but deliberately refrains from any retributive response to it.
He may do so from appreciation of Ralph's merits or virtues in
other respects (cf. the maxim 'You cannot apply ordinary moral
standards to an artistic genius'), from his proneness to tolerate the
'weaknesses proper to human nature' (cf. psychological sophistries
like *Tout comprendre, c'est tout pardonner*, 'We were all young
once', or 'From his point of view, he is perhaps right'), or simply
out of a prudential interest he has in keeping on good terms with
Ralph. Condonation is fairly akin to 'emotional prescription' but is
not conditioned by the 'lapse of time' factor; it relates similarly to
'revised judgement'; it differs from 'indifference' and 'exculpation'
by Fred's being, as stated above, 'clearly aware of Ralph's offensive
conduct'. It is closest to 'finding excuses' for Ralph's conduct in
the one Austinian sense of absolving Ralph in virtue of 'mitigating
circumstances' as opposed to absolving him as 'not guilty', but it
is a more consciously decisional act and so far closer to a *simulacrum*
of forgiveness proper. But it sharply differs from forgiveness in that
it does not presuppose and nullify the original retributive position
but quasi-automatically 'loves' or 'cleaves to' the wrongdoer rather
than 'hating' the sin and placing the emphasis on ideally 'separat-
ing' it from the sinner. Rather than lazily or light-mindedly overlooking it, condonation *acquiesces* in the offence. Condonation is
thus virtually 'conniving' and immoralistic; in its graver forms, it
is not only undignified and self-soiling but also unfair in so far as
it may reveal that Fred is ready to put up with a starkly offending
Ralph while being perhaps mercilessly hard on a far more lightly
offending and possibly even repentant Robert. To condemn *all*
condonation might, however, amount to over-severity; for it seems
plausible that without condoning *some* faults we could not possibly
live together with others nor, for the matter of that, with ourself.
But, just as it is highly undesirable to live at peace with our own
misdeeds and vices, it is, generally speaking, also undesirable to
condone those of others, seeing that it similarly means silencing
and neutralizing the retributive attitude to moral disvalue even
where it particularly concerns us. It is well known that those who
practice submissive meekness before evil, and danegeld-paying to

aggressors and blackmailers often resort to gross or refined techniques of exculpation and also parade the 'sublime' tinge of forgiveness; the point need not be laboured. Thus condonation very
easily takes on the semblance of forgiveness and may therefore be
seen as constituting the first term of the *logical dilemma*: Forgiveness is objectionable and ungenuine inasmuch as there is *no reason
to forgive*, the offender having undergone no *metanoia* ('Change of
Heart') but persisting in his plain identity *qua* offender. The contrast lies between genuine forgiveness with its backbone of a
crystal-clear *pro* response to value and *con* response to disvalue on
the one hand and condonation with its innuendo of spineless
accompliceship, or 'compounding with' disvalue, on the other.

St Augustine's famous dictum 'Hate the sin, love the sinner' is
undoubtedly in focus here. 'Hate the sin' unambiguously precludes
outright cynical condonation; yet 'love the sinner', encouraging
unconditional and as it were instantaneous forgiveness, introduces
an element of ambiguity. It postulates a neat separability between
the sin and the sinner, which is fictitious, and insinuates a wholly
misleading analogy between wrongdoing and illness: in fact, the
sick man is afflicted with his disease, whereas Ralph inflicts a
wrong upon Fred. The Gospel itself often proclaims the special
value and love-worthiness of the *repentant* sinner: and does so not
without a hyperbolical emphasis, for the repentant sinner has a
plus-value over the originally and consistently virtuous person in a
'marginal utility' sense only, as illustrated by the example of the
poor widow who had ten groats, lost one and finally recovered it,
and feels somehow gladder to possess it than any one of the other
'nine'; in fact the 'tenth' groat is not worth any bit more than the
'first' or the 'fourth' or the 'ninth', it is only ten groats that are
worth more than nine. Sometimes, indeed, the Gospel even urges
us to 'love the sinner' without its being made clear whether he is a
repentant, and much less whether he is an efficaciously and endur-
ingly repentant sinner; nay, we are told to forgive and love the
relapsing sinner as well (this was what Tertullian's Montanist
heresy could not swallow). At the one end of its spectrum, then,
forgiveness threatens to collapse in condonation, which perhaps
may be sometimes necessary but is an intrinsically bad thing and
plainly at variance with the condemnation of wrong which appears
to be implicit in the genuine concept of forgiveness, an act supposed to contribute to the eradication of wrongdoing—the
'redemption' from sin—rather than to the fostering of it.

2. *Is Forgiveness a possible response to Change of Heart?*

At the other end of its spectrum, forgiveness seems to collapse in mere *redundancy*, or the mere *registering* of moral value in the place of previous disvalue. Suppose Ralph has clearly undergone a change of heart. He has revoked and disavowed the offence in point and effected a rupture with his past in the given context; he has credibly 'mended his ways', apologized in a manner unmistakably manifesting or firmly presaging such a turn, in an appropriate case has made restitution, and so on. Fred can—and, we may well say, ought to—change *his* attitude to Ralph *à fond*, that is give up and revoke radically his own retributive position. Unless he does so, he appears to be guilty of sheer vindictiveness. This responsible change in Fred's attitude *would* ordinarily be called forgiveness— the central and standard form of it. But is it? The objection arises that forgiveness has now lost its ground and *raison d'être*: that there is no room for it, seeing that *there is nothing to be forgiven*. If Fred, a sensible value-loving man and deeply fond of cats, learns that his friend Ralph, whom he has for many years known as likewise sensible, value-loving and always appreciative of cats, in his early youth repeatedly ill-treated cats, can he now 'forgive' him? When a sluggish debtor has at last paid his debt to his creditor with due apologies, the creditor can still in some—I think, fairly rare— circumstances sue him for compensation on account of *lucrum cessans/damnum emergens* but cannot generously, with a forgiving mind, decide *not* to sue him for payment of the debt which has already been paid. Suppose we formulate the moral principle: 'Respond to value wholeheartedly, condemn and shun disvalue; be grateful for kindness done to you and reciprocate it, retaliate (within the appropriate limits, without overstepping your rights and lapsing into vindictiveness, without disproportionate hostility) for malicious wrong suffered.' Is this not a self-sufficient maxim of interpersonal conduct, with no need to call in the paradoxical complication of 'forgiveness'? Either the wrong is still flourishing, the offence still subsisting: then by 'forgiving' you accept it and thus confirm it and make it worse; or the wrongdoer has suitably annulled and eliminated his offence, and then by harping on it further you would set up a new evil and by 'forgiving' you would only *acknowledge* the fact that you are no longer its victim. Briefly, forgiveness is either unjustified or pointless.

3. AN ATTEMPT TO SALVAGE THE CONCEPT OF FORGIVENESS FROM LOGICAL HAVOC

1. *The role of Degrees and Variants*

I suggest that, as is mostly the case, a careful differential approach offers a 'loop-hole for freedom', the promise of dissolving a rigid alternative. The 'Either-Or' expounded in Part 2 is too mechanical to do justice to the complexities of 'moral life' (i.e. the practice of life seen, as it *also* has to be seen, in a moral perspective). Ralph's 'wronging' Fred may argue very different kinds of attitudes towards Fred and very different forms, however objectionable, of Ralph's moral status. It may be an isolated and uncharacteristic act, episodic as it were, even though not confined to a single unrepeated occasion. It may, on the contrary, be thoroughly symptomatic of Ralph's basic attitude and ingrained character, even if confined so far to a single act or course of action. The classic distinction between the primitive, impulsive and uncontrolled type of behaviour ('incontinence', 'weakness of will') and the depraved ('intemperant', 'vicious') character is far from covering the whole field of possibilities as regards 'wrongdoing', to say nothing of the variety of attitudes that may underlie 'wronging'. Naive amorality is a quite different thing from succumbing to an overwhelming gust of passion; rough impulsiveness is not the same thing as being swept off one's feet by a rising wave of anger (whose intensity may be out of proportion with its slight amount of justification); again, a definite and limited vice may not betray a comprehensive *habitus* of immorality. Further, Ralph's excessive impatience with this or that salient feature of Fred's personality is entirely different from hostility hidden behind a mask of amity, and both from a gnawing resentment of which Ralph himself is but imperfectly conscious, which however may suddenly and unexpectedly break through to the surface; and it may also happen that a change in circumstances engenders an entirely new, perhaps narrowly limited yet passionate rivalry between the two friends.

In its turn, Fred's problem of deciding between putting up with Ralph's defects or ignoring his offensive gesture and turning his back on Ralph, relegating him to a world outside his own (an 'underworld' as it were), is a genuine one and bears most closely on the theme of forgiveness. It cannot be shown that it must be a matter of choosing between exculpation, leniency or cynical condonation and hard-hearted vengefulness. In a somehow similar way, the forgiveness felt and manifested by Fred may be unqualified, hearty and 'full-fledged'; while from its being hesitant, reserved and provisional we cannot securely infer that it is no genuine forgiveness at all but merely a matter of supine cowardice or astute practical expediency. In sum, there *may* be 'something to be forgiven' and yet forgiveness be granted that does *not* reduce to indifference to value and compounding with disvalue. Putting it differently, genuine forgiveness on Fred's part does not *necessarily* presuppose a dramatic and fundamental change of heart evinced by Ralph.[1]

2. *Forgiveness and the permanence of Guilt*

Forgiving is not only *not* 'forgetting'—in spite of the popular use of that metaphor carrying a cheap appeal of picturesque banality—but incompatible with forgetting; yet this massive distinction cuts both ways. On the one hand, it enables Fred to forgive Ralph even in some types of cases when Ralph has not undergone an obvious and credible change of heart; for the object of forgiveness is a subsistent guilt, not a guilt that (in the forgiver's eyes) has ceased to exist. One most important factor is of course Fred's impression and assessment of whether Ralph is engaged in an 'upward' movement or struggle or on the contrary is gliding down the slope; cf. the Schoolmen's *bonum progressionis* and *malum regressionis*, applied I think primarily to 'physical' good and evil. Fred's supine 'softness' or his unpleasing 'hardness' *might* be more ostensible than real and thus perhaps come to be misjudged by a third party, a censorious and insufficiently informed observer. It should also be noted that backsliding on Ralph's part, especially if repeated, casts suspicion on the genuineness of his incipient or hoped-for change of heart but does not exclude it; to forgive the sinner 'seven and seventy times' or forgive an offence again and again is not *necessarily* a sign of feeble-minded indifference or of an inveterate readiness for immoral condonation. Yet, at the other end of the spectrum, even an unmistakable genuine change of heart does not simply *undo* the offence committed and equate forgiveness to automatically 'forgetting' it as if it had never happened or, rather, as if the action that embodied it had not really been an offence. (When *this* occurs the person 'wronged', say Fred, has merely imagined himself to have been wronged, and there he indeed cannot 'forgive' but is obliged to clear the matter up and to tender to Ralph, not his forgiveness but his apologies.)

The fact remains that credible and perhaps 'proven' Change of Heart constitutes the standard occasion to exercise and show forgiveness; it may be argued that genuine change of heart, and it alone, tends to make forgiveness a 'duty'. The Ralph who has undergone this *metanoia* is in one sense no longer identical with

---

[1] For having won through to this admission—which is not congenial to my temper and still to some extent goes against the grain—I am mainly indebted to my conversation on Forgiveness about two years ago, with Mr Kenneth Cohen, then a postgraduate student at Bedford College, University of London. I need hardly say that I am alone responsible for the actual contents of this paper, with much of which Mr Cohen may disagree.

Ralph the offender *qua* offender, but in another sense he is still identical with the Ralph who committed the offence, for he is still Ralph, i.e. the same person; in English verbal idiom, he is the Ralph who *has committed* the offence. Hence there is still 'something to be forgiven' and an *act* of forgiveness on the wronged person's—Fred's—part is required in order to eliminate the offence from the texture of their relationship and in that sense to 'annul' it (while it cannot be undone in the sense of effecting its not having been committed). The present Ralph is not discontinuous with the Ralph who once 'wronged' Fred; our revoking, disavowing, regretting, condemning, repenting, etc., a past act of ours cannot, however decisively it may change our moral status, wish away our responsibility for that act. Fred's forgiving Ralph in such a case, however duty-like, is not a strict obligation like promise-keeping or even certain acts of benevolence, e.g. warning an innocent person of a danger that threatens him. Rather, it is still residually a 'free' act (in the sense of 'freedom from the law'). Fred *might* have legitimate reasons for persevering in merely cool and distant relations with Ralph: thus, Ralph's offence, though deprived of its sting by his change of heart, may at any rate have convinced Fred for good that Ralph, in view of his *dispositions* as a whole, is not the sort of person with whom it would be fit and fruitful for him to maintain a close association. A serious wound when healed leaves a scar behind; it cannot vanish to the point of *restitutio in integrum*. On the other hand, in some sense the 'scar' may prove to be tougher, more solid and resistant, than the intact tissue was. A quarrel 'made up' between friends may in some conditions make their relationship more fragile and vulnerable, but in other conditions make it deeper, more conscious and more valued mutually. It is only too natural to be on one's guard against relapse in a 'converted sinner'; yet it is also a commonplace that *some* 'reformed' poachers turn out to be the best gamekeepers.

3. *Forgiveness and the generous Venture of Trust*

Although Fred's act of forgiveness *may* both extinguish Ralph's hostility or malignancy towards *him* and provoke, promote or stabilize Ralph's moral *purification*, and although it very likely includes Fred's intention to bring about such an effect, the effect is far remote from being certain, and pursuing it as an aim is not the *essence* of forgiveness and by no means constitutes the moral value of forgiveness. Let me take these three points in order.

(*a*) If change of heart *has* indubitably occurred in Ralph, it is indeed highly probable that Fred's manifest forgiveness will exert on Ralph a favourable effect; it will sometimes render the change of heart more explicit, definitive and fruitful, and perhaps melt away the residuum of pride which has still prevented it from being entirely overt, explicit and complete. In cases of this nature, forgiveness is the best policy both in the moral and in the practical sense, though for reasons already stated I would still demur at recognizing it as a strict duty of Fred's; policy, including moral ('educative') policy is never codifiable into hard and fast rules with the same degree of generality as are primary, and especially prohibitive, moral principles themselves ("Thou shalt not swear falsely' and the like). If, on the other hand, Ralph's change of heart is doubtful or if indeed there is no sign of it at all, the reconciling or reforming effect of Fred's forgiveness is utterly dubious; indeed, instead of shaming Ralph into a change of heart calculated to deserve the anticipated forgiveness, it may easily irritate him, harden his resentment and hatred, and encourage him to persist in his line of wrongdoing with which he appears to have got away so cheaply. In such cases, forgiveness is plainly open to practical and even to moral objections; for to increase another person's wickedness, in a sense howsoever alien to complicity, is open to the charge of immorality. But even so, Fred's act may be true forgiveness as distinct from base or at any rate frivolous condonation; perhaps it reposes on an error of psychological judgement, in that Fred has underestimated Ralph's malice or depravity, or mistaken some of Ralph's further actions or attitudes, known to him, for signs of an approaching, though still only virtual, *metanoia*. In such cases, forgiveness, while it is genuine forgiveness, may be foolish, imprudent and objectionable, that is to say far from unequivocally virtuous, but it is still a noble and generous—not a vile or contemptible—attitude.

(*b*) That forgiveness is not a form of moralizing strategy is obvious from the fact that one may—though one need not—also forgive offending persons after their death, when forgiveness or its denial can no longer have any effect on their state of mind and their moral character. The anecdote about General Narváez, who (Prime Minister and semi-dictator of Spain for long periods during Isabel II's reign) on his death-bed in 1868 is said to have answered the priest's question whether he forgave his enemies 'I cannot: I have had all of them executed' does not appear to me authentic, unless perhaps Narváez still retained a grim sense of humour in his last moments. The statement itself was, as he must have known, blatantly false: his chief leftist enemies, who a few months after his demise were to lead the victorious revolution of 1868, were notoriously conspiring in London and Brussels; moreover, the Duke of Valencia, whether a staunch Catholic believer or not, cannot have ignored the fact that men of his faith believed in the survival of the soul and the possibility of our having different attitudes to dead persons. But even if I were perfectly certain that the soul dies with the body, I should see a meaning in, say, forgiving the misdeeds of Napoleon I but not those of Napoleon III, Frederick the Great's but not Hitler's, and so forth. I might also see a meaning in forgiving X, who has gratuitously 'wronged' me, without condoning his offence but also without hoping for an improvement of his character, and particularly for such a possible improvement being brought about by my forgiveness. The sin and the sinner are not separable but they are distinguishable, and this suffices for the *possibility* of one kind of forgiveness. It is possible to 're-accept' somebody—the essence of forgiveness—without exculpating him and without hoping for anything like a thorough-going repentance on his part. That at the same time we should *wish* for such a change of heart seems indeed to *belong* to the essence of forgiveness; but in a less emphatic sense it is a general moral duty to wish an improvement of everyone's defective character independently of whether or not he has in some way 'wronged *us*'.

(*c*) To hold that the moral value of forgiveness resides in its possible improving effect or the forgiver's intention to achieve such an effect would amount to crass utilitarianism, in the sense at least of 'consequentialism' or 'agathistic' utilitarianism. While I deny that a virtuous person forgives every wrongdoer and for any wrong done by him, I suggest that, other things being equal, the more virtuous I am the more *disposed* I am to forgive. This is so simply because forgiving is an exquisite act of charity or benevolence in a meaningful context, that is in a situation which in some way specially concerns the agent, i.e. the forgiver. His hope of achieving a morally good effect merely *adds* to the moral value of his forgiveness. On the contrary, if he expects it to exert a bad ('hardening') effect on the offender, the moral value of his forgiveness is diminished and becomes infected thereby with an element of disvalue but does not reduce to zero. Utilitarianism is right in the modest sense that the foreseeable results of our actions *influence* (not that they determine) their moral value or disvalue. To forgive with the *intention* of proving and aggravating the beneficiary's wickedness would of course itself be a bad act; but whether this variety of forgiveness *is* true forgiveness and not rather an act of crafty and perverse resentment invested with the semblance of forgiveness is at best open to doubt. I am inclined to assume that in this respect marginal cases occur which involve a good deal of self-deception.

To sum up. Whereas a credible change of heart on Ralph's part constitutes the standard situation making forgiveness a *quasi*-obligation for Fred, the standard situation which makes forgiveness legitimate and virtuous is that in which Fred has at least *some* reason to hope for *metanoia* on Ralph's part and for making it easier for Ralph by forgiving him. His being possibly disappointed in his hope does not alter the fact that his according precedence to this hope and aspiration over his straightforward and just retributive attitude will not stamp him with the blighting mark of indifference to Value and Disvalue or with that of a cowardly and base condonation and lack of self-respect. 'Casting one's bread upon the waters' may be highly problematic from the practical and sometimes from the moral point of view; but inasmuch as it springs from, and reveals, virtue, it is a very high virtue indeed. It expresses that attitude of *trust* in the world which, unless it is vitiated by hare-brained optimism and dangerous irresponsibility, may be looked upon, not to be sure as the starting-point and the very basis, but perhaps as the epitome and culmination of morality. It is closely tied up with the demotion of our concern about Certitude and Safety in favour of a boldly, venturesomely aspiring and active pursuit of Value—infinitely remote from a craven acceptance of Disvalue and from the placing of practical success, comfort, 'adjustment', etc., above Right, moral sensitivity, purity and sense of dignity. Offering trust 'in advance' *may* increase the *objective trustworthiness* of the recipient. Fred in the supposed case 'gambles' on this hope, which inevitably involves a *risk*. He may do so wisely ('calculated risk') and then highly morally, or in a less well founded way (still with a definitely moral intent), or frankly unwisely, which yet may not involve, but may easily blend with, immorality and deserve moral reproof. As I was saying above, where depravity and malice hold sway they may all too easily draw nurture from a good-natured approach and batten on forgiveness. (Not always along the line of utilitarian profit and self-interested advantage; resentment at moral superiority as such may play a prominent part. As Karl Kraus once wrote, 'Saints and heroes must not exist, lest slime might become weary of life.') But even in cases where there is no positive sign of a change of heart at all, that adverse effect will by no means always ensue and give the lie to Fred's generous, even gratuitous, confidence. On some occasions, we may *disapprove* of Fred's forgiveness without denying that it *is* genuine forgiveness and without *condemning* it as being, at bottom, base accommodation.

I forbear from discussing the special and not uninteresting problem of *self*-forgiveness. So much is certain that in most of us a tendency to self-exculpation is operative and needs careful watching; the habit of easy self-absolution, even following an act of repentance, is always suspect of being more akin to condonation than to genuine forgiveness. Yet in another sense it is with ourself that we are most irrevocably committed to *patience*; the Gospel, not a little hard on Judas's betrayal of Christ, is right, I think, in not holding up his suicide—allegedly originating from mere 'remorse' rather than from true 'repentance', though I do not quite understand the distinction[2]—as an example for imitation. Forgiveness granted to ourself seems a fairly dubious concept, if only because a person cannot 'wrong' himself, i.e. infringe his own rights, though of course he can harm himself and illegitimately renounce some of his rights. Yet we can have, or lack, patience with ourself: seeing that it is for our own life that we are most integrally responsible and that our total and definitive breech with ourself implies our absolute rupture with, and mistrust of, the world. Thus, while it is an excellent practice to blame our own transgressions and inner disfigurements more severely than those of others, at the same time we may do well to consider the verses of the mediaeval 'Monk of Heisterbach', quoted in Franz Brentano's *Vom Ursprung sittlicher Erkenntnis*:

> Sonne dich an Gottes grosser Huld;
> Hab' mit Allen—auch mit dir—Geduld.

(Bask in the sunshine of God's great bounty; have patience with all—including thyself.)

---

[2] Perhaps it is assumed that remorse is mere regret, be it just practical or even connoting a moral accent, felt by the agent about the deed he has perpetrated, whereas repentance amounts to a loathing and dissolving of the very attitude that has underlain his bad action.

NOTES

SOVEREIGNTY OF THE OBJECT

[a] From 'much as' to 'elementary algebra' is a later addition by the author.

[b] The author appears to have had doubts about this statement. This is indicated by a query written into the margin.

[c] The original text reads 'is' instead of 'may be'. The alteration was made later by the author.

DELIBERATION IS OF ENDS

[a] The author has written into the margin, next to the latter part of this sentence, the words 'then, not derivable'. This seems to be a comment about whether it is coherent to talk about desiring 'true ends' both for their own sake and as 'means to happiness'.

[b] The text from here to the end of the paragraph has been marked by the author in a number of ways. It is difficult to ascertain his intentions and we have amended the text in only one place where the indication is relatively clear.

MORALITY AND PRACTICE I

[a] Instead of 'earlier' the manuscript has 'the more ancient'.

[b] In the original text the author indicates that he intended to return to this topic later.

[c] Instead of 'discussion' the manuscript has 'chapter'.

[d] The word 'good' does not appear in the manuscript.

MORALITY AND PRACTICE II

[a] Instead of 'discussion' the manuscript has 'chapter'.

[b] At the beginning of this sentence instead of "This does not mean that' the manuscript has 'This means simply that it is not'.

[c] The manuscript reads 'how far "Christian ethic" can be'.

[d] At the beginning of this sentence instead of 'I should indeed argue that' the manuscript reads 'I shall indeed argue somewhat later that'.

EXISTENCE AND ETHICS

[a] The author has written the following into the margin: 'cf. another highly important Kierkegaard passage (I borrow it from Maurice Barrès, who quotes it via Unamuno): "If, of two men, one prays to the true God without personal sincerity while the other prays to an idol but with the full passion of infinitude, then the former is in reality praying to an idol, and the latter in reality praying to God".'

[b] The author has written the following into the margin: 'cf. "New Left" and the idea of "authentic community through the experience of violence" '.

MORAL CONSENSUS

[a] A short 'Note on Relativism and "Sociological" Ethics' has been omitted from the end of this paper. It seems to have been an afterthought of the author and does not continue the argument of the main text.

BIBLIOGRAPHY

BOOKS

Psychoanalyse und Soziologie, Wien-Leipzig: Internationaler Psyhoanalytischer Verlag, 1920, pp. 115

Psycho-Analysis and Sociology, London and New York: Allen and Unwin, 1921 (translation of the above)

Der ethische Wert und die Wirklichkeit (Ethical value and reality), Freiburg i. Br.: Herder, 1927, pp. 171

Sexualethik, Paderborn: Schöningh, 1930, pp. 447

The War against the West, London: Gollancz and New York: Viking Press, 1938, pp. 711 (on the doctrines and philosophical roots of German National Socialism)

Errores del Anticomunismo, Madrid: Rialp, S.A., 1952, pp. 167 (translation by Salvador Pons of 'Quelques Erreurs Courantes sur le Communisme'—see under ARTICLES, 1950–1)

La Divinización y la Suma Esclavitud del Hombre (The divinization and supreme enslavement of man), Madrid: Ateneo, 1952, pp. 40

Crítica de las Utopías Políticas, Madrid: Ateneo, 1959, pp. 44 (condensed version of Chapter 1 of the unpublished *The Utopian Mind*)

PAPERS

'Über das Mystische' (On the Mystical), *Imago* (Wien), VII, 1, 1921, pp. 40–70

'Neigung, Pflicht und Gesinnung' (Inclination, duty and moral intention), *Archiv für systematische Philosophie und Soziologie* (Berlin), XXX, 1 and 2, 1923, pp. 55–65

'Max Schelers Kritik der Freudschen Libidolehre' (Max Scheler's critique of Freud's theory of Libido), *Imago*, XI, 1925, pp. 135–46

'Der Aufbau der ethischen Intention' (The structure of moral intention), *Philosophisches Jahrbuch der Görres-Gesellschaft* (München), XLI, 1, 1928, pp. 1–16

'Versuch einer Klassifizierung der allgemein-sozialen Machtideen' (Towards a classification of the general social conceptions of power), *Archiv für systematische Philosophie und Soziologie*, XXXI, 1 and 2, 1929, pp. 125–41

'Die Machtideen der Klassen' (The social classes' conceptions of power) *Archiv für Sozialwissenschaft und Sozialpolitik* (Tübingen), LXII, 1, 1929, pp. 67–110

'Der Ekel' (Disgust), *Jahrbuch für Philosophie und phänomenologische Forschung*, X, 1929, pp. 515–69. Reprinted Tübingen: Max Niemeyer, 1974

'El Asco', *Revista de Occidente* (Madrid), XXVI, 77 and 78, 1929. Reprinted in Serie II, 1950, pp. 243–312 (translation of 'Der Ekel')

'Der Hochmut' (Pride), *Philosophisches Jahrbuch der Görres-Gesellschaft*, XLIV, 2 and 4, 1931, pp. 153–70 and 317–31

'Gegenrevolution' (Counter-revolution), *Kölner Vierteljahrshefte für Soziologie* (München), X, 2 and 3, 1931 and 1932, pp. 171–99 and 295–319

'Der Inhalt der Politik' (The content of politics), *Zeitschrift für die gesamte Staatswissenschaft* (Tübingen), XCIV, 1, 1933, pp. 1–38

'Versuch über den Hass' (Essay on hatred), *Philosophisches Jahrbuch der Görres-Gesellschaft*, XLVIII, 2/3, 1935, pp. 147–87

'Sozialismus und Ganzheit' (Socialism and Totality), *Wiener Soziologisch-Politische Monatshefte*, 1934

'The Problem of Austrian Nationhood', *Journal of Central European Affairs* (Boulder, Colorado), II, 3, 1942, pp. 290–309

'Austria and the Danubian Nations', *Journal of Central European Affairs*, III, 2, 1943, pp. 167–82

'Danubia: a Survey of Plans for Solution', *Journal of Central European Affairs*, III, 4, 1944, pp. 441–62

'The Humanitarian versus the Religious Attitude', *The Thomist* (Baltimore, Maryland), Oct. 1944, pp. 429–57

'Le Mythe des "Enfants de la Lumière" ', *Université Laval Théologique et Philosophique* (Quebec), I, 2, 1945, pp. 199–205

'Le Culte de l'Homme Commun et la Gloire des Humbles', *Université Laval Théologique et Philosophique*, II, 1, 1946, pp. 74–116. Reprinted in English translation as 'The Cult of the Common Man and the Glory of the Humble', *Integrity* (New York), VI, 2, 1951, pp. 3–43

'Les Ambiguités Nationales', *La Nouvelle Relève* (Montreal), Jan. 1946 and June 1947, pp. 533–46 and 644–55

'Les Débuts du Formalisme dans la Philosophie Moderne', *La Revue de l'Université Laval* (Quebec), I, 4, 1946, pp. 269–71

'Necesidad de la Filosofía' (The necessity of philosophy), *Estilo* (San Luis Potosí, Mexico), VII, 1947, pp. 151–64

'The Meaning of the "Common Man" ', *The Thomist*, July 1949, pp. 272–335

'Privilege and Liberty', *Université Laval Théologique et Philosophique*, V, 1, 1949, pp. 66–110. Reprinted in French translation as 'Privilège et Liberté', *Contrepoint* (Paris), 21, 1976, pp. 63–111

'Quelques Erreurs Courantes sur le Communisme', *La Revue de l'Université Laval*, IV, 8, V, 1, V, 4, V, 5 and V, 7, 1950–1, pp. 681–93, 1–19, 323–37, 388–97 and 626–38. Reprinted as *Errores del Anticomunismo* (see under BOOKS)

'Le Conditionnement Historique de la Pensée Humaine et la Philosophie de l'Experience Commune', *Actes, Congrès de Sociétés Philosophiques de la Langue Française*, Geneva, 1952, pp. 91–5

'Revolución y Restauración' (Revolution and restoration), *Arbor* (Madrid), LXXXV, 1953, pp. 125–34

228 BIBLIOGRAPHY

'Notes sur l'Utopie Réactionnaire', *Cité Libre* (Montreal), 13, 1955, pp. 9–20. Reprinted in Spanish translation as 'Notas sobre la Utopía Reaccionaria', *Punta Europa* (Madrid), 10, 1956, pp. 71–86

'The Thematic Primacy of Moral Evil', *Philosophical Quarterly*, VI, 1956, pp. 27–42

'Reflexiones sobre el Alziamento Húngaro y la Crisis de la Utopía Política' (Reflections on the Hungarian uprising and the crisis of political Utopia), *Oriente Europeo* (Madrid), 27, 1957, pp. 259–74

'El Sentido Positivo de la Libertad' (The positive meaning of liberty), *Punta Europa*, 18/19, 1957, pp. 105–22

'Erroneous Conscience', *Proceedings of the Aristotelian Society*, 1957–8, pp. 171–98

'A Note on the Meaning of Right and Wrong', in *Scientiis Artibusque*, Hungarian Academy of Science and Arts, Rome: Herder and Co., 1958, pp. 49–60

'La Filosofía Británica Actual y sus Aspectos Políticos' (Contemporary British philosophy and its political aspects), *Punta Europa*, 41, 1959, pp. 70–90

'Pluralismo y Correlación de las Finalidades' (Pluralism and the correlation of ends), Quinta Semana Espagnola de Filosofía, Madrid, 1959 (presumed published, reference unknown)

'The Sovereignty of the Object: Notes on Truth and Intellectual Humility', in *The Human Person and the World of Values*, ed. Balduin V. Schwarz, New York: Fordham University Press, 1960, pp. 57–81

'The Moral Theme in Political Division', *Philosophy*, XXXV, 1960, pp. 234–54

'La Mentalité Utopienne', *La Table Ronde* (Paris), 153, 1960, pp. 62–84

' "Unanimité" et Neutralité Religieuse', *Cité Libre*, 13, 1961, pp. 5–10

'Deliberation is of Ends', *Proceedings of the Aristotelian Society*, 1961–2, pp. 195–218

'Existence and Ethics', in Symposium: 'Existentialism', *Aristotelian Society Supplementary Volume* XXXVII, 1963, pp. 27–50

'The Concept of the Interesting', *British Journal of Aesthetics*, IV, 1964, pp. 22–39

'Erreur et Verité', *Actes du XIIe Congrès des Sociétés de Philosophie de la Langue Française*, Brussels–Louvain, 1964, pp. 108–11

'Los Intereses Políticos y no Políticos' (Political and non-political interests), *Atlantida* (Madrid), 1965

'Objectividad y Tecnicismo' (Objectivity and technicality), *In* (Información) (Madrid), 22, 1965, pp. 71–8 (contribution to conference at Universidad Internacional Menendez Pelayo, Santander)

'Games and Aims', *Proceedings of the Aristotelian Society*, 1965–6, pp. 103–28

'La Pureté du Langage est-elle Signe de Pureté Morale?', *Actes du XIIIe Congrès des Sociétés de Philosophie de la Langue Française*, Geneva, 1966, pp. 340–3

'Agency and Freedom', in *The Human Agent*, Royal Institute of Philosophy Lectures, I, 1966–7, London: Macmillan and New York: St Martin's Press, 1968, pp. 20–46

'The Justification of Commands', *British Journal of Educational Studies*, XVI, 1968, pp. 258–70

'Moral Consensus', *Proceedings of the Aristotelian Society*, 1969–70, pp. 93–118

'A Defence of Intrinsicalism against Situation Ethics', in *Situationism and the New Morality*, ed. R. L. Cunningham, New York: Appleton-Century-Crofts, 1970, pp. 232–71

'The Concept of Hierarchy', *Philosophy*, XLVI, 1971, pp. 203–22

'Aesthetic and Moral Experience', *British Journal of Aesthetics*, XI, 1971, pp. 178–88

'Contrasting the Ethical and the Aesthetical', *British Journal of Aesthetics*, XII, 1972, pp. 331–44

'The Dream as Artist', *British Journal of Aesthetics*, XII, 1972, pp. 158–62

'Konservatives und revolutionäres Ethos' (Conservative and revolutionary ethos), in *Rekonstruktion des Konservatismus*, ed. G. K. Kaltenbrunner, Freiburg i. Br.: Rombach, 1972, pp. 95–136

'La Función Moralizadora del Derecho' (The moralizing function of Law), in *Anuario de Filosofía del Derecho*, Instituto Nacional de Estudios Juridicos, Madrid, 1973, pp. 205–9

'Forgiveness', *Proceedings of the Aristotelian Society*, 1973–4, pp. 91–106

'Dignity', *Philosophy*, LI, 1976, pp. 251–71

BOOK REVIEWS

(This list is almost certainly incomplete, and possibly contains one or two inaccuracies, particularly as regards the period before 1956.)

'*Németség és democrácia* by R. Charmatz' (German democracy), *Huszadik Század* (Budapest), Dec. 1918, pp. 345–7

'*Valláslélektani kérdesek* by T. K. Österreich' (Questions in the psychology of religion), *Huszadik Század*, Dec. 1918, pp. 347–8

'*Pacifista nevelés* by W. Börner' (Education towards Pacifism), *Huszadik Század*, Dec. 1918, pp. 348–9

'*La doctrine d'Émile Durkheim* by Maurice Halbwachs', *Huszadik Század*, Dec. 1918, pp. 349–50

'*Az értekelés filosófiája* by Ambró Czakó' (The philosophy of evaluation), *Huszadik Század*, 1919, pp. 111–20

'*The Austrian Economy* by R. Kobatsch', '*Causal and Conditional View of Life* by M. Verworn', '*Socialism and the Intellectuals* by M. Adler', *Huszadik Század*, April 1919, pp. 247–8

'*Adalék a tudományos szocializmushoz* by E. Bernstein' (Contribution to Scientific Socialism—League of Nations or League of States), *Huszadik Század*, April 1919, pp. 300–1

'*A vallásoktatás helyetesitése* by L. Heilmaier' (Substitute for Religious Instruction—Moral Instruction in French secular schools), *Huszadik Század*, April 1919, pp. 301–2

'*Australian Totemism* by Geza Róheim', *Századunk* (Budapest), 1926, p. 150

'*Geist und Gesicht des Bolschewismus* by René Fülöp-Miller' (The spirit and face of Bolshevism), *Das Neue Reich* (Wien), 38, 1927, pp. 793–4

'*Kleine Philosophie für Jedermann* by August Forel' (A little Philosophy for Everyman), *Volkswohl* (Wien), xix, 7, 1928, pp. 267–9

'*Fundament der Volkswirtschaftslehre* by Othmar Spann' (Foundations of the theory of social economy), *Das Neue Reich*, Heft iii, 1929, p. 64

'*Wespennester* by Oscar Schmitz' (Wasps' nests), *Századunk*, 1929, pp. 185–6

'*A Labour Party és az 1929-i választások* by Egon Wertheimer' (The Labour Party and the election of 1929), *Századunk*, 1929, pp. 194–9

'*Der Geist der Englischen Politik und das Gespenst der Einkreisung Deutschlands* by Hermann Kantorowicz' (The spirit of English politics and the ghost of Germany's encirclement), *Századunk*, 1930, p. 431

'*Ideologie und Utopie* by Karl Mannheim', *Századunk*, 1930, pp. 361–4

'*Der Kampf um die Österreichische Verfassung* by Ignaz Seipel' (The struggle for the Austrian constitution), *Századunk*, 1930, pp. 371–2

'*Wert, Person, Gott. Zur Ethik Max Schelers, N. Hartmanns und der Philosophie des Ungegebenen* by Otto Kühler' (Value, Person, God. On the ethics of Max Scheler, N. Hartmann and the philosophy of the Ungiven), *Századunk*, 1932, pp. 458–9

'*Hösök, tudósok, emberek. Az utolsó 70 év története 1860–1930, Vilmos Juhász* by György Kovács' (Heroes, Scholars, People. The last 70 years of history 1860–1930), *Századunk*, 1933, pp. 47–8

'*Weltgeschichte von der Urzeit bis zur Gegenwart* by Ernst Gombrich' (A history of the world from primitive times to the present day), *Századunk*, 1936, p. 352

'*Methodenlehre der Sozialwissenschaften* by Felix Kaufmann' (Method in the social sciences), *Századunk*, 1936, pp. 351–2

'*Les Paradoxes du Bouddhisme* by Fr. Taymans d'Eypernon, S.J.' and '*Hindu Philosophy* by Theos Bernard', *Thought* (New York), xxiii, 91, 1948, pp. 742–5

'*Man and the State* by Jacques Maritain', *Integrity* (New York), v, 11, 1951, pp. 40–5

'*Liberty or Equality* by Erik von Kuehnelt-Leddihn', *The Tablet*, 17 May 1952, p. 397

'*The Corporative State* by Joaquin Azpiazu, S.J.', *Integrity*, vi, 4, 1952, pp. 43–4

'*Ethics* by Dietrich Bonhoeffer', *The Tablet*, 18 Feb. 1956, p. 156

'*Moral Values in the Ancient World* by John Ferguson', *Philosophy*, xxxv, 1960, pp. 76–7

'*Diccionario de Filosofía* by José Ferrater Mora', *Philosophy*, xxxvi, 1961, pp. 85–6

'*The Concise Encyclopaedia of Western Philosophy and Philosophers* edited by J. O. Urmson, *Philosophy*, xxxvii, 1962, p. 184

'*Political Messianism: the Romantic Phase. The History of Totalitarian Democracy vol. II* by J. L. Talmon', *Philosophy*, xxxvii, 1962, pp. 368–9

'Findlay on Ethics', *Philosophy*, XXXIX, 1964, pp. 75–9 (Review of *Values and Intentions*, by J. N. Findlay)

'*Untersuchungen zur Ontologie der Kunst* by Roman Ingarden' (Investigations in the ontology of art), *British Journal of Aesthetics*, IV, 1964, pp. 164–6

'*Rationalism in Politics* by Michael Oakeshott', *Philosophy*, XL, 1965, pp. 263–4

'*Die Lebenswelt: eine Philosophie des konkreten Apriori* by Gerd Brand' (The life-world: a philosophy of the concrete A priori), *Journal of the British Society for Phenomenology*, IV, 1973, pp. 76–8

'*Reason Revisited: the Philosophy of Karl Jaspers* by Sebastian Samay', *Mind*, LXXXII, 1973, pp. 453–6

ARTICLES

(Dr Kolnai published numerous articles, especially during the inter-war period. Many of them are attacks on various aspects of Nazism. The following list is incomplete. It has not proved possible to ascertain or check thoroughly every reference. Articles are listed under the periodical in which they appeared.)

Volkswohl, Wien, 1928–1930

'Eine Illusion der Zukunft' (An illusion of the future) [critique of Freud's theory of religion], XIX, 2

'Ist Othmar Spanns Ganzheitslehre mit dem Katholizismus vereinbar?' (Is Othmar Spann's theory of Totality compatible with Catholicism?), XX, 3 and XX, 4

'Thomas Mann, Freud und der Fortschritt' (Thomas Mann, Freud and progress), XX, 9

'Autorität und Demokratie' (Authority and democracy), XX

'Die christlichen Gewerkschaften im Kampf gegen den Kapitalismus' (The Christian trade unions in the fight against Capitalism), XX, 11

'Sozialreform gegen Demokratie' (Anti-democratic social reform), XXI, 9

'Geistige und politische Voraussetzungen der Wirtschaftsdemokratie' (Spiritual and political presuppositions of economic democracy), XXII, 1

Nord und Süd

'Entwurf eines Verhältniswahlsystems nebst persönliche Bezirksvertretung' (Project for a system of proportional representation with personal representation of districts), April–June, 1920

'Ist das Volk zur Demokratie reif?' (Is the people mature enough for democracy?), July-Sept. 1920

Schönere Zukunft, Wien, 1928–1930

'Max Scheler und der Kapitalismus' (Max Scheler and Capitalism), June 1928

'Hilaire Bellocs "Sklavenstaat" ' (Hilaire Belloc's vision of the 'servile state'), Nov. 1928
'Chestertons Distributismus' (Chesterton's Distributism)

Der Kampf

'Kritik des Ständestaates' (Critique of the corporative state), 1933

Der Deutsche Volkswirt, Berlin

'Fascismus und Bolschewismus' (Fascism and Bolshevism), 25 Oct. 1926
'Rechts und Links in der Politik' (Right and Left in politics), 25 Feb. 1927
'Die Ideologie des Sozialen Fortschritts' (The ideology of progress), 22 April 1927
'Kritik des Sozialen Fortschritts' (Critique of the creed of progress), 29 April 1927
'Der Aufbau des Kapitalismus. Die Soziallehren G. K. Chestertons' (The structure of Capitalism. The social theories of G. K. Chesterton), 29 July 1927
'Tote und lebendige Demokratie' (Democracy dead and alive) [G. B. Shaw's ideas on the decay of democratic idealism], 30 March 1928
'Max Scheler als Sozialphilosoph' (Max Scheler as sociologist), 22 June 1928
'Jugend und fascistische Reaktion' (Youth and fascist reaction), 13 Feb. 1931

Der Österreichische Volkswirt

'Das Weihnachtsmanifest der österreichischen Bischöfe' (The Christmas manifesto of the Austrian bishops), 9 Jan. 1926
'Gegen den Ständerat' (Against the corporative council), 24 July 1926
'Listenwahl und Diktatur' (Selective election and dictatorship), 8 Jan. 1927
'Die Ehrenrettung des Liberalismus' (The rehabilitation of liberalism), 15, 22 Oct. 1927
'Das Recht der Parteien' (The justification of parties), 27 July, 3 Aug. 1929
'Ständestaat ist Absolutismus' (Corporative state means Absolutism), 18, 25 Jan. 1930
'Herrschaft und Wirtschaft' (Government and economy), 20 Sept. 1930
'Das Remarque-Manöver der Rechten' (The 'Remarque manoeuvre' of the Right), 17 Jan. 1931
'Von der Universität durch den Universalismus zum Untermenschentum' (From university through universalism to sub-humanity), 1 Jan. 1932
'Ständeverfassung in Österreich' (The corporative constitution in Austria), 17 June 1933
'Österreich und die Demokratie' (Austria and democracy), 19 Aug. 1933
'Der Sinn des Liberalismus' (The meaning of liberalism), 3 Sept 1933

'Totaler Staat und Zivilisation' (The Total state and civilization), 28 Oct. 1933

'Katholizismus und Demokratie' (Catholicism and democracy), 23 Dec. 1933

'Demokratie und "Geldherrschaft"' (Democracy and the 'rule of money'), 27 Jan. 1934

'Persönlichkeit und Massenherrschaft' (Personality and mass-rule), 10 Feb. 1934

'Der Sinn des Rassenwahns' (The meaning of racial obsession), 17 March 1934

'Rückblick auf die Demokratie' (Looking back on democracy), 21 April 1934

'Volkswille und Zifferzauber' (Popular will and the magic of figures), 19 May 1934

'Das Problem des Konservatismus' (The problem of Conservatism), 14 July 1934

'Die Aufgabe des Konservatismus' (The task of Conservatism), 28 July 1934

'Das System Dollfuss' (The Dollfuss regime), 1 Sept. 1934

'Volkswille gegen Freiheit' (The popular revolt against liberty), 5 Jan. 1935

'Die Gesellschaftskrise der Gegenwart' (The contemporary social crisis), 30 March 1935

'Objektive Staatsgewalt' ('Objective' state power), 16 Nov. 1935

'Klarheit in den Sozialwissenschaften' (Clarity in the social sciences), 15 Aug. 1936

'Neuösterreichische Staatslehre' (The neo-Austrian theory of the state), 17 Oct. 1936

'Aussenpolitik und "Ideologien"' (Foreign relations and 'ideologies'), 16 Jan. 1937

Der Christliche Ständestaat: Österreichische Wochenhefte

(This magazine was founded and edited by Dietrich von Hildebrand as a weapon in the ideological war against Nazism in Austria. The articles Dr Kolnai wrote for it were published under the pseudonym *Dr A. van Helsing*.)

'Marxistisches und Liberalistisches im Nationalsozialismus' (Marxism and Liberalism in National Socialism), 24 June 1934

'Der Missbrauch des Vitalen' (The abuse of the Vital), 26 Aug. 1934

'Othmar Spanns Ganzheitslehre' (Othmar Spann's theory of the 'Total state'), 11 Nov. 1934

'Othmar Spanns organische Staatslehre' (Othmar Spann's theory of the organic state), 18 Nov. 1934

'Einfallspforten des Nationalismus' (The entry-points of nationalism), 27 Jan. 1935

'Langbehn und der deutsche Katholizismus' (Langbehn and German Catholicism), 17 Feb. 1935

'Entschuldigtes Christentum. Glossen und Notizen' (Christianity pardoned. Notes and comments), 6 Oct. 1935
'Chesterton', 28 June 1936 (an obituary)
'Heideggers Nihilismus' (Heidegger's nihilism), June 1934
'Staatsidee und Staatsform' (The idea of the state and the form of the state), 19 Aug. 1934

The World Tomorrow, New York
'Will German Catholics go Left?', 1 Feb 1933

The Nation, New York
'The Ghost of Versailles', 15 April 1939
'Must Democracy Use Force?', 21 Jan. 1939
'Fate or Freedom', 31 May 1941

The American Teacher, New York
'The Techniques of Fascism', May 1941

Free Europe, London
'German and Western "Imperialism"'
'Is there an Austrian Nation?', 23 April 1943
'The Problem of Austrian Nationhood', 18 June 1943
'Frontiers are Important', 10 March 1944
'The American Mind and the Problem of Europe', 30 June 1944

Liberation, New York
'Collective Insecurity', July 1943

The Voice of Austria, New York
'The Axis Plays "Empire"', Aug. 1941
'The Problem of Germany', Oct. 1941
'Our Fight for Democracy', Nov. 1941
'Führers and Kings', Feb. 1942
'Can Catholics be Fooled by Hitler?', March 1942
'Is "Federation" a Solution?', May 1942
'National Liberty in Danubia', Oct. 1942
'The Calling of Catholic Europe', Dec. 1942
'Victors and Gainers', April 1943

Rheinischer Merkur, Bonn
'Das unvollendete Völkerreich: die hundertjahres Feier eines fünfzigjährigen Reiches' (The peoples' empire that was never completely destroyed: the hundredth anniversary of a fifty-year empire), Sept. 1967

Huszadik Század, Budapest
'Aktivitás és passzivitás a kulturfejlödésben' (Activity and passivity at different levels of civilization), Dec. 1918

'Az állandó és változékony álláspont lélektanáha' (Psychology of the variability of political attitudes), April 1919
'A fejlödés raktár—optimum—elméletéhez' (The theory of the store of (optimum) development), 1919

Századunk, Budapest (continuation of *Huszadik Század*)
'A bécsi szociológiai kongresszus' (Negotiations of the 5th Vienna Congress), Sept. 1927
'A német választási harc' (The German electoral fight), April 1928
'Hozzászólás "A demokrácia 'válsága'?" körkérdéshez' (A contribution to the discussion "Crisis of Democracy?")
'Osztály hatalom és osztály ideál' (Class power and Class ideal), Nov. 1929
'Az osztrák democrácia sorsa' (The fate of Austrian democracy), Dec. 1929
'Jászi Oszkár fejtegetéseihez a bolsevizmusról hozzászól Kolnai Aurél (Aurel Kolnai comments on Oszkár Jászi's analysis of Bolshevism), 1930
'Ifjuság és fasiszta reakció' (Youth and Fascist reaction), Nov. 1930
'A német állam harca a fasizmus ellen' (The struggle of the German state against Fascism), May/June 1932
'Az emberek egyenlöségéröl' (On the equality of man), Aug./Sept. 1934
'Demokrácia és valóság' (Democracy and reality), Sept. 1935
'A józan ész mágusai: K. Kraus és G. K. Chesterton' (The magicians of sober reason: K. Kraus and G. K. Chesterton), July/Aug. 1936

Aurora, Budapest
'Nyugat pusztulása' (on Spengler's *Decline of the West*), July 1920
'A liberális szocializmus erkölcsi kiindulópontjai' (The moral principles of liberal socialism), Feb. 1921
'A liberális szocializmus társadalomtudományi kiindulópontjai' (The principles of social science in liberal socialism), 1921

NACHLASS

Apart from the completed chapters of *Morality and Practice*, which are printed in this collection, Dr Kolnai left two books completed, two books partly completed, and numerous papers, articles, sketches and notes, from which the list below has been compiled. There are also a number of other items, including poems, letters and children's stories, not all of which are in English.

BOOKS

The Fallacies of Pacifism, 1938, pp. 271
Liberty and the Heart of Europe, 1943–4, pp. 373. (Written during world war two; an historical, political and cultural survey of the Danubian

countries with suggestions for their reconstruction after the war. The work includes substantial contributions to political philosophy. Unfinished owing to the changing political situation.)
Twentieth Century Memoirs, 1952–5, pp. c. 700
The Utopian Mind, c. 1957–c. 1967, pp. 153 (Chapter I (Critique of Utopia), Chapter II (The Utopian Idol of Perfection and the Non-Utopian Pursuit of the Good), and part of Chapter IV (The Utopian 'Godhead of Man') were completed)

PAPERS, ARTICLES AND NOTES

(The following list must be regarded as incomplete and provisional, and includes handwritten as well as typewritten manuscripts. Dates are supplied wherever known.)

'Democracy and Value', 1936, pp. 25
'Moral Truth', c. 1937, pp. 19
'The Moral Dilemma of Patriotism', pp. 14
'The Pivotal Principle of National–Socialist ideology', c. 1938, pp. 12
'The Austrian Coffee-house', 1942, pp. 14
'Rehabilitierung Preussens?' (Rehabilitation of Prussia?), 1944, pp. 6
'Seinskreise, Seinskreiszeichen, Traum' (Notes on 'spheres of being' in connection with the published paper 'The Dream as Artist'), pp. 6
'Random Political Reflections meant to be "Provocative" ', pp. 4
'Racialism and Cultural Implications', pp. 1
' "System" and Consistency', pp. 2
'Sur la Coupabilité du Cardinal Mindszenthy', 1949, pp. 8 (Communication to the International Anti-Communist Congress, Montreal)
'La dialectique de l'extrémisme et la dialectique de la moderation', pp. 3
'Textes choisis' (Selected texts for two courses in the history of modern philosophy, from the renaissance (Laval, Quebec)), 1945–7, pp. 76
'Progress and Reaction', c. 1950, pp. 8
'The Three Riders of the Apocalypse', 1950, pp. 25 (On Communism, Nazism, and Progressive Democracy)
'Voluntas per se est liberum arbitrium', 1952, pp. 17 (On free-will)
'My Experience of Canada', pp. 28 (From last chapter of *Twentieth Century Memoirs*)
'Nuestra actitud delante de la "Sociedad Moderna" y del progresismo industrialista y humanista' (Our attitude towards "Modern Society" and industrial and humanistic progressivism), pp. 14
'Ocho tesis: En Torno a la Restauración' (Eight theses: About the Restoration), pp. 24
'Memorias del siglo Veinte, Indice y Comentarios' (Twentieth Century Memoirs, Index and Commentary), 1956, pp. 24
'Memoria' (Memorandum on monarchism and the restoration), 1956, pp. 38
'La Dignidad Humana, Hoy' (Human Dignity Today), pp. 12

' "Physical Premotion" versus Human Responsibility and Divine Judgement', 1955, pp. 21 (On predestination and Thomism)
' "Waste-book": Political Philosophy', 1957, pp. 22 (Assorted notes, including reference to the relation between morality and practice)
'The Universality of "Loyalty" Rules', 1957, pp. 6
'Are there Degrees of Ethical Universality?', pp. 15 (Plus supplement, p. 2)
'The Concept of Practical Error', pp. 19
'Existentialism, Libertarian or Anti-libertarian?', pp. 10 (Plus supplement, pp. 10)
'Testability, Universality: "Emphasis on the Individual" (Existentialist Ethics)', pp. 9
'The Contrast between "Universalizability" and "Totality" Types of Ethics', pp. 2
'Existentialism Notes', pp. 3 (Comments on a paper by Iris Murdoch)
'The Utopian Mind', pp. 15
'Utopia and Alienation', pp. 10
'Political and Non-political Interests', 1960, pp. 9 (Read at the Royal Institute of Philosophy)
'Religious Naturalism Re-furbished', 1963, pp. 16
'Universality and Political Attitudes', 1964, pp. 17
'Intuitionism, Deontologism', pp. 15
'Notes on two opposite ways of using descriptive-evaluative terms and "apparent" good or extra-moral good', 1965, pp. 22
'Games, Practice and Politics', pp. 11
'Game: Paratelic Intention and Agonistic Structure', 1965, pp. 12
'The Ghost of the Naturalistic Fallacy', 1966, pp. 16
'Identity and Division', 1967, pp. 28 (Paper on politics)
'The Standard Modes of Aversion (Fear, Disgust, and Hatred)', 1969–70, pp. 18
'Actions and Inactions,' 1970–1, pp. 29
'Advising', 1966, pp. 12
'Some Features of Phenomenological Ethics', pp. 9; 'Brentano's Ethics', p. 10; 'Brentano's Place in the History of Recent Philosophy', pp. 14 (Notes for inter-collegiate lecture courses), 1970–3

LOST

A considerable amount of material has been lost, including a textbook of phenomenological ethics entitled *Ethik* completed in 1932.

INDEX

abominatio, 193n.

'absoluteness' and moral laws, 10, 157, 160f.; two senses of, 157

actions and inactions, 106f.; and types of action, 128

Acton, Lord, 18, 185

Aesthetic, the, and the Moral, 143, 187–210; 'non-existential' character of, 208–10

aesthetic, argument, 203

consensus, 145, 204

discussion, *ad hoc* nature of, 203

judgement, 145f., 203f.; distinct from taste, 204

objects, 'dispensability of', 210

perversion, 191

principles, 202, 206; compared with moral, 202–4

qualities, 15, 73, 180, 209

response, 206, cf. 199

rules, 202

tastes, 145f. (*see also* taste)

theories of ethics, 192n., 201

valuation, 195; absence of criteria in, 202f.; priority over moral, 199–210; universal range, 197, 206

values, 73, 145, 180f., 184, 187–210 (esp. 190, 194, 196, 200, 207, 210)

Aisthesis, 203

alienation, 132–4, 136, 138–41, 143; of conscience, 16, 20; (*see also* self-alienation)

alterity, 132–4, cf. 135f., 138–40

amor benevolentiae, 200; *complacentiae*, 200; *concupiscentiae*, 200

amoralism, 91

angels, 177, 197, cf. 173

anguish (anxiety), existential, 124, 126, 131f.

animals, 8, 169, 197

annulment of a wrong, 220

Anscombe, G. E. M., 61

Anselm, St, 61

antinomianism, 126, 158

appetite and 'the good', 67, 72–6

appreciations, moral, 13, 156; non-moral, 93, 136, 141, 171, 175, 195, 207

Aquinas (*see* Thomas, St)

Arendt, Hannah, 76

aristocracy, 165, 170f., 177, 185

Aristotle, 11, 30, 38, 41, 42&n., 43&n., 44–6, 48f., 49n., 51f., 54–8, 60, 65f., 70, 73–6, 78, 90, 96, 120, 144, 165, 174, 175&n., 179, 182, 196, 198, cf. 88; Aristotelian thought, 85, 99, 104

art, and beauty, 187, 189, 195, 209; and morality, 189, 195, 201; and perfection, 193; and representation, 189, 195, 209; and utility, 190; purpose of, 195; works of, 187, 189f.

artistic creation, 202, 208

atonement. 214

Augustine, St, 38, 56, 67, 126, 163, 216

Austin, J. L., 214f.

authenticity, 52n., 60, 96, 124–9, 139, 142f.; as second-order moral concept, 129–31

authoritarianism, 32, 151f.

authority, 139, 158; an (the authorities), 18, 118, 152, 163, 212–14; divine, 113–15; established, 134, 184; intellectual, 24, 28f., 32, 34f., 37–9, 41n., 66, 147; moral, 7, 14f., 18, 91, 101, 142, 152, 159; social, 140, 171, 184f., 211, cf. 169

'autonomous legislation', 152

autonomy, of intrinsic non-moral good, 71; of the Moral, 61, 91, 100, 105, 121, 156, 200; personal, 138, 152, cf. 133

axiology (the Axiological), 165, 170f., 183, 189, 193f., 196f.; axiological ethics, 66; axiological primacy of

240

INDEX

axiology (the Axiological) *cont.*
 the ethical and aesthetical, 187,
 189–97

bad faith, 12, 126, 128
badness, and evil, 79–87; intrinsic,
 216
Bainville, Jacques de, 40
Barrès, Maurice, 225
Beautiful, the, 187–93, 195–7, 201,
 203f., 206, 209; and existence, 208–
 10; and the Pleasant, 204; gratuitous nature of, 207; priority over
 the Ugly, 206–8
being and goodness, 77, 83, 85, 95
Beneficial, the, 191f.
Bergson, Henri, 181
blame, 1, 12, 106, 224 (*see also* moral
 reproof); and praise, 42, 76, 205,
 cf. 96; -worthiness, 1, 96, 146, 207
Bolshevism, 135, 141
Bonaventura, St, 67
Bonum delectabile, 50, 196; *honestum*,
 43, 50, 73, 196f.; *progressionis*, 219;
 utile, 50
Bossuet, J. B., 156
Bourgeois, the, 127, 135–7
Brentano, 43, 67, 73, 174, 193&n., 224
British Moralists, 42, 147f., 175, 192n.
Broad, C. D., 151
brutishness, 77f.
Buddhism, 13
Burckhardt, J., 140, 156
Burke, Edmund, 140
Butler, Bishop, 104, 191

Carritt, E. F., 67
Categorical Imperative, 104, 113, 117
Catholicism, Roman ('The Church'),
 18, 29–41, 180, 198
change of heart (*see Metanoia*)
character, 71, 101, 111–13, 117f., 131,
 151, 191f., 197, 218, 221f.
choice (choosing), 10, 48–50, 51n.,
 52n., 52–61, 74–6, 82, 89, 93, 97f.,
 109, 123, 125f., 128f., 138, 140–2,
 154, 181, 197, 199
 and free-will, 48, 54, 141
 between ends, 53–5, 58; criteria for,
 53
 free, reification and alienation, 141
 gratuitous, 124, 129
 'grounds' for, 140
 intellectualist theory of, 61

irrationality and rationality in, 58,
 60, 69
 of ends, 48–51
 (*see also* wise choice)
Chomsky, N., 188
Christ, Jesus, 37, 173, 224
Christian (-ity), 13, 18f., 30, 33, 41f.,
 61, 75, 82, 109, 117, 126f., 130, 133,
 138, 158f., 165, 174f., 197, 200, 202,
 208, 211; ethics, 42, 114; ethos, 42,
 158f.; intellectual and artistic
 achievement of, 174f.
Cicero, 155
circularity, 149
civilized life, 134–6, 169
Clarke, Samuel, 148
Codreanu, Zelea, 135
cognitive, acts, 128; satisfaction, 208;
 values (*see* values, intellectual)
Cohen, K., 219n.
Coleridge, 18
command and futurity, 79
commendation, 95, 107f., 117 (*see also*
 praise *and* moral condemnation)
commitment, 21, 101f., 125, 129, 132f.,
 142
common sense, 7, 28f., 37, 61, 69f.,
 99, 125, 144, 153, 189, 201
Communism, 18, 20, 125, 142, 169,
 171
community, 135, 138–40; Heidegger's
 interpretation of, 138f.
compensation, 207, 210, 217
compromise, 141
Comte, 174
concerns, 10f., 15, 19, 22, 49n., 52&n.,
 54–7, 65, 69, 73, 76, 78, 89, 92, 101,
 103f., 107, 111–13, 116, 119f., 128f.,
 137, 141, 157, 204; relation to the
 'self', 52n.
condonation, 215f., 218f., 221–4
conflict of principles, 3, 11, 21, 163
conscience, 1–22, 63, 69, 71, 78, 85,
 101, 103f., 112, 114, 116–18, 121,
 126, 129, 138, 149–53, 156f., 162–4,
 177, 183, 201f., 205
 and authority, 7
 and consensus, 19, 149–52, 157, 162f.
 and principles, 3f., 6f., 16
 and the moral emphasis (q.v.), 103
 and will, 10
 composite nature of, 11f.
 development of, 201f.
 dissentient, 1, 3f., 162–4